MANY ARE THE HEARTS

MANY
ARE THE
HEARTS

The Agony and the Triumph of
ULYSSES S. GRANT

Richard Goldhurst

READER'S DIGEST PRESS
DISTRIBUTED BY
THOMAS Y. CROWELL COMPANY
NEW YORK
1975

Maps by George Buctel

Designed by Abigail Moseley

Manufactured in the United States of America

Library of Congress Cataloging in Publication Data

Goldhurst, Richard.
    Many are the hearts.

    Bibliography: p.
    Includes index.
    1. Grant, Ulysses Simpson, Pres. U. S., 1822–1885.
I.   Title.
E672.G64   973.8'2'0924 [B]   75–8698
ISBN 0–88349–050–1

1   2   3   4   5   6   7   8   9   10

Grateful acknowledgment is made for permission to quote from:
The Captain Departs, by Thomas Pitkin, Southern Illinois Univer-
sity Press, 1973; *Patriotic Gore*, by Edmund Wilson, Oxford
University Press, 1962; *Mister Clemens & Mark Twain*, by Justin
Kaplan, Simon and Schuster, 1966; *Mark Twain: Business Man*,
by Samuel Clemens Webster, Little, Brown, 1946; *Remembered
Yesterday*, by Robert Underwood Johnson, Little, Brown, 1923;
Ulysses S. Grant and the American Military Tradition, by Bruce
Catton, Little, Brown, 1954; *Four in America*, by Gertrude Stein,
Yale University Press, 1941; *Mark Twain: A Biography*, by Albert
Bigelow Paine, Harper's, 1912.

by Richard Goldhurst

This book is for Mary Lehn Knox,
my wife's aunt, whose generous gift
financed the original research.
Every writer ought to have such a wife
and every writer's wife such an aunt.

CONTENTS

ACKNOWLEDGMENTS

STANLEY CRANE OF THE PEQUOT LIBRARY IN SOUTHPORT, CONNECT-icut, never failed in helping me to locate references in the early runs of American magazines catalogued there. His assistant Grace Donaldson was equally gracious with time. Miss Louise Jost of Red Bank, New Jersey, researched the Long Branch material. Traditionally the contribution of an editor goes unremarked. I cannot perpetuate such an injustice against Steven Frimmer, senior editor of the Reader's Digest Press, whose enthusiasm and expertise helped bring this book into print. I also owe a debt to William Craig of Westport, good friend and esteemed war historian. Many of his casual observations became salient points in this story. Dr. Shelly Orgel also of Westport was a friend to this work, and so was Dr. David Beck. Lastly, I must acknowledge my dependence on Grant's biographers: Hamlin Garland, Adam Badeau, Owen Wister, George Childs, W. E. Woodward, Horace Porter, Ishbel Ross, Allan Nevins, William Hesseltine, and especially Lloyd Lewis, Thomas M. Pitkin, and Bruce Catton.

A NOTE ON SOURCES

THE FACTS OF GRANT'S LIFE AND CAREER ARE SO INDISPUTABLE AS TO need no documentation.

At the end of the book, however, I have appended a bibliographical essay in which I cite and comment upon those books and authors on whom I relied. I felt some comment necessary because many of the biographies about Grant reveal as much of the time in which they were written as they do of the time about which they were written.

I quote Ulysses S. Grant frequently. None of this dialogue is invented or imagined. I quote Grant both from his correspondence and his memoirs; and I quote him as well on the authority of those who heard what he said.

Many are the hearts that are weary tonight,
Waiting for the war to cease;
Many are the hopes, the hopes once high and bright,
That sleep with those at peace.
　　Dying tonight, dying tonight;
　　Dying on the old camp ground.
Walter Kittredge
Tenting on the Old Camp Ground

INTRODUCTION

From the depths of failure began the road to Appomattox. . . . To the host of biographers and historians who have attempted to account for it, the reasons for this meteoric rise have proved an enigma.

William B. Hesseltine
Ulysses S. Grant: Politician

THE LAST YEAR OF ULYSSES S. GRANT'S LIFE WAS THE SHORT CAREER of a once-great old man dying and, in dying, becoming great again.

When the Civil War ended, Grant, along with George Washington and Abraham Lincoln, was one of the heroes in the American pantheon. He was the general who had won the war. But there had been pitfalls since Appomattox—a disastrous presidency, a humiliating defeat while seeking a third term in office, and total personal bankruptcy. Now, at the end of his life, Grant rallied his strength in a way that those generations who had fought under him knew he would do. And so his glory was resplendent when thousands filed past his catafalque in 1885.

Only twelve years later, when William McKinley, the last President to have served in the Union army, dedicated Grant's Tomb in 1897, the ranks of the veterans of the Civil War were thinning out. With the demise of these generations there was a transformation in the way people looked at Grant. Washington and Lincoln remained constant stars. Grant did not.

In 1900—the year is significant—the popular novelist Owen Wister wrote the first openly critical biography of Grant. It was an objective work offering a moral assessment unencumbered by military considerations or political partisanship. Neither hostile nor defamatory, it insisted convincingly that Grant drank himself out of the army in 1854 and that he left no legacy as President. "Great will and indolence," wrote Wister, "met equally in Grant. There-fore he stood still, needing a push from without to move him. We Americans have passed a century in abusing our Army and in electing every military hero we could get for President . . . [but] as

President, Grant was no more himself than he had been when tanning leather."

In 1906, Henry Adams ventured the opinion that Grant had had no right to exist, that he should have been extinct for ages. In *The Education of Henry Adams* he stated: "That, two thousand years after Alexander the Great and Julius Caesar, a man like Grant should be called—and should actually and truly be—the highest product of the most advanced evolution, made evolution ludicrous."

It was true that Grant had behind him a scandal-ridden presidency, a presidency in which the nation for better and for worse took the shape it bears now. Things that might have been done were not done; things that ought not to have been done were. The result was that in the historical reassessment of the post-Civil-War years, Grant fared badly. Even the most eminent of Grant's biographers, Bruce Catton, has said it was Grant's misfortune never to transcend the national character but instead to embody it.

What Grant's critics have overlooked, however, is that while his embodiment of the national character precluded making Grant a great President, it did not preclude making him a great man. And he was a great man because he was capable of massive concentration, which enabled him to see military means and ends as an integral unit. He was great because his restraint and reserve in tumultuous moments inspired greatness in others. "Ulysses don't scare worth a damn," said a Union soldier when the General exposed himself to enemy fire. And William Tecumseh Sherman wrote that his confidence in Grant during the war could be likened "to nothing else than the faith a Christian has in his Saviour."

There was a heroic quality to the course of Grant's life, and something more, too, something at his core that reflected the rough divinity that is America. He was a son of the frontier with the frontier virtues of self-reliance and common sense. He knew intuitively that the way to accomplish a task was to get at it. In his presence others recognized a will and a power that admitted no obstacles. The frontier also invested him with that plastic, surging restlessness belonging to a race of men always wanting to move on. He was, in fact, too restless ever to be wily or devious or dissembling.

He had a dry, perceptive wit. Tone deaf, he said he knew only two tunes: "One of them is 'Yankee Doodle' and the other one isn't." He was the first American to remark that Venice would be a nice little town as soon as they got it drained. Privileged to view the unveiling of "The March to the Sea," by Theodor Kauffman, an artist then in vogue, Grant studied it intently. In the foreground a campfire blazed. Moonlight filled the background. Centered in the picture, in front of a tent in a white shirt without coat or hat, sat General William Tecumseh Sherman. Finally Grant said, "It looks like Cump all right, but I never knew him to wear a boiled shirt."

He had an arresting voice with singular powers of penetration. Speaking in an ordinary tone, he could be heard at surprising distances in an army camp. When he had anything important to say, he would raise one hand, with his fingers at right angles to his other palm, and chop with it as he spoke. He said "immejetly" instead of "immediately" and "Confound it!" instead of "God damn it!" and "chippermonk" instead of "chipmunk."

His spelling was notorious, even subversive. "Sweeping" was "sweaping," "vegetables" was "vegitables," "paralyzed" was "par- lised," "vamoose" was "vamouse," and "in two" was "into." In his letters, the Mexican town of Tepeyahualco became Tipping Ahualco.

War brought out the best in him, as did his wife and family and horses. He was an incredible horseman. He swung from horses' tails when he was three and he managed a team at eight. They said the only way a horse could get rid of young Grant was to lie down and roll over on him. As a young lieutenant in Mexico, he kept the best string of horses in Zachary Taylor's army. And as a Union general he kept the best string in either army. He rode mounts named Jack, Fox, Kangaroo, Egypt, and Jeff Davis, who was named by the Union soldiers who seized him when they overran Jefferson Davis's Mississippi plantation. Grant's favorite charger was Cincinnati, perhaps the most valuable horse ever ridden in battle. He later gave it to the Northwestern Fair in Chicago for the benefit of sick and disabled soldiers, where it brought $10,000 at auction.

His greatness surprised him as much as it did others. He was never a man to put himself forward. He was the last man anyone would spy in a room. He was not ambitious nor did he maneuver for rank. Certainly part of his greatness emanated from his courage. Not everything he attempted was a success, but everything was attended by a magnificent courage, a courage rooted in a clarity of mind and an indifference to physical danger. To have run a fleet of gunboats and transports past the fearsome batteries at Vicksburg when only two of the steamboat masters were willing to encounter the danger, undertaking this with volunteers, accompanying them himself; to have crossed the Mississippi below Vicksburg and, though outnumbered, put his forces between two Confederate armies, one in Vicksburg, the other coming to its relief; to have whipped one and captured the other required rare courage—a courage that accepted responsibility while inviting disastrous failure to achieve success.

Lastly, though he may have been the embodiment of the national character, his life was by no means typical of his times. He came from a two-room Ohio cabin to the White House, but he rode no meteor. He failed as an army captain and he failed as a farmer. The first was the profession for which he had been trained; the second was the profession he said he preferred above all others. Yet, when a West Point classmate once pitied him as a down-and-outer, Grant still took heart in that he was doing the best he could to provide for his wife and children.

His character never weakened. Out of a vast fund of moral reserves he was always able to fight his way back. But his last battle, when he was old and there was only his personal honor to be won, was a harder struggle than his battles in the other times had been. But he did it. He fought and won against incredible odds, and he left no doubt that his courage was imperishable.

PART I

GRANT AMONG THE MILLIONAIRES

The average American is a man who has risen.

William Dean Howells
in a letter to James Russell Lowell

HARD TIMES HAD GATHERED AGAIN FOR ULYSSES S. GRANT. ON SUNDAY afternoon, May 4, 1884, he left his brownstone at 3 East 66th Street and rushed by carriage under hazy skies to see William Henry Vanderbilt, the president of the Pennsylvania Railroad. Grant wanted to borrow $150,000; he needed it immediately, and he was going to the man he knew would give it to him.

William Henry Vanderbilt lived in a mansion at 640 Fifth Avenue that occupied the entire block between 52nd and 51st streets. It had cost so much to build in 1879 that its construction materially benefited the then depressed economy of New York City. Vanderbilt also was the most admiring of the millionaires who boasted they were the friends of Ulysses S. Grant. In 1872, William Henry had helped Henry Clews circulate a petition calling for Grant's reelection as President. "We believe," said the petition, "the sacredness of contracts, the stability of wealth, the success of business enterprise and the prosperity of the whole nation depends upon the election of President Grant." The petition added: "Of course, we expect to share in Wall Street's subsequent prosperity."

Now, on this Sunday afternoon in 1884, Grant explained to Vanderbilt that the city chamberlain of New York had made a sudden withdrawal from the Marine Bank of Brooklyn. The bank was one of the city's depositories, but, more to the point, it held the cash reserves for Grant and Ward, a private investment house of which Grant was a nominal partner. Thus the city's withdrawal imperiled Grant and Ward's ability to conduct business.

William Henry was a cranky man. People suspected it was because his father, "Commodore" Cornelius Vanderbilt, had always referred to him as a "footless boy," even though he had owned a railroad before his father did. William Henry folded his hairy hands over his little round stomach and said, "I care nothing for the Marine Bank, General Grant. To tell the truth I care very little about Grant and Ward. But to accommodate you personally, I will draw my check for the amount you ask. I consider it a personal loan to you and not to any other party."

Vanderbilt later explained that he had tendered the loan simply because the man who asked for it was Ulysses S. Grant. "He is one of us," William Henry said.

Indeed the General was one of the recent millionaires the booming economy of the 1880s had produced. Grant and Ward had catapulted the General's investment of $100,000 into securities worth $750,000, for the use of which the firm paid him monthly interest and reinvested his profits and dividends. Grant had recently boasted to his friend and Civil War biographer General Adam Badeau that for the first time in his life he was able to make withdrawals from his account without worrying about an overdraft. He gave his wife, Julia, $1,000 a month and asked no questions. He wanted for nothing. He had the money to indulge without caution his two extravagances, horses and cigars. He loved big, black cigars. The press had once called him "Smoky Caesar." The cigars were poisonous.

And at sixty-two, he looked like a millionaire. When the Civil War ended he had weighed 140 pounds; in his enlisted man's blouse he was skeletal. Now his shoulders filled out his tailored broadcloth suit and he looked much as he does on a fifty-dollar bill. Clear blue eyes that betokened determination, aggression, and a first-rate intelligence redeemed a face covered by a close-cropped beard and a graying mustache. He had a Cromwellian wart on his right cheek. Thin lips formed a horizontal line and the square, heavy jaw was rigid and tenacious.

He was not, however, prepossessing. His five feet eight inches were shortened by a slight horseman's stoop, and he was retiring. Grant would rather not enter a crowded room than try to command it. Many found him at first shy. But, obviously, he was still a man who could meet emergencies, and he left Vanderbilt's mansion with the money.

By Monday noon the crisis was presumably over. Grant's partner, Ferdinand Ward, assured him of this by saying he had deposited Vanderbilt's check in the bank. The General went back to his work. Actually he did not participate in the transactions of Grant and Ward. His private offices were above those of the firm, which were located on the ground floor of a building on the corner of Wall Street and Broadway. On the second floor, Grant presided as the unsalaried president of the Mexican Southern Railroad. Mexico had enthralled him since he had first seen it as a young lieutenant in Zachary Taylor's invading army. He spent much of his time, too, lobbying for an isthmian canal between the Atlantic and Pacific oceans. He also spent time surrounded by friends at the chattering stock market ticker downstairs. Now he returned to these preoccupations unconcerned.

But the Vanderbilt loan had by no means secured the situation. Ferdinand Ward confided the still-desperate plight of the bank to the General's son, Ulysses S. Grant, Jr. He was called "Buck" because he had been born in Ohio, the Buckeye State. Far from securing the Marine Bank, $150,000 was only a drop in the bucket in terms of the bank's immediate needs. What the bank had to have was another half-million dollars, and it needed the money within the week.

The working Grant of Grant and Ward was Buck, and on hearing Ward's latest statement, he betook himself to the offices of the financier and speculator Jay Gould. The sharklike Gould looked over the list of stocks owned outright by Grant and Ward and said he wouldn't lend hatpins on such securities. This blunt refusal worried the ever-trustful Buck. Leaving Gould's office, Buck decided the Grants could not do more borrowing on behalf of the Marine Bank.

Buck was also a junior member of a prestigious law firm. He consulted that Monday afternoon with the senior partner, Samuel D. Elkins. Elkins represented the interests of Buck's father-in-law, Senator Jerome Chaffee, who owned silver mines in Colorado and who had helped capitalize Grant and Ward with an investment of $400,000. Elkins said he and Buck had better pay Ferdinand Ward a visit.

That evening Mrs. Ward admitted them to the parlor at 81

Pierrepont Street in Brooklyn but said her husband was not at home. Elkins and Buck said they would wait. Servants offered them cakes and wine. Ward did not show up until after midnight. Then he agreed that the Marine Bank had to take care of itself. He was annoyed when Elkins, on Senator Chaffee's behalf, demanded $400,000, but he promised to pay the money in the morning.

On their way home, Buck ingenuously asked Elkins why the demand for the senator's security. Elkins stared at the young innocent and said, "The whole thing is suspicious. Did you observe Ward had his slippers on? He was in the house all the time and was afraid to come down and see us."

Complying with Elkins's demand, Buck drew a check on the account of Grant and Ward and sent it to the Marine Bank on Tuesday morning. The officers of the bank refused to pay it. Then they lowered the great iron shutters on the Wall Street entrance, shut and locked the doors at the other end, and announced that the Marine Bank had suspended. A last depositor was just out the door when the shutters slammed down behind him. He had the consolation of standing on the bank steps and describing his experience to a rapidly gathering crowd.

Before noon, another institution, the First National Bank, threw out three checks drawn by Ward on his personal account in the amounts of $85,000, $80,000 and $25,000, because he had a balance of slightly more than a thousand dollars.

The General was unaware of these events when he arrived at his office and alighted from his hansom cab late Tuesday morning. The city was crystalline under a benign sun. But an earthquake was shaking the offices of Grant and Ward. The General made his way with a cane to the entrance; he still limped from a bad fall on the ice on Christmas Eve. The doorway was crowded with angry, gesticulating men. Inside, other men were clamoring for their money and their investment certificates. Buck stood near, coatless and harassed. When he saw his father he said, "The Marine Bank closed this morning. Ward has fled. We cannot find our securities."

The old warrior wordlessly took in the scene. Without a quiver, he limped past the milling crowd and slowly ascended by elevator to his office. Suddenly he knew that he was ruined, swindled, not only a pauper but hopelessly in debt. What had made him a masterful general was his ability to gauge precisely the worth of his subordinates. During the war, he could issue clear, direct, bold orders and *know* that Sherman or Sheridan or Meade would be in the right place at the right time. But it is one thing to know whether a man can soldier and another to know whether he is honest. And Grant made more wrong guesses than right ones about men's honesty.

Nor was this the first time he had been swindled. The General had an unfortunate history as a victim. He was a man easily swindled, easily used—a mark. Swindlers and users will find a mark even though he is a continent away and living in a cave. Grant was never that hard to find. As a thirty-two-year-old first lieutenant at Fort Vancouver in the Oregon Territory, and later at Fort Humboldt in California, Grant had earned $480 a year, to which the government added $197 to meet the costs of boom times in the West. This was hardly enough money to transport a wife and two children from Ohio, let alone support them when they got there. Seeking more money, Grant and three fellow officers formed a partnership on a visit to San Francisco. Pooling their earnings, they leased the Union Hotel on Kearney Street and renovated it as a billiard club and boarding house. But the agent they hired to run the establishment collected the rents and promptly decamped.

On another occasion, in 1859, Grant swapped sixty cleared and cultivated acres in Missouri for a house in St. Louis. It was a narrow clapboard structure with two tiny upstairs windows and a side porch askew. It was also a house whose title was unclear and whose mortgage was in default. He had, of course, to surrender the house a few months later and find another. It took eighteen years, until he became Andrew Johnson's Secretary of War, for Grant to recover the farm whose possession he had lost.

These were the swindles he could laugh about when he became a four-star general. But then the swindlers became more acute, more cunning. He tolerated three notorious brothers-in-law without a murmur of reproach. As President he discovered some friends so insidious they made the brothers-in-law seem like boyish pranksters. Men he trusted swindled the United States government out of millions of dollars. And there was not one group of friends who did so, there were several.

[7]

Still, they had never swindled him of his reputation. The constituency always saw him as the general who had held the muddy blue lines together at Shiloh. But now a swindler had made off with his good name. For Grant had accepted for investment not only the sizable sums of friends who called him "General," but also the small pension checks of hundreds of old soldiers who once called him "Sam." The money was gone. He knew it. Worse, there was no way he could redeem their trust. That, too, was gone—plus his money and the mite of two widowed sisters, the life savings of two sons, and Mrs. Grant's inheritance.

The day was ending when George Spencer, the cashier of Grant and Ward, quietly came into the General's office to tell him that Buck had finally located the firm's securities, which were worthless, and that the Vanderbilt check had been cashed by Ward but the money not deposited.

"Spencer," asked Grant, "how is it that man has deceived us all in this manner?"

Spencer could offer no explanation.

Grant's hands convulsively gripped the arms of his chair. "I have made it a rule of life to trust a man long after other people gave him up. I don't see how I can trust any human being again."

The General fell silent. Clutching his useless ledgers, Spencer withdrew. He saw Grant bury his head in his hands. It was not the first time circumstances had gotten the better of Ulysses S. Grant, but it was the first time they made him bow his head.

Like most men able to master the storm centers, Grant could do with very little sleep, and when he needed rest he could fall asleep straightaway in the most uncomfortable of circumstances. Now he was wakeful at night. He was silent in his wakefulness but his mind was a chaos of "hows" and "whys."

The "how" of the ruin lay in the trust he and his second son, Buck, the Columbia law school graduate, had placed in Ferdinand Ward. Ward had induced the General to move from Galena, Illinois, to New York City in 1880 to establish the banking house of Grant and Ward, which numbered four partners, two of them special partners who did not direct the business. These were the General and James D. Fish, president of the Marine Bank of

Brooklyn, on whose reserves the firm could depend for financing in any amount. The two active partners were Buck Grant and Ferdinand Ward. The four partners capitalized the firm at $100,000 apiece. Ward guaranteed a return of 3 percent a month. It never dawned on either the General or Buck that the Grant name and reputation were in themselves a handsome capital investment for a well-secured, reputable firm.

Presidents had retired to their plantations and some had returned to the practice of law. John Quincy Adams had served another seventeen years in the House after leaving office, and Andrew Johnson had returned to the Senate. No ex-President had ever gone into business, and no ex-President had ever joined or started a Wall Street firm. Grant later confessed he should have been more dubious about what he was putting in and more thoughtful about what he was taking out. But he wasn't. In 1880, the prospect of joining a banking house founded on his name and reputation simply overwhelmed him.

He also accepted the partnership with Ward because of Buck. The Grants were indulgent, reasonable, decent, humorous, and loving parents. Matthew Arnold, who had dined with Grant in London, explained Grant's move in a little book about the General. "Like Grant," he wrote, "you may have a son to whom you are partial, and like Grant, you have no knowledge of business. Had you been, like Grant, in a position to make it worth while for a leader in business and finance to come to you, saying that your son had a quite exceptional talent for these matters, that it was a thousand pities his talents should be thrown away, 'Give him to me and I will make a man of him,' would you not have been flattered in your parental pride, would you not have yielded?"

To the silent, wakeful General, the "hows" were obvious. The "whys" were more complex. They had to do with money, about which he had never cared much nor whose possession did he ever seem to need. But money had become a raw force in post-Civil-War America, and Grant admired the clever, savage men who cornered and controlled markets, railroads, industries, and shipping. The making of money had always been a deep mystery to him, and he had a too tolerant sympathy for the men who possessed money without the burden of culture.

[9]

When William Henry Vanderbilt characterized the General as "one of us" he was more accurate than he knew. Commodore Cornelius Vanderbilt started as a ferryboat skipper, Daniel Drew as a cattle drover, Jim Fisk by selling cotton candy in a circus, and Jay Gould as a grocery clerk. They were none of them patricians. Grant did not need money as an entrée to the company of these men nor did he need money to enjoy their friendship. But he thought he did. He wanted to keep up appearances and he said as much.

The final reason why he said yes to Ferdinand Ward was that by now he was a man used to a cornucopia of rewards, a man who had developed the habit of taking things for nothing. It was a habit, he was to find, that cost too much.

In 1861 when Governor Richard Yates made Grant a colonel of the Twenty-first Illinois Volunteers, the new colonel had to return to Galena from Springfield to borrow the money to buy himself a uniform. When he next returned to Galena in 1865 the townsfolk met him *en masse*. The length of Galena's main street supported dozens of garlanded arches on which were inscribed the names of his famous victories. On the last arch was inscribed, "General, the sidewalk is built." Grant had once remarked that the only political office to which he aspired was mayor of Galena, so that he could repair the streets and crossings. Grant passed through this arch followed by a procession of thousands from the surrounding countryside. At the end of the new sidewalk was a home built for the General by the citizens of Galena, paid for through a popular subscription of $16,000. The home was furnished, too, with plush chairs, a gilt clock, a kitchen stove, a portrait of Lincoln on the wall, and even a Bible on a marble-topped table.

Not to be outdone, the city of Philadelphia also presented Ulysses S. Grant with a house worth considerably more than $16,000. When Grant found that his duties as general-in-chief of the army required residence in Washington, he offered to return the gift, but the Philadelphians released him from all obligations.

The Grants' house on I Street in Washington was also purchased through popular subscription. The chairman of the committee was A. T. Stewart, who had started by importing Irish lace and now ran the largest mercantile establishment in the country. Grant sold the house when he became President. He nominated A. T. Stewart as Secretary of the Treasury.

The Union League Club in New York, at a dinner and reception for the General in February, 1866, presented him with a portrait of General Winfield Scott by William Page. The affair was one of the most prestigious and noteworthy ever staged by the Union League Club, and elite clubs and organizations elsewhere hurried to emulate it. Boston gave the General a library reputedly worth $5,000.* The library, incidentally, had the serendipitous result of transforming the General's oldest son, Fred Grant, a West Pointer, into a noted bibliophile. By 1881 Fred owned the most extensive collection of Samuel Johnson and Alexander Pope first editions and pamphlets in the United States, which he sold at auction in order to buy his way into his father's new firm.

There were also fourteen horses that admirers gave him at different times, blooded horses so valuable that once two kidnappers tried to steal several of them from the famous Martin's Farm in Maryland and hold them for ransom.

There is every reason to believe Grant looked upon the presidency itself as a reward rather than a responsibility. He thought nothing of summoning a navy cruiser to transport him from Washington, D.C., to Long Branch, New Jersey. And he was out- raged that people accused him of a salary grab when he signed a bill raising his pay from $25,000 to $50,000 a year. Grant pointed out that he had affixed his signature to the bill on March 3, 1873, but that it was not to take effect until the following day, when his second term commenced. In other words, he did not receive an increase during the term in which he signed the pay raise. He also pointed out he was not receiving a retroactive raise, as were congressmen. And finally he explained that he signed the bill only to raise the salaries of cabinet officers and Supreme Court jus- tices.

* Grant was always proud of the collection and kept it in the White House. The books were in the best leather bindings with marbled sides and edges. They ranged in content from a John Audubon portfolio through Cervantes, Schiller and Harriet Beecher Stowe to Zschokke's *Meditations on Death and Eternity*. Buck inherited the library and took it with him to San Diego in 1893. In 1952 Dawson's Book Shop purchased the collection and offered the volumes for sale individually. The Audubon went for $500, the Zschokke for $3.50.

He had been elected because he won the war and deserved the appreciation of the American people. That is what the millionaires told him, what the generals in politics told him, and the politicians seeking patronage told him. And that is what Grant believed, that things were coming to him.

So Ferdinand Ward was just another in the train of important men who wanted to assure the General of a comfortable old age. The Wall Street venture was made more enticing to the General by two more subscriptions raised by the millionaires that were meant to secure him for as long as he needed security. The first of these, started in 1880, was headed by George Childs, publisher of the Philadelphia *Public Ledger*, a partner and intimate of the Drexels, later a biographer of Grant, and the donor of the Grant, Sherman, and Sheridan portraits that hang in Grant Hall at West Point.

Childs collected $100,000 from twenty millionaires, among whom were J. Pierpont Morgan, Anthony Drexel, Thomas Scott, and Hamilton Fish, who, as Grant's second Secretary of State, was the only member of the cabinet to serve through both of the General's administrations. Fish wrote to Childs that he was on principle opposed to such gifts, thinking that Congress, in all decency, ought to give an ex-President a pension of $25,000 a year. Fish, however, included his contribution because he was glad to have Grant as a neighbor in New York. The $100,000 raised by Childs purchased the brownstone house on East 66th Street.

Made of a reddish-brown limestone, the house was typical of the upper-middle-class row dwellings in the city. It was four stories high with a mansard roof covering an attic. On the sidewalk level were the kitchen, pantry, milkroom, and servants' quarters. A steep stone staircase with filigreed iron bannisters led to the front door, on either side of which were two big bay windows. Past the foyer to the right was the dining room, in communication with the kitchen by dumbwaiter. To the left was the living room, antimacassars on the sofa, ottomen at the ready by the chairs. To the rear was the conservatory, a room the family inhabited when there were no visitors. On the next story was the library to one side, the sewing room to the other. Behind each of these was a short row of bedrooms and utility rooms. More bedrooms occupied the fourth story.

The house carried a $50,000 mortgage. The trustees of the

Childs subscription had paid $48,000 for the title. They deposited the remaining $52,000 with Grant and Ward to be applied toward the purchase of gilt-edged stocks that Ward never bought.

A second subscription, initiated in the same year, was the project of George Jones, co-founder of *The New York Times*. In November, 1880, the *Times* appealed for a popular subscription of $250,000, the interest from which would be paid to the oldest ex-President. The *Times* hoped to match the quarter dollar of the laborer with the $10,000 of the millionaire. "Were it for no other reason than the evidence it gives of the generous and patriotic impulses of men who control a large share of the wealth of the United States, the raising of the fund for the benefit of General Grant would deserve to be reckoned among the most encouraging of recent public achievements," commented Jones windily.

The mechanics of a public subscription proved so formidable that Jones undertook to raise the $250,000 himself from 168 individuals, among whom were men as diverse as Vice President Chester A. Arthur, who contributed $500, and Jay Gould, who contributed $25,000. "I'd give $1,000,000 to have Grant as President again," Gould remarked to Jones.

The trustees invested the fund in Wabash Mainline Railroad, which guaranteed $15,000 a year in interest. Neither of these subscriptions were anomalies. Not too long before, the Congress had finally determined upon retirement pensions for army and navy officers; and in 1881 Cyrus Field, promoter of the transatlantic cable, headed a subscription to raise $325,000 for the penniless widow and children of the assassinated James A. Garfield.

Thus, when Ulysses S. Grant moved from Illinois to New York City, he had an income of $10,000 from rental properties, $15,000 from the Jones subscription, and a house of his own. And he had an investment of $100,000 in the firm of Grant and Ward. Buck had also invested $100,000, plus the money from his father-in-law, Senator Chaffee. What neither the General nor his son realized when they collected their interest, which often amounted to $3,000 a month for each, was that they were collecting their own money. Ferdinand Ward and James D. Fish also collected $3,000 apiece. But they had not put up any money to capitalize Grant and Ward;

they had put up only securities, mere paper—paper on which they fraudulently printed nonexistent holdings.*

The son of a Baptist minister from Geneseo, New York, Ferdinand Ward came to the city in 1875. Through a friend of his father he secured a clerkship on the Produce Exchange that paid $1,000 a year. He also made some marginal speculations in flour that proved successful. Then Ward met and married Henrietta Green, daughter of Sidney Green, cashier of the Marine Bank. Through this connection, he was able to borrow money from James D. Fish, with which he purchased Produce Exchange seats for $200 to $300. Within a year, these seats sold for $3,000 and $4,000. He bought and sold elevated railway securities, another profitable speculation. Before he was thirty Ward was considered one of the sharpest financiers on Wall Street. Tall and handsome, he was magnetic, persuasive, and infinitely polite. The sharks said he knew how to lend money at high rates without risk, that he could buy cheap and sell dear, and that left to his own devices he could probably reduce the national debt.

Every morning Ferdinand Ward put twenty-five Havana cigars on the General's desk. He stopped in three or four times a day with papers for the General to sign, and at the end of the month Ward answered any question Buck or the General put to him about the books. That was the extent of the General's participation in the business.

Both Ward and the General had agreed not to lend money on government contracts. As an ex-President, Grant thought it was unseemly for him to solicit government business; he knew also there were no large profits in government contracts except by dishonest methods. Ward agreed. Government contracts in those days were let to a large variety of suppliers and speculators who agreed to furnish the army, the trading posts, the settlements, or the federal agencies with oats, wheels, meat, barrels, or bricks at a stipulated price. The suppliers then borrowed money at high rates of interest to fulfill their agreements. These contractors defaulted on their payments as often as they cheated on their supplies. But govern-

* Buck testified later that he discovered this deceit, but at the time of his discovery things were going so swimmingly he didn't want to lose his temper.

ment contracts constituted a large commerce, highly speculative and somewhat notorious.

Actually, Ward was telling Grant's friends and colleagues that, of course, the firm was lending money on these contracts, but lending it covertly; that because of the General's influence and his contacts, the payments were virtually assured; that Ward and the General were willing to let a friend in on a particularly promising deal. Grant had a wide circle of wealthy friends on whom Ward called and an even wider circle of would-be friends. When Ward finished his litany of the firm's growth, the friends and the would-bes were certain the General was doing them a service by accepting their money.

Ward was an especially gifted confidence man. He had perfected the technique whereby the victim acquiesces in his own fleecing. The confidence man—the term is of American not European coinage—was a denizen of Wall Street and the Mississippi riverboats, and he was already by this time a staple of American fiction. Washington Irving wrote about the Dutch burghers conning the Indians of Manhattan, and Edgar Allan Poe wrote stories in the 1830s and '40s describing small-time con men tricking innocents out of small change by elaborate means. The con man in frontier literature often served as the personification of Andrew Jackson and his wiles were seen as the result of Jacksonian democracy. Herman Melville constructed an elaborate metaphysic in his novel *The Confidence Man: His Masquerade*, published in 1857. The apotheosis of the confidence man was realized in the characters of the Duke and the King in Mark Twain's *The Adventures of Huckleberry Finn*, published in 1884. Many of the authors who described "cons" were themselves victimized by confidence men, Mark Twain included.

When one of Grant's friends stopped by and asked what had transpired with his investment of $50,000, the General tapped a little silver bell on his desk and Ward materialized as quickly as if he had been the sentry at the door. When Ward produced the report, he invariably accompanied it with a check for $100,000. No one but a foolish investor would have withdrawn his money from Grant and Ward at that instant. "Set that hen again," the investors said. Their money appeared to be doubling and quadrupling on loans advanced to the Erie Railroad, on the purchase of city bonds, and by astute stock manipulations.

But the money was not doubling or quadrupling at all. Ward was running a "bucket shop," a phrase his machinations helped popularize.* Ward never bought the stocks he promised. He never bought any stocks with the money entrusted to him. He used the money to return dividends to earlier investors. He was pyramiding debt. He was also, in the jargon of the day, "rehypothocating" loans, which is to say he lent money on securities he accepted as collateral and then borrowed more money than he had lent by using the same securities. The firm survived as long as it did because Ward could draw money at will from the Marine Bank. James D. Fish accepted promissory notes from the clerks and messengers at Grant and Ward's in the amount of $50,000, $60,000, and $80,000. These he discounted, which is to say he sold them and entered the transactions as a legitimate profit. Clerks and messengers could not possibly repay $50,000, $60,000, and $80,000 loans. The duped clerks and messengers handed the money over to Ward, who collected more than $2 million this way.

At his Brooklyn home Ward stabled five horses. He maintained as well a palatial home in Stamford, Connecticut. There he entertained General and Mrs. Grant on summer weekends, and such other luminaries as the General's presence could attract— Chester A. Arthur, James G. Blaine, and J. P. Morgan, among others. He might well have gone on forever but the Marine Bank could not.

James D. Fish, president of the Marine Bank, came from Stonington, Connecticut, and had achieved his eminence in finance by hard work, diligence, and acuity. A widower, he lived in a suite above the bank and was a warm patron of the arts, the artists, and especially the artistes. He confessed that he realized earlier than most that Ward was gulling him. By the time he realized this, however, he was in too deep to get out and he went along taking his payoff every month, holding to the illusory hope that one of Ward's schemes would succeed and they could pay off a dangerously growing list of suckers.

* The con man accepts money and an order. He spends the money as he chooses and throws the order in the bucket.

Fish deceived his board of directors by "cooking" the books—listing promissory notes, loans, and worthless stock as cash reserves. The bank was a depository for municipal funds, and when the city chamberlain withdrew $1 million he drew out every dime the bank had.

The failure of the Marine Bank annoyed rather than threatened other reputable banks and investment houses. Whatever the General and his friends thought about the firm of Grant and Ward, the smart money had never rated it one of the powers of Wall Street. Its operations had always excited more skepticism than admiration.

The public had no such sophistication, and the failure of the bank and the firm set off a small panic. Other shaky houses collapsed. There were runs on several of the banks. The newly incorporated City of Long Island had collected two thirds of its taxes and placed these on deposit with the Marine Bank. The Long Island City Common Council met hurriedly and passed a resolution that hereafter it would deposit its money in a local bank and assign the entire police force to guard it.

At least twelve members of the Union League Club had contributed over $500,000 to a "blind pool" run by Ferdinand Ward, who had paid back a small proportion in dividends and used the rest in wildcat speculation. Congressman Freeman Clark found that of the $50,000 he had deposited, $40,000 was immediately negotiated. "The failure is the most colossal that ever took place among merely private firms in the United States," editorialized the *New York Post*, "and the next bank president who wants to live over his bank will have to show that the bank does not suffer by his too close application to its affairs." It went on to say that, "The conclusion is irresistible that a large number of persons were drawn into the maelstrom by a belief held out to them that General Grant's influence was used in some highly improper way to the detriment of the government and the benefit of Grant and Ward." The papers were to point out that Ward lived at a rate of $50,000 a year but they did not add parenthetically that the General lived far more modestly.

The sleeplessness produced a decision. On Wednesday morning the General and Buck went downtown for the last time. In the now deserted office of Grant and Ward they themselves began to go over the books.

Grant sent for his trusted friend ex-Senator Roscoe Conkling, political boss of one faction of the Republican Party. Conkling was a noted corporate lawyer. "Conkling Dumb as the Deeps," reported the *Times* on his visit to Grant's office, but inside the office Conkling had a lot to say to the General and Buck. He told them that they were as liable to the investors as Ward and Fish. As far as Conkling could ascertain from Ward's books, the firm owed at least $3 million. The only succor Conkling could offer was that no investor thought for a second that Ulysses S. Grant had $3 million.

But serious charges were about to be leveled at the General. On Friday, May 9, when the police arrested Fish, he released to the press two letters signed by Ulysses S. Grant. These letters suggested that the General was criminally as well as financially liable. The letters, written in 1882 and addressed to Fish, read:

> . . . Your understanding in regard to our liabilities in the firm of Grant and Ward are the same as mine. If you desire it, I am entirely willing that the advertisement of the firm shall be so changed as to express this.

And again:

> In relation to the matter of discounts [on promissory notes] kindly made by your bank for the account of Grant and Ward, I would say that I think the investments are safe, and I am willing that Mr. Ward should derive what profit he can from the firm that the use of my name and influence will bring.

Fish's argument was that he had committed himself and his bank because he had trusted the word of Ulysses S. Grant, and that Grant had misled the Marine Bank as he had misled the investors in Grant and Ward. It wasn't a good argument. Fish had committed himself and his bank to Ward's depredations long before Grant signed the two letters; in fact, long before there was a Grant and Ward. But the *Sun*, a longtime enemy of Grant, headlined: "Is Grant Guilty?"

The man who could answer that question was Ferdinand Ward, but he had disappeared from his home in Brooklyn. Mrs.

Ward opened the door to police, who made a thorough search of the premises. The police posted a guard at 81 Pierrepont Street day and night to apprehend Ward if he appeared. Until he did so, the question of Grant's complicity went unanswered.

Then, on May 26, Ward turned himself in to a Manhattan precinct. He was ashen, shaken, and his ears seemed to hang from his head. He was able to post bail the next day. He asked the sheriff's deputy who released him to drive him around to Grant's home on East 66th Street. The deputy was kind enough to wait for Ward because the Grants refused to see him.

Before he was indicted by a United States Court, Ward admitted to a prosecutor and to newsmen that he had gotten Grant's signature on the damaging letters by a ruse. He had simply slipped the letters in a pile of correspondence ordinarily prepared for the General's signing. This was confirmed by George Spencer, the cashier, the only honest businessman at Grant and Ward— Buck could hardly be counted as a businessman. Spencer testified that on Fridays the General would sign anywhere from ten to fifty letters at a sitting.

Ward was eventually tried by New York State on a charge of grand larceny. At his trial he admitted he had been insolvent for two years. He was unable to recall when he had bought either his houses or the furniture for them. He tried to define the differences between the "books of the firm" and the "books of the office." The "books of the firm" were the books the General never saw. Ward also admitted having deposited the Vanderbilt check in his personal account. But he said for the life of him he could not remember what he had done with the money. He confessed to borrowing money for pretended investments, paying profits out of principal, inducing lenders to leave the remainder in his hands. Finally, he confessed that he could no longer decipher his own books, the "books of the firm." After two years of careful analysis, a receiver of Grant and Ward announced the liabilities of the firm amounted to $16,792,640 and its assets amounted to $67,174.

Grant was left in the middle. Despite Ward's revelations, some charged him with complicity. He had heard such charges before, when he was President. They were not demoralizing then, but they were now. Those who defended him made him out the fool. "That General Grant never had an aptitude for the kind of business in which the firm was engaged," editorialized the *Tribune* in May, 1884, "and was of such nature as to trust his business affairs absolutely to those who seemed competent to take care of them was well known before a breath of suspicion had fallen on the firm."

There were other, more considered judgments. General Phil Sheridan said it had tried his heart sorely to hear Grant discussing stocks and bonds and debentures in Wall Street. And William Tecumseh Sherman said that the rich men Grant cultivated would have given all their money to have won one of the General's battles.

The truth is that some men are equipped by nature to consort with millionaires. Grant was not. Millionaires were to the General in his late years what alcohol had been to him in his early ones.

He was the first general in the modern age to know instinctively how to deploy effectively armies numbering hundreds of thousands of men. And he could carefully plan the transportation of hundreds of thousands of tons of matériel to keep those armies moving. He could inspire men to hew roads around the treacherous cone of a mountain and he could plan for other men how to move matériel through bayous where the water breasted the caissons' wheels. But he was sometimes inept when it came to providing for a wife and four children. He never understood that day-to-day life often demands the same ruthless pragmatism war demands.

"Financially, the Grant family is ruined and by one of the most stupendous frauds ever perpetrated," wrote Grant to his niece, Clara Cramer. "But your Aunt Jennie [Grant's sister] must not fret over it. I still have a home and as long as I live she shall enjoy it as a matter of right; at least until she recovers what she has lost. Fred [the General's eldest son] is young, active, honest and intelligent and will work with a vim to recuperate his losses. Of course his first effort will be to repay his aunts."

The failure of Grant and Ward devastated the entire family. The sister that Grant mentioned, Virginia Corbin, had lost her widow's mite of $5,000. His daughter Nellie, who lived in London with her English husband, Algernon Sartoris, had lost $12,000. Buck, besieged by creditors and challenged by a phalanx of plaintiffs, was destitute and unemployable. With his wife, Fannie, he had to seek refuge in his father-in-law's house. Frederick Dent Grant, who had resigned his army commission in 1881 to become a vice-president of a furniture company, lost his savings and more— within the week creditors repossessed his home in Morristown, New Jersey, and he, his wife, and two children were forced to move in with the General at the East 66th Street house.

On the evening he was ruined, Ulysses S. Grant had $81 in his wallet, and Julia Grant had $130 between her purse and the cookie jar. Checks the General had written so confidently in the past weeks began coming back.

What made the failure catastrophic for the Grants was that, a year before, the Wabash Mainline Railroad had ceased paying dividends on the investment made by the Jones subscription. The Wabash owed Grant between $30,000 and $40,000 in interest. Jones had made the investment in the Wabash on the recommendation of ex-Governor Edwin Morgan of New York, who had personally guaranteed both the capital and the return. In fact, the trustees of the subscription had paid Morgan 2 percent over the market price of the bonds in return for his guarantee. But Morgan had died and the executors of his estate were not particularly anxious to reimburse the fund. They argued that, since the Wabash was in default, they had the right to hand over the coupons to the Wabash and have it settle with the trustees. Grant had received $18,000 from this subscription. The munificence of the millionaires rewarded the Wabash, not the General. In fact, the munificence was never to reward him.*

Julia Grant had in her name two small houses in Washington, D.C. She wrote W. J. McClean, a family friend, and asked if he would buy them. McClean promptly paid her the market price, not quite $3,000 apiece, but the money didn't reach her for several weeks. In the meantime, stripped of all cash, General and Mrs. Grant had to depend upon miracles for sustenance and daily expenses.

The first of these was bestowed by a complete stranger, Charles

---

* Eventually the trustees of the Jones subscription, who came to number any who had contributed $5,000 or more, received $188,000 from Morgan's estate, which they reinvested and many years later divided among Grant's descendants *per stirpes*.

Wood of Lansingburg, New York, who sent the General a check for $1,000. Wood wrote that the money was a loan "on account of my share for services ending in April, 1865."

The second was bestowed by Mathias Romero, the Mexican ambassador, who came directly from Washington to New York when he learned of Grant's misfortune. Romero was a cultivated, European-educated *criollo*, a Spaniard born in Mexico. He had fought with Juárez, and arrived in Washington in 1865 as the emissary of a burgeoning republic that was still struggling against Maximilian. "Their friendship was the more remarkable," wrote Adam Badeau, the General's most compulsive biographer, "because Grant as a rule was not fond of foreigners."

The United States recognized Romero as the Mexican representative in 1866. However, for political reasons, he could exchange no courtesies with the ministers of France, Austria, and England, which lessened his diplomatic consequence in Washington. To enhance Romero's position, General-in-Chief Grant showed him deference and attention. Romero enjoyed the gratification of introducing Mexican President Benito Juárez to Washington at a reception at General Grant's home. Romero found Ulysses S. Grant an ardent champion of Mexican independence and the affection between them was an abiding one. At fetes honoring one, the other was always called upon for a testimonial. Romero was a small man, bald, with popeyes, a pencil mustache, and gracious manners.

Romero tried to press money upon the General, who told him he needed nothing. The General was invariably imperturbable during crises, and it is a measure of their friendship that Romero quickly saw through this. He surreptitiously left $1,000 on the foyer table when he departed. Grant recognized Romero's desire to help, and took the money because he needed it. Besides, Romero's money was not as troubling a debt to the General as the one he owed William Henry Vanderbilt.

Vanderbilt, on the eve of departing for Europe, dispatched a lawyer to the Grants. That gentleman politely told Ulysses and Julia Grant that Vanderbilt considered the $150,000 a debt of honor, and that in his heart Vanderbilt was assured the General would repay him when convenient. The millionaire was trying to forgive the debt, at least for the immediate present.

Grant, however, considered a debt of honor a presumptive debt. He told the lawyer that he still had resources, which he would use to redeem his honor. The lawyer, to whom the boasts of bankrupts were no novelty, left it at that.

Grant proceeded to strip himself of everything. Literally everything. He owned a farm on the Gravois River outside of St. Louis, a farm he had reclaimed from virtual wilderness. The farm was worth $60,000 in 1884. He also owned his house in Galena, another in Philadelphia, and two undeveloped lots in Chicago. But all told, these properties did not add up to $150,000. So the Grants included in their transfer to Vanderbilt various household effects and personal possessions which had a value far beyond their monetary worth.

These consisted of swords presented to Grant by citizens and soldiers; the maps he used in his campaigns; fifteen buttons Julia had snipped from his uniforms after victories; engraved cards ordered struck by Congress to express the nation's gratitude; a gold medal from Congress to celebrate the reopening of the Mississippi after Vicksburg; the shoulder straps from coats worn as he besieged Richmond and Petersburg; the pen he used to write his orders during the Battle of the Wilderness; and canes and medals. There was also a gold lacquer cabinet, given to the General by the Mikado; teakwood cabinets, jade and porcelain from Li Hung-chang, a Chinese statesman, "the Bismarck of Asia"; malachite and enamels from Russia; a gold model of the table in the McLean house on which the surrender terms were signed; a collection of Japanese coins, the only duplicate of which was in the Japanese treasury; elephant tusks from the King of Siam; and a Coptic Bible taken by Lord Napier from King Theodore of Abyssinia.*

Upon his return from Europe, Vanderbilt found all these items in his expansive foyer, where his lawyer had wisely elected to store them. The deeds for the Grant properties were on his desk. Immediately Vanderbilt tried to return the assignment to the General. More than refusing, Grant insisted that Vanderbilt enter a

---

* The General used to hoist his grandchildren piggyback to let them look at the encased trophies, and even let them play with the medals, the gold table, and the coins, until grandmother Julia shooed them away and put the artifacts back into their cases, saying they were not playthings.

judgment against his estate to secure the properties and valuables without encumbrances. Annoyed rather than satisfied, the millionaire grudgingly went to court. Grant appeared, allowing a judgment to be taken against him in the amount of $155,417.20, the loan plus interest.

"Now that I am at liberty to treat these things as my own," wrote Vanderbilt to Julia Grant after the judgment, "the disposition of the whole matter most in accord with my feelings is this: I present to you as your separate estate the debt and judgment I hold against Grant; also the mortgages upon his real estate and all the household furniture and ornaments coupled only with the condition that the swords, commissions, medals, gifts from the United States, cities, and foreign governments and all articles of historical value and interest shall at the General's death, or if you desire it sooner, be presented to the United States Government at Washington where they will remain as perpetual memorials of his fame and of the history of his times."

To this the General replied that Mrs. Grant could not accept his offer in the whole, although she would make sure that the articles of historical value would be delivered to Washington as soon as possible. "I have only to add," concluded the General, "that I regard your giving me the check for the amount without inquiry as an act of marked and unusual friendship."

Stubbornly, Vanderbilt persevered. "I must insist," he wrote back, "that I shall not be defeated in a purpose to which I have given so much thought and which I have so much at heart. I will, therefore, as fast as the money is received from the sale of real estate, deposit it in the Union Trust Company . . . and will create with that company a trust with proper provisions for the income to be paid to Mrs. Grant during her life."

Grant conceded. "Your generous determination compels us to no longer resist." But, if Vanderbilt thought that was the end of the matter, he was wrong. Julia Grant wrote to him:

> Upon reading your letter of this afternoon General Grant and myself felt it would be ungracious to refuse your princely and generous offer. Hence his note to you. But upon reflection I find I cannot, I will not accept your munificence in any form. I beg that you will pardon this apparent vacillation and consider this answer definite and final.

The situation distressed Vanderbilt. On the one hand, colleagues whispered that he was avaricious; and on the other hand, he genuinely admired and loved the General. In the end, he prevailed upon Grant to let him publish their private correspondence, so that he could still the rumors which, if they were not blackening his name, at least were sullying his willingness of heart. The exchange of notes between Vanderbilt and the Grants consequently appeared in the *New York Tribune* of Monday, January 12, 1885, under the headline "A Generous Creditor." It was something of an epitaph for William Henry Vanderbilt, who had less than a year to live when the paper made plain his generosity.

It is reasonable to conclude that Grant wanted to quit the millionaires on his own terms and leave their company the same man he was when he met them. At the end of the war, George Jones had called him the "Hero of Heroes," and William Backhouse Astor had once introduced him as the "Idol of a Nation." The General was going to have to scrimp and save in order to live. But living was less important than somehow salvaging his self-respect. He sold his horses and carriages and sadly paid off the groom. Julia let the servants go, providing them with severance pay and letters of recommendation. The General still retained the services of his valet, Harrison Tyrell, a black man who had attended him for many years. Julia and the General called him "Faithful Harrison."

At best there was very little time left for a new start. The Grants determined to spend what was to be the last full summer of the General's life in Long Branch, New Jersey. Long Branch was then at its height as a summer resort, hardly the place for contemplative planning. But Grant was no ordinary man. Since the first year of his presidency, Long Branch had offered him surcease from the worry and tedium of his office. After the Grant and Ward failure, New York was a torment. Living in Long Branch was also cheaper and many of the General's friends would be there. Penniless, the Grants left New York for Long Branch on the last day of May. They had been penniless before. Once again, armed with only their own moral resources, Julia and Ulysses S. Grant faced the uncertain future.

PART II

SING IT AS WE USED
TO SING IT FIFTY
THOUSAND STRONG

When asked what state he hails from
Our sole reply shall be
He hails from Appomattox
And its famous apple tree.

Senator Roscoe Conkling
to the delegates of the
Republican National Convention
of 1880

ULYSSES S. GRANT WAS BORN ON APRIL 27, 1822, IN POINT PLEASANT, a small town on the Ohio River, twenty-five miles east of Cincinnati. His father, Jesse, born in 1794, was a transplanted Connecticut Yankee, and his mother, Hannah Simpson, born in 1798, came from Pennsylvania people.

Point Pleasant was a frontier town, no more than a clearing in the forest. Grant was born in a rude clapboard, one-story, saltbox house with two rooms and a shingled roof. The house had two windows, but no porch, veranda, or trimmings. Hannah cooked in one of the rooms, using the fireplace as a stove, and the family slept in the other.

Jesse Grant was a tanner by trade, converting hides into leather and leather goods. The two-room shanty was a temporary affair for him, in the way log cabins generally were temporary for other pioneers. These settlers accepted hard work and privation because they believed unprecedented opportunity awaited them. They were an energetic, muscular people wanting freedom. Freedom was not only the promise that the land would yield to their efforts to clear it, but also that its produce would one day fill their pockets with cash.

By 1822, "Ohio Fever" had brought 450,000 people into the state. Within a year of his son's birth, Jesse Grant moved his family to Georgetown, in Brown County. Twenty-five miles to the east, on the banks of the White Oak Creek, Georgetown was a growing community only four years old. Jesse chose this site because it was back from the Ohio River, in the midst of an oak forest which reached for miles in every direction. From oak bark comes tanbark,

[29]

which, mixed with water, yields tannic acid, the pickle used to cure or tan hides.

New settlers poured over the old Forbes Road to Pittsburgh, and from Pittsburgh into the Western Reserve. Many of them spilled south into Brown County. The forest rang with the sound of axes as the settlers resolutely diminished it, forever enlarging a cleared perimeter. Within a generation Ohio was the fourth most populous state in the Union, and the forest had become rolling farmlands, the stumps of trees yanked from the land like so many infected teeth.

Jesse Grant was enterprising. He had made a good guess and he capitalized on it. In Georgetown he employed hidesmen to transform his trade into a business, a small industry that attracted several more settlers. He acquired two small farms and a fifty-acre tract of forest. He became a contractor when he built the Georgetown jail, and a politician when he became the town's mayor for a two-year term. With Ulysses's help, he operated a carriage service for travelers to other Ohio towns. Eventually he was to own four leather goods stores in Ohio, Kentucky, and Illinois.

Jesse built a two-story brick house in which more children were born over the next seventeen years—Simpson, Clara, Virginia, Orvil, and Mary. He added dormers and rooms, a stable and a tool shed, and eventually a separate dining room so that the house achieved majestic proportions. A wide hall ran the length downstairs and a landing ran the length upstairs.

Another age might have called him the Leather King of Southern Ohio. By 1860, he was worth $150,000, which made him a substantial citizen by the standards of any generation. He was able to put together this fortune and secure his own importance despite his reputation as a disputatious man. Constantly involved in litigation with his customers, Jesse was held in little esteem by his neighbors.

This area of Ohio was populated by Southerners, whose chief crop was tobacco. There was never a time, Ulysses S. Grant remarked later, when the citizens of Georgetown wouldn't have voted for Jefferson Davis over Abraham Lincoln if they could. Jesse Grant was an irritant among them because he was an abolitionist.

In his youth he had worked for Owen Brown, whose son John was to seize the arsenal at Harpers Ferry in October, 1859. Jesse Grant left Kentucky, where he had served his apprenticeship, because he would not own slaves or live in a place where other men owned them.

He was also a Whig in a Democratic community; constantly arguing politics with his customers, reading pamphlets to them to prove his points, bombarding the local newspaper with letters fulsome in their disagreement. He was a braggart, vain and egotistical, a know-it-all who had the added disadvantage among his neighbors of being right more often than wrong on the issues of the day.

Jesse Grant wore gold-rimmed glasses and a Sunday coat every day of the week—affectations in a county that only grudgingly forgave its congressman for shaving daily while in Washington. A man of many affectations and quirks, he would, in the late 1860s, finance the first séances ever held in Ohio. But it must also be said of him that he was inordinately proud of his first son.

Hannah Simpson Grant, though a dutiful mother, was an undemonstrative woman. She never kissed her children, nor was she ever unduly worried about any of the dangers they might encounter. When a neighboring housewife rushed in to tell Hannah that three-year-old Ulysses was playing under the hoofs of the horses in the stable, she remarked that the boy could take care of himself. She never visited a home in which Ulysses lived, not even the White House. When Ulysses S. Grant returned to see her after the Civil War as the first four-star general in his nation's history she said only, "Well, Ulysses, you've become quite a great man, haven't you?" and returned to her household chores. As Georgetown noted Jesse's disagreeable pugnacity, it gossiped about Hannah's indifference.

She was a Methodist, as pious in her faith as Jesse was fierce in his politics. She wanted to live "unspotted from the world," as the brethren put it. In 1822, Methodism was not forty years old in America, but its itinerant preachers had made it the popular religion in the West. Its revivalist tradition and its simple theology, which promised that God would save "those whom he foresaw

[31]

would persevere to the end" and punish "those who should continue in their unbelief," made it the religion of the pioneer.

Hannah Grant abjured worldly things and passions. The one letter of hers that survives, written in her old age, after Ulysses had been President, exults that a grandson who had been "under conviction" had at last "been converted." Her husband converted when he married her, and though the other five children were baptized, Ulysses was not. Nor was he a punctual churchgoer. Hannah herself shrank from the frenzied, uninhibited tent meetings. Perhaps she exempted Ulysses from attendance because the tent sings and the Sunday hymns were a riotous cacophony to his ears, producing in the boy a nervous revulsion. The last thing that would have brought Ulysses S. Grant nearer to his God was music.

Neither Jesse nor Hannah were parents a sensitive boy could easily respond to, nor were they parents an intelligent boy would care to imitate. Their influence induced in Grant a lifelong reticence and modesty. Until he went to West Point he made ineffective contact with people. Instead, he found satisfaction among horses, and in daring to surmount physical obstacles.

He was named Hiram Ulysses; Hiram to honor a maternal grandfather and Ulysses because his father and an aunt had been excited by the mythical Greek hero after reading a translation of François Fénelon's *Telemachus*. The family always called him "Lyss" or "Ulyss," which the neighbors transformed into "Useless" in mockery of his father's boasts. Useless young Grant was not: out of his love of horses, he did all the farm work; and he ground the bark that made the tannic acid, an ever-continuing process. He could sling wet hides along with the strongest hidesmen.

But as a boy growing up in Georgetown, Ulysses paid heavily for his father's braggadocio. When Jesse wrote a lengthy and pointless account of a trip to Texas for the newspaper, *The Castigator*, the other boys nicknamed Ulysses "Tex." Though he often recalled his boyhood and described it as a happy one free from punishments and scoldings, the stories Grant told usually revealed heartbreak.

Georgetown laughed about his bargaining for a horse he dearly wanted when he was eight. The colt belonged to Robert Ralston, a local farmer, who wanted $25 for it. Ulysses pressed his father, but

Jesse said the colt wasn't worth $25. After more of his son's pleading, however, Jesse relented and sent Ulysses to buy the colt. But first he instructed the boy in how to deal for it. Ulysses rode to the Ralston farm and said, "My father says I may offer you twenty dollars for the colt, but if you don't take that I am to offer twenty-two fifty and if you won't take that, twenty-five."

Grant told this humorous story on himself many times, adding, "I certainly showed very plainly I had come for the colt and meant to have him." There is a key phrase he always included in the story, revealing a more profound sentiment than an eight-year-old's naïveté. That phrase is "My father says . . ." The eight-year-old understood that his father was devious, and the grown man who told the story insisted on the same fact. Indeed, Jesse Grant *was* devious.

Several times during the war Jesse Grant tried to exploit his son's fame. On one occasion Ulysses insisted that Jesse stop circulating and publishing letters he had written to him from the battlefield in confidence; on another occasion he demanded that his father stop importuning the Secretary of War for saddle orders. The Secretary of War was not going to place the order with Jesse and the reason he was not was that Ulysses S. Grant was a major general of the United States Army.

Ulysses S. Grant was a man of great restraint. Nevertheless, several times in his life he consciously disassociated himself from his father. In his early teens he told Jesse he did not like tanning. "I'll work at it though, if you wish me to, until I am twenty-one," he said. "But you may depend upon it, I'll never work a day longer at it after that." Jesse took the boy at his word, and said he didn't have to work at it now if he didn't mean to stick to it.

Throughout his life, Grant had a strong aversion to animal blood, which he never overcame. He wanted his meat charred to a crisp, and he did not like fowl, saying, "I could never eat anything that went on two legs." Nor could he bring himself to hunt, though firearms never frightened him and he handled them well enough. It was a curious aversion in a hardened soldier. The knowledge that soldiers bled before they died never deterred him in his plan of battle, nor did the sight of a bleeding dying soldier turn him from his duty.

[33]

There is an obvious wellspring for this aversion. Tanning is bloody, smelly work. Fresh hides come to the tanner glutinous with animal blood and fat, which must be scraped off before curing. The hair is removed by soaking the hide in a tub of lime. Just as Grant didn't want to work in a tannery, following in his father's footsteps, so animal blood became a symbol of those characteristics in Jesse with which he could not sympathize and of which he could not approve.

After the Civil War, when the Congress made his rank permanent, Ulysses S. Grant publicly forswore any share of his father's wealth and therefore wanted no share of the inheritance. It was admittedly a generous move that benefited Grant's brothers and sisters; but it certainly did not benefit his own children, whose interests he usually guarded assiduously. More to the point, Jesse frequently came to Washington at that time, and Grant always put him up in a hotel.

Ulysses grew up in some reaction to his parents—shy, lonely, unimaginative, and prudish. He rarely swore and never told an off-color story. As a general in the field, he always pinned the flaps of his tent securely when he took a bath, where the other generals stood in a tub and asked a fellow officer to splash water over them.

Despite ague—malarial chills, the bane of the pioneer west—Grant grew up with remarkable physical strength. Slinging a wet hide develops knotty back, shoulder, and arm muscles, and when he was forty Grant could still throw a hide with one hand. Farming, too, in a time when the settlers still had to bust the sod with wooden plows or, at best, small iron ones, made him strong.

Boyhood produced in him a fortitude, an ability to bear misfortune and bad luck without crippling self-pity or self-defeating complaint. A boyhood such as his, passed without the influence of an understanding and admirable adult can produce rough bullies—Jesse's boyhood, which was passed in similar fashion, made him a bully and a braggart. But Grant's boyhood, while it eventually made him bold and courageous, also made him tender and gentle. That he later looked upon his boyhood as mischievous and carefree, and upon middle-aged failure as somehow purposeful, demonstrates that fortitude is probably the only effective enemy against despair.

Jesse Grant's inordinate pride yielded many compensations.

Grant was one of the few boys in Georgetown to receive anything more than a rudimentary education. He went to Thomas Upham's village school, where John White, one of the teachers, patrolled the classroom with a long beech switch, flicking it constantly. White made the boys cut and bind these switches into bundles and often exhausted a bundle in a day. White's pedagogical methods were anything but sophisticated; yet what he and teachers like him set out to do, they brought about to pass. They taught boys and girls to read and write and do sums with nothing more at their disposal than a room, a book, and themselves. Of this education Grant said, "They taught me that a noun was the name of a person, place or thing so often I came to believe it."

When he was thirteen, Ulysses lived with an aunt in Maysville, in Mason County, Kentucky. There he attended Richeson and Rand's "subscription" school, so called because the parents of the students subscribed to a salary guarantee for the teachers. A year later Jesse enrolled him in the Presbyterian Academy at Ripley. The milieu at Ripley, on the Ohio River midway between Georgetown and Maysville, was one of ferment and tumult. Ripley was one of the stops on the underground railroad along which slaves were spirited from the South to Canada. Abolitionists met there nightly and the antislavery society staged mass meetings.

Ulysses was marked "studious" by his teachers. The books at Ripley consisted of an *English Reader* and its sequel, Lindley Murray's *English Grammar*, Haven's *Speller and Definer*, Comstock's *Philosophy*, and a geography with pictures of Indians and Chinese. Ulysses got hold of an algebra book, but with no one to tutor him, it remained impenetrable.

Ulysses Grant was also a widely traveled boy. Most boys ventured no farther than Maysville, ten miles distant. But Grant drove teams to Cincinnati, Louisville, and as far south as Flat Rock, Kentucky, on errands for his father. He always loved travel—different places, different sights, new people calming restlessness.

He told his father he wanted to become either a farmer or a down-the-river trader. Though Jesse had extensive farmland, most of it was rented and he was cultivating the rest. He offered none to Ulysses. As for the down-the-river life, it simply wasn't respectable. Certainly it would add no luster to Jesse. Many boys left the farms along the Ohio River to work on the side-wheelers that made for St. Louis, Memphis, Vicksburg, Natchez, and New Orleans. They either made money or got thrown in jail, but they rarely came home once they left.

What Jesse wanted for his son was a college education. It was what Ulysses wanted, too. But Jesse was too thrifty and tight-fisted to pay for it. Moreover, a depression had set in in 1837, and Jesse had five children besides his firstborn. So he determined on West Point, the United States Military Academy, where an education was free. Jesse did more than make this determination, he secured Ulysses's appointment.

When Hannah learned that a neighbor's son had failed his examination at the Military Academy, she told Jesse, who wrote immediately to Senator Thomas Morris asking for an appointment for Ulysses. Morris replied he did not have an appointment to give, but that Congressman Thomas L. Hamer did. Hamer and Jesse had once been staunch friends and political allies. Jesse had stumped for Hamer's election to the Ohio State House. But in 1833 they disagreed over President Andrew Jackson's withdrawal of funds from the United States Bank, and Jesse, standing on principle, steadfastly refused to make peace with Hamer. On Ulysses's behalf, however, he relaxed his principles and wrote Hamer for the appointment.

The letter reached the congressman on March 3, 1839, the last full day of his term. Hamer seized upon the chance to lay aside the old quarrel, and hastily filled out the appointment papers. He knew the boy was named Ulysses, but he could not remember his other name. Then Hamer recalled that Mrs. Grant's maiden name was Simpson, and that settled the matter. It settled the matter for Ulysses, too. Cadet Grant, protest as he might, learned that Ulysses S. would have to do him for the rest of his life as far as the army bureaucracy was concerned.

After forwarding the application to the Secretary of War, Hamer wrote Jesse, "I received your letter and have asked for the appointment of your son which will doubtless be made. Why didn't you apply to me sooner?" The friendship was quickly resumed and lasted until 1847, when Brigadier General Hamer succumbed to dysentery in Mexico. Some of his last hours were spent with Lieutenant Ulysses S. Grant.

Some in Georgetown were outraged by the news that Ulysses would go to West Point. This shy, almost withdrawn boy didn't seem to them capable of military command. Though Ulysses had proved himself an apt enough worker, though he could teach a horse to pace in a single afternoon, though he was certainly brave, the Ohio settlers considered West Point an academic citadel for which the boy was unqualified. One neighbor told Jesse, "I'm astonished Hamer did not appoint someone with intellect enough to do credit to our district." But Jesse, remembering that Ulysses had once named a particularly dumb horse after the man, did not lose his temper. Among those who thought that the appointment would come to no good end was Ulysses himself. The prospect of going off to West Point and consequent failure dismayed him. When, without warning, Jesse told him about the appointment, he replied that he wouldn't go. But as the General put it many years later, "My father said he thought I would, *and I thought so too if he did.*"

On May 15, 1839, he left Georgetown for Ripley, there to catch the steamer to Pittsburgh, then to proceed by boat and train to Philadelphia, New York, and West Point. He was barely past his seventeenth birthday, weighed 117 pounds, and stood five feet one inch high, just one inch over the Academy's minimum requirement.

When the adjutant posted the list of plebes entering the Academy, the upperclassmen gathered around the bulletin board and pinned nicknames on the newcomers. William Tecumseh Sherman, whose own name had been transformed into "Cump" by this process, recalled forty-six years later that he had volunteered "United States" for U. S. Grant. Another upperclassman overruled him by suggesting "Uncle Sam." "Sam stuck," said Sherman, "although a more unpromising boy never entered the Military Academy."

If Sam Grant was unpromising, perhaps it was partly due to his fear of failing, the worry that he would not measure up to a standard that had nothing in common with his hopes and aspirations, ill-formed though they were. He was going to West

Point because his father pushed him into it. And it did not occur to him that thousands of other American boys have gone to school for no other reason than that their fathers pushed them into it, even into West Point.

Small, round-faced, Grant arrived at the Academy wearing yellow, big-toed work shoes and a worn black field hat. He walked with the awkwardness of the veteran horseman, shoulders stooped forward, knees slightly bowed. He was a rustic, a country boy, and as such he had every reason to worry about failure. At that time, half the corps of cadets was composed of Southerners and 45 percent of Easterners. Only 5 percent of the corps came from the West—Ohio, Illinois, Indiana, Michigan, and Wisconsin. Proportionately as many of these Western boys failed the entrance and subsequent examinations as Southerners, roughly half. Easterners did better because their schooling more adequately prepared them for the West Point curriculum.

But Grant did pass his entrance examination, which was not so hard after all. He was asked questions in reading, writing, spelling, and arithmetic through decimal fractions. Having passed, he was issued a uniform, ". . . as tight to my skin," he wrote his mother, "as the bark is to the tree."

Though an obvious rustic—he was often called "Country Sam"—he survived his first year without undue agony or trial. As a plebe, which is short for "plebian," he was expected to attend an upperclassman, hauling and fetching, sometimes without reason. He was also expected to bear without complaint the hazing and humiliation inflicted by all cadets senior to him. The process was supposed to instill discipline, though in many plebes it elicited stubborn disobedience and anger. But not in Grant. He never incurred a demerit for disobedience or resentment. He did incur demerits for inattention and untidiness. A dreamy streak often possessed him, and laziness, as he himself once offered, was his besetting sin.

He spent a good portion of his plebe year eagerly reading the debates in Congress over whether or not to abolish the Military Academy. The proponents of a bill that would close West Point charged that it was "a school of art," "that it had never produced a military genius and never would," and that "it was a breeding ground for snobbery and a waste of money."

There was an element of truth in these charges. West Point in those years resembled a New England educational institution. Its faculty was composed principally of Easterners not always alert to the needs and virtues of the rest of the country. It had adopted a sectarian religion, Episcopalianism, and the cadets were required to attend services every Sunday. Episcopalianism was the one established religion at the time that frowned on antislavery agitation. Thus the issue that was beginning to obsess the nation was never discussed at the Academy.

Grant, who still anticipated failure, saw an honorable escape from West Point in the possible congressional action. The abolition of the Academy would leave his integrity and confidence in himself still reasonably intact. A year later, he was glad the bill had failed. He had not come to love the Academy more—he was never a general who revered the Academy, though he loved the corps of cadets—but he had found his place within it. Grant, a genius at reading maps and assessing facts, had certainly discovered that West Point was not a citadel of intellect. There was, of course, no reason for the Academy to be one. Its purpose was to educate a cadre of officers to staff the United States Army.

What helped Grant find his place was his flair for mathematics. Mathematics came to him quickly, almost as though by intuition. He discovered this precocity in his plebe year; and then, in his second year, the Academy introduced a thoroughgoing course in horsemanship. "Mules and mathematics was what Sam Grant was good for," commented one of his less sympathetic classmates. Sam Grant was often detailed to bust the wild broncs.

When General James B. Fry was a plebe he mistakenly wandered into one of the graduation exercises. The last event of the riding demonstration was Cadet Grant taking a great white horse, York, to an Academy high jump record. Fry wrote that, as they went over the bar, it seemed as if man and beast had been welded together.

The curriculum Grant pursued included French, geology, mineralogy, engineering, political science, geography, English grammar, tactics, and mathematics through trigonometry, analytic geometry, and calculus. He also studied physics, chemistry, and drawing. His sketches and paintings were more than creditable, though Grant never thought so.

He was a quick study, and rarely read his lessons over more than once. To occupy himself during the hours he was required to spend studying he read novels. His plebe-year roommate, Rufus Ingalls, summed him up as ". . . so quick in his perceptions that he usually made very fair recitations even with little preparation. In scientific studies he was very bright, and if he had labored hard he would have stood very high in them."

Grant was far from marking time, however. He planned to finish West Point's four-year course and, upon graduation, secure an appointment there as a mathematics instructor. When the remaining four years of his enlistment were up, he planned to resign and seek a professorship at some respectable college.

"A military life had no charms for me," he said, "and I had not the faintest idea of staying in the army. In a class of more than one hundred I was behind in almost everything. I was within three of the foot in languages and within five of the head in mathematics. I was at the head in horsemanship, but that did not count."

Throughout his life he remained unaffected and was often made uncomfortable by the traditional pomp and heraldry of the soldier's career. Only twice did military panoply inspire him: once when the corps of cadets marched in review for General Winfield Scott, a six-foot-four colossus, resplendent in blue uniform with red sash and a sword that glinted diamondlike; and much later, as general-in-chief, when he took the salutes of the Army of the Potomac, led by Meade, and the Army of the Tennessee, led by Sherman, during the Grand Review of May, 1865.

Among the cadets at the Academy in the early 1840s were Longstreet, Buckner, Hardee, Pope, Ewell, Buell, Rosecrans, Halleck, Hancock, and Thomas. Of these, Grant was a lifelong friend of James Longstreet, called "Pete," later Lee's second-in-command, and Simon Bolivar Buckner, who surrendered Fort Donelson to him and, after the war, served as Governor of Kentucky. Other friends were Rufe Ingalls, who served as commissary general during the war; George Deshon, from Connecticut, nicknamed "Dragon," who later took vows as a Paulist father; Isaac Quinby, called "Nykins"; William B. Franklin, who was graduated number one in the class of 1843; and Fred Dent, from Missouri, with whom Grant roomed in his last year and whose sister he married.

The circle was small. The Southerners excluded Grant because of his Western crudities, and thought him an "uncle-ish" sort of boy. The intellectual leaders generally ignored him, though one of them specified "he was a good fellow and no dullard." Curiously, he was president of the Academy's literary society, in 1843, and a member as well of the Twelve-in-One, a collegiate secret society disguising its name behind the initials T.I.O.

Preferring the middle is not in itself unsoldierly. No one particularly relishes walking point to find the fight, or bringing up the rear to defend against an ambush. Though the undistinguished man in the middle, Grant nevertheless left an impression; more than fifty years later people could vividly recall him as a cadet. One classmate remembered him as a plain, common-sense, straightforward youth; quiet, shunning notoriety, contented while others were grumbling; performing his duties in a perfunctory way; not prominent in the corps, but respected by all. General Joseph J. Reynolds recalled Grant as unassuming, modest, not disposed to assert himself, candid, self-reliant, and never inclined to lead. "He was not a hard student, though he neglected nothing, always held a safe place about the middle of the class and proved proficient in the more difficult and practical studies."

Zealous B. Tower, one of his instructors, wrote in 1897 that Grant ". . . though possessing undoubted capacity to excel, did not evince that strong desire to attain high class standing. The stimulus of ambition seems to have been lacking, otherwise one so mentally strong would not have been content with medium success among his classmates." Another instructor, Dennis H. Mahan, wrote, "Grant was what we termed a first section man in all his scientific studies—that is, one who accomplishes the full course. He always showed himself a clear thinker and a steady worker, belonging to the class of compactly strong men who went at their task at once and kept at it until finished. . . . That Sherman should accomplish something great, I was prepared to learn. But not so in Grant, whose round, cheery, boyish face, though marked with character and quiet manner, gave none of that evidence of what he has since shown he possesses."

Seventy-seven boys entered West Point with Grant in 1839. Thirty-nine were graduated in 1843. Among these, Grant stood twenty-first in the class. Class standings were important. The very top of the class could choose a commission in the Corps of Engineers, the elite branch of the service; those next to the top could choose a commission in the dragoons, as the cavalry was then known. The sad commentary on Grant's class was that not one attained the academic excellence to qualify for the Engineers; and the best horseman in the army was shuffled off to the infantry.

In *Meet General Grant*, W. E. Woodward suggests that Grant's years at the Academy and his indifference to maintaining a surpassing record bespeak more than lack of ambition. Boys from the western frontier were fatigued at seventeen and eighteen. They were forced into an early physical maturity by dawn-to-dusk work in their childhood. Certainly this goes a long way toward explaining the prevalence of ague, consumption, and other debilitating afflictions on the frontier. Grant suffered from both ague and consumption in his early years. When he left the Academy in 1843 he still weighed only 117 pounds, though he had grown seven inches. Until military service in Mexico healed his lungs, Grant worried that his constant cough would do him in. Two of his uncles had succumbed to consumption, as tuberculosis was then called.

Grant confided to John Russell Young, whose *Around the World with General Grant* is one of the primary sources for Grant biographers, "I think West Point is the best school in the world. I do not mean the highest grade, but the most thorough in its discipline. A boy to go through four years in West Point must have the essential elements of a strong, manly character. Lacking any of these he must fail. I hear army men saying their happiest days were at West Point. I never had that experience. The most trying days of my life were those I spent there and I never recall them with pleasure."

If his West Point days prove anything, they prove there was nothing inevitable about any of his career, either the best or the worst. Had he not attended West Point, certainly he would never have commanded the Union forces. But West Point did not make him Lincoln's general any more than it made him Ferdinand Ward's patsy.

General Benjamin F. Butler, himself no West Pointer, served under Grant in the Virginia campaign and was relieved by the General for failing to take Fort Fisher. In his memoirs, Butler wrote: "Grant evidently did not get enough of West Point into him to hurt any; he was less like a West Pointer than any officer I ever knew. . . . The less of West Point a man has the more successful he will be. We see how little Grant had. . . . The whole thing puts me in mind of an advertisement I saw in a newspaper in my youth. It contained a recipe for making graham bread out of unbolted flour mixed with sawdust. The recipe ended as follows: 'N.B.—The less sawdust the better.' "

While Ulysses was at West Point, Jesse Grant entered into a partnership with E. A. Collins, a tanner who lived in Bethel, twenty-five miles nearer Cincinnati. Jesse sold out his Georgetown holdings, and he and Collins established a large wholesale tannery in Bethel and an equally large retail leather goods store in Galena, Illinois. The store prospered enough for Simpson Grant, Ulysses's younger brother, to settle in Galena to help manage it.

The newly commissioned Ulysses S. Grant arrived in Bethel in June of 1843, followed a few weeks later by his uniform. He donned the blousy cap, the knee-length blue tunic with silver buttons running from its priest's collar to waist, and the sky-blue trousers with a one-inch-wide white strip running the length of the seams. Proudly he set off for Cincinnati, where a barefoot urchin announced his entry by running alongside Grant's horse bawling, "Soldier, will you work? No siree, I'll sell my shirt first."

It was worse when he returned to Bethel. The drunken stableman was amusing pedestrians by prancing in the street in a pair of blue trousers on which he had sewn a strip of white cotton sheeting. It was a huge joke to the neighbors, but Grant said he did not value it so highly. His efforts and accomplishments were attended by teasing and humiliation in Georgetown and Bethel, but the truth was that he *had* accomplished something. He had succeeded where many before him failed, and he had succeeded despite an indifference to army life, and without any intellectual or physical headstart. He had vindicated his father's faith in him, a faith that had occasioned ridicule among his neighbors. Grant always loathed ridicule; his seemingly thick skin was only supreme restraint. Men who ridiculed him politically were counted as sworn enemies, and he never forgave them, no matter how profoundly they apologized later or tempered their views.

The early ridicule is supposed to have prompted in Grant a lifelong distaste for formal military dress. In his Civil War photographs, however, he is unquestionably dressed to weather conditions in the field. And though his staff would never win compliments for sartorial splendor, they always looked soldierly. The chances are Grant preferred his comfort. A saber got in his way on horseback, his trousers were constantly tucked within his boots.

But he had a moment of glory in Bethel when he was asked to drill the local militia. Sword flashing in the sun, the young lieutenant bawled the first command, and within minutes the men were keeping step and following precisely the convoluted maneuvers of the manual of arms. The drillmaster knew what he was doing and did it well.

When his furlough was over he went off to active duty as a brevet second lieutenant. A brevet was a commission that promoted an officer to higher rank without the commensurate pay.

Sam Grant joined the Fourth Infantry at Jefferson Barracks, nine miles north of St. Louis, then the largest military reservation in the West, a seventeen-hundred-acre tract with barracks, officers' housing, mess hall, hospital, and ammunition buried in underground magazines.

St. Louis was a thriving Mississippi city with a decided French style. Within the decade, however, thousands of Germans would flow into the city and change its character. Named for the Crusader King of France, St. Louis had been a small trading post when Lewis and Clark left it in 1803 on their expedition to span the continent. When Ulysses S. Grant saw it for the first time, forty years later, it was the gateway city to the Far West, the largest river port in the United States. Paddleboats crowded its piers and slaves were sold at auction from the steps of the city's red courthouse.

The Fourth Infantry numbered 21 officers and 449 enlisted

men, counting musicians, blacksmiths, and mule skinners. Among the officers were Grant's classmates "Pete" Longstreet, Don Carlos Buell, Charles Jarvis, and Richard Ewell. They each earned $64 a month. Grant reported for duty on September 4. By November, accustomed to his routine, he filled his time with a regimen of studies. William Conant Church, head of the West Point mathematics department, had assured him of an appointment to the faculty as soon as the first vacancy occurred.

Not far from the post was White Haven, the home of Fred Dent, Grant's roommate of the year before. Fred, posted to a Great Plains reservation, had stopped off in Bethel to urge that Ulysses call on the plantation. Though it was worked by slaves, White Haven was not a plantation in the traditional sense. It was a farm of 952 acres, much of it wooded, owned by Fred's father, Colonel Frederick Dent, a colonel by courtesy not by rank. The farm produced wheat, corn, legumes, pork, milk, and eggs. It was a losing proposition for the Colonel because the slaves and their children had to be fed, clothed, and sheltered all year round. But the Colonel, who was descended from an old Maryland family, was aristocratic in attitude, if not in manner and sentiment, and never questioned the wisdom of squandering a patrimony.

Smooth-shaven, white-haired, crusty, and garrulous, Colonel Dent was fifty-six when Grant first met him. He was as contentious and litigious as Jesse Grant. He had fathered eight children, four boys and four girls, all but one of whom reached adulthood. The fifth child and first girl was Julia, born on January 26, 1826. She was at a girls' finishing school in St. Louis when Lieutenant Grant paid his first call.

Young officers from Jefferson Barracks were no novelty at White Haven. The Dents entertained often, and the Colonel was related to "Pete" Longstreet. Grant was quiet, the Colonel was opinionated; but they got along well enough for Mrs. Dent to invite the young man back many times. On one of these visits, Grant met Julia. She became the only woman in his life. Not even the most jealous of his military opponents or the most bitter of his political enemies ever suggested otherwise.

At seventeen, Julia Dent was well-formed, plump, almost voluptuous. She was black-haired, fair-skinned, had small hands, and stood just an inch over five feet tall. She could prattle delightfully, and was an excellent horsewoman. Julia was her father's darling, and spoiled by him. But she was also well schooled by her mother in what were then the feminine disciplines. She never represented herself as a Southern belle—she knew well enough that the plantation was a farm—but all her homes, no matter what the circumstances, revealed taste and refinement.

The only thing that marred her features was a squint in her left eye, a residual defect from a disease in infancy. As she grew older it sometimes distorted her face, so that she appeared to be cross or grumpy. Confederate soldiers unkindly called her "Cock-eyed Mrs. Grant." In later years she steeled herself to have the squint surgically corrected. However, as she was about to leave the White House for the hospital, Grant took her hands and said he liked the way she had first looked at him, and he liked the way she looked at him now, and why didn't she unpack her bags?

It was Julia who first noticed Ulysses's interest in flowers, and she picked bouquets for him to carry back to the post. On the other hand, she was a vivacious dancing partner, and Grant did not dance. He said he could dance pretty well if it wasn't for the music. Still, he escorted her to enough balls so that on one occasion when he did not, an officer asked, "Miss Julia, where is the little man with the large epaulets?"

The ways in which they offset each other were to be important in their later lives. Where he had immense reservoirs of morale, she had immense reservoirs of optimism. She would need her optimism often enough in the years ahead, and it would serve Grant well through crises and discouragements. Julia was not only optimistic, but invariably even-tempered. She shunned unpleasant people, a trait that would have one unexpected consequence. It was the prospect of spending an evening with Mrs. Lincoln that made her insist that the General break off their date to attend Ford's Theater with the President.

Above all, she believed in Ulysses S. Grant, and in their fortunes together. He was her cause—a cause equal to her powers of hard work, faith, and devotion.

In wooing her, Grant attempted to keep her on horseback as much as he could. Unfortunately, more than once this made him late at the officers' mess. Traditionally, when a man arrived late, he paid a fine of one bottle. On one such occasion the president of the mess, Captain Robert Buchanan, greeted Ulysses with the order "Another bottle of wine, sir."

"Mr. President," replied Grant, "I've been fined three bottles of wine within the last ten days, and if I'm to be fined again, I shall be obliged to repudiate."

"Young people should be seen and not heard," retorted Buchanan, rankled by the hint of insubordination. Grant paid the fine. Neither man forgot the incident, and the martinet Buchanan eventually made Grant pay for it.

Grant's courtship might have continued leisurely for years, but for the imminence of war with Mexico. In April, 1844, the Third Regiment was ordered from Jefferson Barracks to Fort Jesup, Texas. The Fourth expected to follow in the late summer. In May, Grant left on a twenty-day furlough to visit his parents. On the day he left, the Fourth Infantry was ordered to Louisiana. The news reached Grant in Bethel. Fellow officers had packed his gear and advised him by mail to enjoy his furlough. The realization that war with Mexico would separate him from Julia Dent convinced Grant how much he wanted her.

Reporting back to Jefferson Barracks, Grant asked Lieutenant Richard Ewell, the remaining duty officer, for a few days' extra leave to clear up some urgent personal matters. Ewell recognized urgency when he heard it and granted the permission. Grant saddled a horse and galloped for White Haven. Between him and his destination lay the Gravois River. Most of the year it was a creek without water enough to turn a coffee mill, but spring rains had turned it into a torrent. Constitutionally incapable of retracing his steps, Grant struck into the rapids and swam the horse to the other side.

Julia accepted him, and Grant left immediately for Louisiana. Colonel Dent told his daughter she was too young and Grant too poor to get married. But Julia replied that she was poor, too; and the Colonel may have sensed he was getting into a losing battle.

A year later, in May, 1845, just before Congress annexed Texas and finally precipitated war with Mexico, Grant rode up to White Haven on his yearly furlough. He was harder now and bronzed. It was obvious that he had come to ask formally for Julia's hand.

In her old age Julia recalled that Grant walked into the parlor and, without clearing his throat, said, "Colonel Dent, I want to marry your daughter, Miss Julia."

The Colonel thought for a while, then offered, "Mr. Grant, if it were the younger girl, Nelly, you wanted, I'd say yes."

"But I don't want Nelly, I want Julia."

"Oh, you do, do you? Well, then, I suppose it will have to be Julia."

"I do not think," Grant stated long afterward, "there was ever a more wicked war than that waged by the United States on Mexico. I thought so at the time, when I was a youngster, only I had not the moral courage to resign: I had taken an oath to serve eight years unless sooner discharged and I considered my supreme duty was to the flag. I had a horror of the Mexican War, and I have always believed that on our part it was most unjust." On another occasion Grant wrote, "To us Mexico was an empire and of incalculable value; but it might have been obtained by other means. The Southern rebellion was largely the outgrowth of the Mexican War. Nations, like individuals, are punished for their transgressions. We got our punishment in the most sanguinary and expensive war of modern times."

The direct cause of the war was the annexation of Texas by the United States Congress in 1845. The Americans who began to colonize Texas in 1820 were mostly Southerners who brought slaves with them. These Southerners won their independence from Mexico in 1836. The admission of Texas to the Union was a major issue in the election of 1844. It threatened a breach of the 1821 Missouri Compromise, which guaranteed that slave and free states would enter the Union simultaneously, so as not to upset the numerical balance between the two.

Abolitionist sentiment opposed annexation, but it was to some degree muted by the territorial ambitions of the young American republic. These ambitions found concrete expression in James K. Polk's doctrine of Manifest Destiny. Put simply, Polk advanced the conclusion many Americans had reached, that it was their historical role to dominate the North American continent from the Atlantic to the Pacific Ocean.

While the Americans debated annexation, the Mexicans insisted the southern boundary of Texas was the Neuces River, not the Rio Grande, as Texans thought. The Neuces River emptied into the Gulf of Mexico at the small adobe village of Corpus Christi. One hundred and fifty miles to the south, the Rio Grande emptied into the Gulf of Matamoros. The disputed area between the rivers was not only unpopulated, but virtually uncharted, a plain where windblown chaparral piled so thickly as to become impenetrable.

Congress voted to annex Texas on March 1, 1845. President John Tyler signed the bill three days before he left office. His successor, President Polk, promised the people that diplomacy would resolve the dispute with Mexico.

Ulysses S. Grant was then stationed at Camp Salubrity, in western Louisiana. In July, the Fourth Infantry was ordered from this camp to New Orleans. Then, in September, it sailed for Corpus Christi, where it joined what was then called the Army of Occupation. This army was commanded by Brevet Brigadier Zachary Taylor, affectionately called "Old Rough and Ready" by his troops. Taylor had been a soldier since the War of 1812. He was a battlefield commander with little respect for the niceties of the parade ground. He wore blue jeans and a palmetto hat, usually sat sidesaddle on his horse, chewing tobacco while he discussed crop prices to be realized from his Louisiana plantation. But he instantly commanded respect from junior officers like Grant.

When the Mexican government (there were to be twelve Mexican governments during the war) proved obdurate to Polk's offer of arbitration, the President ordered Taylor to occupy the disputed territory and do what he could to prompt the Mexicans into an act of war. Taylor marched his three-thousand-man army down the coast to the north bank of the Rio Grande, halting the main body at Port Isabel, to take on supplies from ships. He detailed a small guard to throw up a hastily built fort opposite Matamoros, twenty-five miles away. The Mexicans on the south bank of the river promptly shelled the fort. In the process they killed its commandant, Major Jacob Brown, for whom present-day Brownsville, Texas, is named.

[49]

This was exactly the provocation Polk had sought. Congress declared war. The President called for fifty thousand volunteers.

Mexico is traversed by two mountain ranges—the Sierra Madre Oriental, on the east coast, and the Sierra Madre Occidental, on the west. Taylor proposed to occupy Matamoros, then work his way west along the Rio Grande to Camargo, a town in the middle of these two ranges. Here he would turn south to capture the strategic city of Monterey. This would secure the disputed territory behind him and open the road to Mexico City in front of him.

To occupy Matamoros, the Fourth Infantry fought first at Palo Alto. It was a sad day for the Mexican lancers, Grant wrote Julia. They were so sure of success that the Yankee *gringos* who overran their camp found dinners still cooking over their fires. The Fourth moved on to fight at Resaca de la Palma and then entered Matamoros unopposed. By modern standards these battles were little more than skirmishes. Mexican soldiers were equipped with blunderbusses and the Americans with flintlock rifles. "At the distance of a few hundred yards," Grant remarked, "a man might fire at you all day without your finding it out."

In spellbinding heat, so hot that the soldiers marched in their underwear, Taylor gained Camargo unopposed and, in September, after a fierce fight, took Monterey. This resounding and quick success transformed Taylor into a national hero, a transformation that worried Democratic President Polk. Taylor was a Whig, a member of the political party directed by Daniel Webster and Henry Clay, who opposed his policies. Rather than conspire in making Taylor an unbeatable opposition candidate in the next election, Polk ordered him to hold at Monterey. To undercut Taylor's popularity, Polk commissioned Winfield Scott, then the general-in-chief, to mount an invasion of Mexico from the south. Scott was to take Vera Cruz, and, by marching over the mountains, to end the war at Mexico City. Scott, nicknamed "Old Fuss and Feathers," was a soldier in the classic mold. He was always military, always surrounded by his aides, and he was a supreme strategist rather than a battlefield leader.

The Fourth Infantry was detached from Taylor's command and joined the ten-thousand-man army under Scott. Grant was in the wave of troops that invested Vera Cruz, after an amphibious landing. Vera Cruz surrendered without much of a fight, and Scott marched up toward Jalapa, a city high in the mountains, guarding the pass through the Sierra Madre Oriental. General Santa Anna, who had decimated the Alamo in 1833, defended this pass by concentrating well-armed troops and artillery on the peaks of Cerro Gordo fifteen miles east of Jalapa. Winfield Scott judged a frontal attack against this position suicidal.

Scott's engineers, led by Captain Robert E. Lee, cut a mountain road up to the enemy's rear. Under the cover of night, a division scaled the precipices, hauling artillery by rope. At dawn on April 18, 1847, Scott attacked the Mexicans from behind and quickly and decisively routed them. The surprise was so complete that the fleeing Santa Anna left behind several bags of gold and his wooden leg.

Once he secured Jalapa, Scott abandoned his base of supplies and marched his army over the mountains and down to the tableland, where Mexico City, the last prize of the war, awaited his coming.

Mexico City was protected by a moat formed by three lakes, and behind this natural barrier a series of walled suburbs. These battlements were manned by seven thousand Mexican regulars and fifteen thousand reservists. Attacking with flanking movements mapped by Robert E. Lee, Scott fought his way through the suburbs. One wing of his army entered the city and took the Alameda, a park near the east. Another took the Palace, a mass of official and administrative buildings known popularly as the "Halls of Montezuma."

Scott was aided immeasurably by Taylor's unexpected victory at Buena Vista in the north. When the Mexicans learned that Taylor's position at Monterey had been weakened to bolster Scott's army, they marched upon the city. A Mexican general offered Taylor three minutes in which to surrender. Taylor replied that eternity wasn't long enough, and in a fierce and bloody battle at nearby Buena Vista, he convincingly defeated the Mexicans. Mexico sued for peace, and in February, 1848, ceded Texas, New Mexico, and upper California to the United States in return for $15 million.

Mexico was a proving ground for the Civil War. Young officers like Ulysses S. Grant learned that the new light artillery severely inhibited the thrust of mounted soldiers. The cavalry charge was a maneuver of the past and the use of the cavalry in war was much diminished. They learned that many of the rules of war were antiquated. A general who could keep the enemy busy needn't worry about his rear, and a general who could make a shrewd appraisal of the countryside could feed his troops from it, and free men from protecting supply lines.

They also learned that discipline and training were more important than numerical superiority in attacking a fortified enemy for in every battle of the war, Mexican troops outnumbered Americans. And they learned that volunteers could fight as well as regulars. The volunteer who didn't run in the first fifteen minutes never ran.

The Mexican War established the reputations of Robert E. Lee, Albert Sidney Johnston, "Fighting Joe" Hooker, the artillerist Braxton Bragg, and Thomas J. Jackson, later called "Stonewall." It also enhanced the reputation of New Hampshireman Franklin Pierce, General of the Volunteers, one of three Mexican War veterans to serve as President. Ulysses S. Grant began the war as a brevet second lieutenant and ended it as a brevet captain. He participated in every one of its battles except Buena Vista.

Grant was among the line officers in the first wave against Chapultepec, one of the outlying suburbs of Mexico City. In the middle of the battle he came across his old roommate and brother-in-law-to-be, Fred Dent. Fred, whose courage had just won him a second brevet promotion, was wounded in the leg. Solicitously, Grant lifted Fred to the flat top of a low wall, so that the surgeons wouldn't miss him, and moved on. Renewed firing, however, forced Fred to roll off the wall, and in falling he broke his leg in two places. In later years Fred never thought the story as funny as the General did.

Later, in street fighting at San Cosme gate, Grant spotted a strategically placed church. He commandeered a howitzer, which he and his men disassembled and piece by piece carried to the belfry. There they reassembled the gun and opened fire on the Mexicans lying behind barricaded rooftops below.

General Worth saw the confusion this maneuver had wrought

among the Mexicans and sent his aide, Lieutenant John C. Pemberton, to bring Grant to him. Grant wanted to stay in the belfry but Pemberton insisted an order was an order. Grant followed Pemberton as reluctantly as, some years later, Pemberton would surrender Vicksburg to him. Worth congratulated Grant on his derring-do and ordered more guns into the belfry. Grant, knowing there wasn't room for another howitzer, led a battery captain to the church but did not use the gun. When the war ended, Grant had been mentioned in the dispatches of his colonel and his general, and the brevets he won took him from the middle of his class academically to the top third in rapidity of advancement.

The war took the lives of many soldiers, and Mexican casualties were double or perhaps triple those of the Americans. Out of 90,000 volunteers and regulars mustered for duty in Mexico, Texas, New Mexico, and California, 2,500 died in action and 11,300 succumbed to cholera, typhoid, dysentery, and other diseases. Another 16,000 were sent home disabled by these afflictions. "My regiment," Grant wrote, "lost four commissioned officers, all senior to me, by steamboat explosions. The Mexicans were not so discriminating. They sometimes picked off my juniors."

In 1848, Zachary Taylor became the second Whig to be elected President of the United States. During July 4 celebrations in 1850, at ceremonies dedicating the Washington Monument, Taylor was taken ill. On July 9 he was dead of cholera, the second Whig President to die in office. Winfield Scott was the Whig candidate in 1852. He was defeated by Democrat Franklin Pierce. Scott, however, did not retire from the army until well after the Battle of Bull Run.

The only prospect Ulysses S. Grant came home to in 1848 was marriage to Julia Dent. The other wished-for prospect, the chance to teach at West Point, was lost to him. The vacancy had been filled while he was in the field.

On August 22, 1848, at eight o'clock in the evening, Lieutenant Grant married Julia Dent. The ceremony took place in Colonel Dent's St. Louis town house, a modest two-story, four-chimneyed brick structure on Fourth and Cerre streets. Julia wore a bridal gown that came from Paris. Grant was in uniform, and his sword kept getting in his way during the ceremony. "Pete" Longstreet, Cadmus Marcellus Wilcox, and Bernard Pratt, who had fought with Grant in Mexico, flanked him. All three would fight for the Confederacy.

Colonel and Mrs. Dent sponsored the candlelight ceremony, which was an event in St. Louis society. The Colonel was barely reconciled to the marriage of his favorite daughter and wept as Julia repeated her vows. Jesse and Hannah Grant did not attend—Jesse because he would not be seen in the company of slaveowners, and Hannah because she would not be seen in company. Once he met Julia, Jesse forgave her her background, though in his old age he was inclined to mutter about the "tribe of Dents" his son had married into.

The young couple honeymooned in Bethel. Jesse thought his son had done so well he would stop people, even in the rain, to talk about "My Ulysses." Afterward Grant rejoined the Fourth Infantry at Fort Wayne, a recently built fortification in Detroit. The army had been pared to eight thousand men, with most of the regiments sent west to facilitate the passage of pioneers. For a time Grant was shifted to Sackets Harbor, New York, on the eastern shore of Lake Ontario. Madison Barracks at Sackets Harbor consisted of old blockhouses designed for Indian fighting, but there Julia held her first dinner party. Then, in March, 1849, they were back in Detroit, where Grant took up his duties as regimental quartermaster. "I was no clerk," he said, "nor had I any capacity to become one. The only place I ever found in my life to put a paper so as to find it again was either in a side coat pocket or the hands of a clerk more careful than myself."

In May, 1850, Julia returned to White Haven to bear her first child, Frederick Dent Grant. A year later the Fourth abandoned Fort Wayne, and the Grants found themselves back at Sackets Harbor. Madison Barracks offered a sparse life, but it was spring and the blossoms and the greenery relieved the tedium. Best of all, the young family was together.

It was at Sackets Harbor that Grant joined the Rising Sun Division of the national fraternal order of the Sons of Temperance. He wore its emblems and regalia, including a white sash, and assumed the presidency of the lodge. It was noted, however, that he sometimes neglected his vows at officer balls.

Julia expected her second child in the summer of 1852, but in the spring the army ordered the Fourth Infantry to the Far West. Julia could not make the trip when Grant left with the regiment. She would be unable to join him until the baby was a year old. Grant sent her to his father's Bethel home, and Buck was born there in July, 1852. Jesse welcomed her, but after a while Julia returned to White Haven, because Hannah Grant disapproved of the way she disciplined the children.

The Fourth Infantry was ordered to New York, from there by steamer to the east coast of Panama, then across the isthmus of Panama, and finally by clipper ship to San Francisco. It was the first such passage ordered by the War Department, which hoped to cut three months from the usual route around Cape Horn. Lieutenant Colonel Benjamin Bonneville was in command of the Fourth—seven hundred officers and men, accompanied by more than one hundred wives and children. Bonneville was strict, testy, crochety, and old. He was sorely tried when he discovered in New York that the side-wheeler *Ohio* was overbooked and there was not room aboard her for all his command. The impasse was remedied by Quartermaster Grant, who built tiers of cots on the deck, transforming the *Ohio* into an open-air troopship. Bonneville's bad temper lasted throughout the voyage. He was constantly at odds with the captain and crew, who relied on Grant to smooth over these differences. At night Grant would pace the deck alone, puffing his pipe, trying to overcome his loneliness.

The Fourth disembarked at the Panamanian town of Aspinwall. It was a gerrybuilt, hastily constructed port, thrown up by an American, William Henry Aspinwall, who proposed to build a railroad across the isthmus. In summer the town lay under a foot of water. The sun was scorching as soon as it rose, heavy rains inundated the streets every noon, and the nights were steaming. "I wondered," said Grant, "how any person could live many months in Aspinwall and wondered still more why anyone tried."

The troops were moved to the town of Cruces by railroad and huge dugout canoes, poled by Panamanian natives. From Cruces,

Bonneville led them over jungle roads to Panama City, where the clipper ship *Golden Gate* lay at anchor. Bringing up the rear was Quartermaster Grant, with the women and children, the regimental band, and the arms and ammunition.

Cholera was rampant in Cruces that July. Learning of the epidemic, Bonneville marched his men out of the town, but not quickly enough to spare them. Soldiers began dropping on the march, some of them sinking beneath the roadside mire before anyone could pull them out.

When Grant arrived in Cruces, he found that Bonneville had preempted all the mules. He managed to dispatch the healthy members of his party on foot, some of the women marching off into the jungle in army coats and pants. Then he procured whatever transportation he could for the remainder, and set out for Panama City. Cholera killed one third of them, and Grant buried the dead along the roadside, beneath a canopy of tropical blossoms.

At Panama City, Bonneville boarded the women and children with the stricken men on the *Golden Gate*. When the regimental surgeon, Dr. Charles Tripler, ordered them off, because the ship was in quarantine, Bonneville threatened to have him court-martialed. Tripler replied that was the Colonel's privilege, but the living would have to get off the ship. Then Tripler and Grant found an old hulk, which they leased to serve as a hospital, while others fumigated the *Golden Gate*.

Soldiers and civilians sequestered on Flamingo Island called the hulk a "death ship." From the shore they could see healthy men walking the decks, felled suddenly by intestinal cramps, which signaled probable death. One day Grant was playing cards with Major John Gore, who had fought beside him in Mexico. Suddenly Gore started to shake. "My God!" he cried. "I've got the cholera." He was dead within hours.

At last the disease abated and the *Golden Gate* sailed for San Francisco. The Fourth Infantry had left behind more than one hundred of its men and over forty of their wives and children. The army learned a dreadful lesson, and it was not lost on Grant. Disease could decimate an army more effectively than enemy guns and soldiers. Grant always described the terrors of Panama to his junior officers to impress upon them the need for sanitary and healthful conditions for their troops. Though other generals scoffed, Grant never turned a deaf ear to a doctor. More of his men survived because of this than for any other reason.

In September, 1852, Grant was the quartermaster at Fort Vancouver, on the Columbia River, not far from present-day Portland. The fort was in the midst of a small settlement of woodsmen, and docile Indian tribes lived in the surrounding forests. Grant lived in the quartermaster's barracks with his plebe-year roommate, Captain Rufus Ingalls. But neither Rufe nor day-long gallops through countryside could dissipate the loneliness of an isolated garrison existence. He carried in his breast pocket a worn sheet of paper on which Julia had traced the hand of their infant. Grant's eyes watered when he proudly showed it to his friends.

It was impossible on his pay to bring Julia to the Far West, so Grant tried to augment his income. He and Rufe Ingalls cultivated a hundred acres in which they planted potatoes, but the Columbia River rose and flooded the land, washing away most of their crop. He and some other officers cut ice from the river and shipped it to San Francisco. Headwinds delayed the ship. By the time it made port, luckier ice cutters from Sitka had broken the market. Next he and a partner tried shipping cattle and hogs. Grant rounded up the stock from the Indians, whom the government was instructing in the ways of agriculture, and his partner took the stock to Frisco. They made several trips before they lost their investment. So they switched to chickens, which died at the first whiff of an east wind.

On August 9, 1853, Grant was promoted to captain and took command of a company stationed at Humboldt Bay, California. It was 240 miles north of San Francisco, in the heart of a redwood forest. The nearest town was Eureka, which consisted of a sawmill and twenty houses. At Humboldt he must have come to the realization that he was about to enter early middle age in a profession in which there was virtually no advancement. Not only could he not support a wife properly, but he didn't like army life. And he was miserable without Julia.

He had learned about liquor during the Mexican War, and now he took to drink. Neither did he drink very much nor did he drink every day. Still, it always showed on him. For the knowledgeable the conclusion is inescapable: Grant was an alcoholic.

Whenever or how infrequently he drank, he drank to excess. Alcoholism has been defined both as a disease and as a behavioral disorder. Whatever it may be clinically, pharmacologically it is an addiction. Liquor can come to dominate life.

Total abstinence suppresses this addiction and frees the alcoholic from domination. Throughout history the most successful therapy to help the alcoholic to abstinence has been through social interaction with other men and women, firm yet sympathetic about the nature of the disease, who understand that the alcoholic is compelled and who try to coax and persuade him away from his addiction.

The key word for this therapy in Grant's time was "approachability," coined by Abraham Lincoln in his speech to the Washingtonian Temperance Society in Springfield in 1842. In this speech Lincoln also suggested that the man who could best "approach" the drunkard was the drunkard who had stopped drinking. Only he, thought Lincoln, could persuade that sobriety was salvation rather than punishment.

To insist that Grant understood none of this is naïve. He had joined a temperance society whose purpose was not to break bottles of whiskey but to discuss drinking and how to forswear it. While heavy drinking was habitual in the old army, Grant had seen that though other officers mastered it, liquor was mastering him. Drinking was visiting upon him the spite of his superior officer, who held him in low esteem.

That officer was Colonel Robert Buchanan, to whom Grant had sounded off in Jefferson Barracks about the wine penalty. Buchanan didn't like sloppy soldiers, and Grant was sloppy. And he didn't like introspective drunks, and Grant was that, too. Grant would sit on the porch of Ryan's general store in Eureka, refreshing himself from the whiskey barrel, staring at the quagmire that passed for a street. The desolation and dreariness of frontier life would propel him back to the barrel.

The confrontation with Colonel Buchanan came one day when Grant, acting as paymaster, was too drunk to count money. Buchanan ordered the adjutant to place Captain Grant under arrest.

Rufus Ingalls summed up the episode:

Grant, finding himself in dreary surroundings, without his family, and with but little to occupy his attention, fell into dissipated habits, and was found, one day, too much under the influence of liquor to properly perform his duties. For this offense Colonel Buchanan demanded that he should resign, or stand trial. Grant's friends at the time urged him to stand trial, and were confident of his acquittal; but, actuated by a noble spirit, he said he would not for all the world have his wife know that he had been tried on such a charge. He therefore resigned his commission, and returned to civilian life.

This was a shameful episode but not on that account without its blessings. Had he remained in the old army he probably would have patrolled the Far West during the Civil War as so many other West Pointers were forced to do. Going home to Julia was a giant step toward sobriety. Julia was the crucial and determining figure in this fight. He never drank when she was near, which is a reasonable explanation of why he brought her so frequently to the battlegrounds. Her love for him and her pride in him represented a supreme value. He beat alcoholism with her to help him. Beating alcohol does not require great will, it requires great thought.

Grant wrote a letter of resignation to the War Department dated April 11, 1854, and told his sympathetic fellow officers, "Whoever hears of me in ten years will hear of a well-to-do old Missouri farmer."

Three weeks later, Major Robert Allen, chief quartermaster of the region, found Grant broke and in despair in the attic room of the What Cheer House in San Francisco. Grant confessed that he hadn't the money for his passage to New York. Allen obtained a free ticket for him as a courtesy from the Pacific Mail Steamship Company. Other officers raised enough money to get Grant to New York, taking in exchange an improperly drawn certificate for per diem services legitimately owed.

He wrote to Jesse for money to get him from New York to Bethel, but no money was forthcoming. In desperation he called then upon his friend from West Point and Mexican days, Captain Simon Bolivar Buckner. They would meet twice more in surpassing dramatic moments. Grant asked the Kentuckian to lend him money to pay his hotel bill. Buckner, fearful that Grant might spend the cash on liquor, went instead to the hotel and guaranteed

Grant's debt. Until money from Jesse finally arrived, Buckner saw to it that Grant had enough to get by.

Grant's resignation was a cruel blow to his father. Jesse learned of it even before Grant had left San Francisco, from Congressman Andrew Ellison, who noticed the routine announcement. Jesse himself wrote to Secretary of War Jefferson Davis, asking him to withdraw his acceptance of the resignation and issue Captain Ulysses S. Grant a six months' leave of absence instead. But Jefferson Davis had himself resigned from the army after the Mexican War, and routinely processed numerous resignations.* He was not disposed to beg a captain to stay on. The captain had resigned for his own reasons and that was the end of it. He would not reconsider, he wrote Jesse.

Jesse no longer stopped people in the sunshine, let alone the rain, to talk about "My Ulysses."

To the son who had to start over again at thirty-two, Jesse said bitterly, "West Point spoiled one of my boys for business."

"I guess that's about so," replied that son.

Because she didn't know when he would come home, Julia wore a freshly starched muslin dress each day. She primped and prettied herself as though she expected him through the front door before sunset. At last, toward the end of the summer of 1854, Grant drew up in a buggy in front of White Haven, threw the reins over the dashboard, and came in to her embrace. He was greeted by the son he never knew and the father-in-law he knew too well.

He came home empty-handed, but they had a start. Colonel Dent had given Julia sixty uncleared acres for a wedding present, and Grant proposed to set up as a farmer. Before he could stock and farm the land, he had to clear it. Clearing meant not only felling trees and hauling them away, but also busting the sod. It would take two summers to get the land ready.

For the next year the family lived at Wish-ton-wish, a nearby cottage owned by Julia's brother, Louis, who lent it to them while he went to California. The Grants' third child, Ellen, called "Nellie," was born at Wish-ton-wish on July 4, 1855.

---

* He was at that time processing one from William Tecumseh Sherman, who wanted to go into banking.

As he cleared, Grant also cut then squared some logs with an adze, split the shingles for a roof, dug a cellar, and hauled the stones for a foundation and chimney. He paid a neighbor to fashion frames and sash for windows and to fit together the panels for a door. After the wood had seasoned over a winter, Grant was ready to raise a house.

The neighbors pitched in for a traditional house raising. Later Grant laid the floor and filled the wall chinks with mortar, which he smoothed over with plaster. When he finished, he named his place Hardscrabble. Grant intended an ironic comment on Colonel Dent's pretensions as well as a descriptive comment on his own. It was a farmer's house and a farmer had scrubbed hard to build it. On the ground floor was a wide hallway, a living room to one side, a dining room to the other. Upstairs were three bedrooms with two long windows. The kitchen and slave quarters were in cabins to the rear.*

To support his family, Grant hauled cordwood into St. Louis by wagon. A cord, which measures eight feet long by four feet high by four feet wide, brought $4. These ten-mile trips to the city consumed the day, but by them Grant earned $50 a month, enough to feed and clothe his wife and children.

The young lieutenant who had been decked with braid and medals was now a bearded man in an old blue army overcoat, wearing a battered army hat, his pants stuck into his boots, a quiet man who went about his business. Undeniably, a man who had seen better days. Captain "Pete" Longstreet was depressed by a meeting with Grant. He saw at once that Grant was in needy circumstances, the realization made more painful when Grant insisted on repaying an old $5 debt. Another former colleague spotted Grant atop his wagon and asked what in blazes he was doing. Matter-of-factly, Grant replied he was hauling wood.

William Tecumseh Sherman, himself a virtual bankrupt, ran into Grant on a street corner one day in 1857. Sherman was returning to Ohio to manage the salt wells of his father-in-law, a

* It still stands. After Grant's presidency, Hardscrabble was moved to a nearby setting called Old Orchard. Later it was exhibited at the St. Louis Louisiana Purchase Exposition. Now known as the Grant log cabin, it is on the Anheuser-Busch estate and open to the public.

prospect he dreaded. "West Point and the Regular Army are not good schools for bankers and for farmers," Sherman said as they parted.

A few of Julia's dearest friends came to visit her at Hardscrabble, though none of them came too often, and a great many dear friends never came at all. The Grants had virtually no commerce with the society they knew when they were first married. Whatever St. Louis thought of ex-Captain Ulysses S. Grant, whether pity or superiority or indifference, had no effect on Julia. "We will not always be in this condition," she insisted to her Dent relatives. Whatever St. Louis thought had even less effect on Grant. Hard times rubbed him hard, they bent his shoulders, lined his face, made his hands grow big with calluses, and, on occasion, embittered him. But he never gave in to them.

His misfortunes in St. Louis may not have depressed him as much as later generations imagine. Neighbors and others lived in meaner circumstances. His narrowed world occupied all of his energy, mind, and labor. And Julia's presence continually sustained him. Moreover, he believed that healthy children were a reward. Before they left Hardscrabble, Fred Grant was as good with a team of horses as his father.

Grant planted oats and corn the first summer, but realized little profit. "If they bear a high price," he wrote to his father, "it is because the farmer had raised scarcely [sic] enough for his own use. If abundant, they will scarcely [sic] bear transportation." The panic of 1857 made that crop worthless. In 1858, an early frost reduced his yield of wheat from 500 bushels to 75. By this time he did not have the money to buy seed for another crop. When his third son and last child, Jesse Root, was born on February 6, 1858, hard times were as habitual to Grant's condition as the old blue army overcoat.

He auctioned off his wagon and his team, his tools and his meager supplies, and moved into St. Louis to go into business with Henry Boggs, a cousin of Julia. Nominally, he was a partner in Boggs and Grant, a firm dealing in realty, loans, and rent collections. Actually, he was a clerk.

He traded his farm for a house in St. Louis, only to find the title to the house wasn't clear. And he was no salesman or rent collector. He could figure discounts and interest rates in his head, but he never sold a house and only rarely did he collect rents. He was, friends said, like a man thinking on an abstract subject all the time. Nothing reveals more tellingly his business acumen than the following letter he wrote to his brother Simpson:

> I have been postponing writing you hoping to make a return for your horse; but as yet I have received nothing for him. About two weeks ago a man spoke to me for him and said that he would try him the next day, and if he suited give me one hundred dollars for him. I have not seen the man since; but one week ago Saturday he went to the stable and got the horse, saddle and bridle; since which I have seen neither man nor horse. From this I presume he must like him. The man, I understand, lives in Florisant, about twelve miles from the city. . . . The man that has your horse is Captain Covington, owner of a row of six three-story brick houses in this city; and the probabilities are that he intends to give me an order on his agent for the money on the first of the month, when the rents are paid. At all events, I imagine the horse is perfectly safe.

The arrangement with Boggs was that Grant would bring in new business through his contacts with army officers at Jefferson Barracks. But the truth was that officers who knew Grant were avoiding him. It wasn't long before Grant was trying to make himself invisible in the office. He was a man who knew he wasn't wanted.

By mutual consent, Grant and Boggs dissolved their partnership and Grant applied for the post of county engineer. It paid $1,500 a year, and Grant was eminently qualified to fill it. Though he forwarded with his application a petition signed by thirty-four reputable citizens, the county commissioners passed him over for a German immigrant. Two of the commissioners had voted for him, but the other three were Republicans, ardent for the cause of Union. Grant's association with Colonel Dent precluded their absolute faith in his loyalty.

Grant was not a political man. Up to this point, he had voted once in his life, in 1856, for Democrat James Buchanan. Grant was not insensitive to events of the late 1850s and knew well what they portended. The first talk he heard of secession chilled his blood. Slavery could not be worth this terrible division. In March, 1859, in fact, Grant manumitted the one slave he owned, whom he had acquired somewhat reluctantly from Colonel Dent.

One of his thirty-four petitioners found him a post in the United States Customs House. The job paid $1,200 a year, but his employment lasted only a few weeks. The Customs Collector died and the new appointee swept the old house clean.

He was thirty-eight years old, with only one prospect left, that of working for his father. Jesse agreed to take him on as a clerk in the Galena store, at $600 a year, until something better turned up. Jesse was thrifty, but he was not in this instance unfair. Orvil and Simpson Grant also worked in the store on salaries, and the profits from the store went into a trust fund for their sisters.

In April, 1860, Julia led the four children off the paddleboat *Itasca* at the Galena landing. Grant followed carrying two chairs. Galena is the oldest city in Illinois. Though its great days were over, it was still a center of wealth. It had been a thriving commercial center when Chicago was a swamp. Lead made Galena's fortune. In fact, the town derived its name from the Latin word for lead sulfide. Galena was the largest river port north of St. Louis. It had a population of about 12,000; housed wholesale firms that marketed products in neighboring states; and had gristmills, iron foundries, lumberyards, lime kilns, and breweries.*

The Grants rented a home on High Street for $125 a year. The neighborhood was called Cemetery Hill, because a graveyard stretched behind it. The rent was low for Galena because the only access to the house was by two hundred wooden stairs, which climbed like a fire escape. At the base of the hill was a small Methodist church at which Julia punctually appeared with the children every Sunday.

---

* It is a town of 4,400 today and its chief industry is tourism. The city has re-created itself as the typical river port city of the 1850s. It contains a large collection of Grant memorabilia, the center of which is the Grant Home on Bouthillier Street, carefully restored by the Illinois Division of Parks and Memorials. While Galena concentrates on Grant the General, the drawing room of the Grant Home still has the original table at which the General counted the electoral votes he won in 1868 and 1872. Almost nothing has happened to Galena since Grant left for Washington in 1872, or, for that matter, since he got off the *Itasca* in 1860.

The Grant store bought untanned leather and cured it. It also dealt in leather goods, harnesses, trace chains, bridle bits, whips, saddles, stirrups, axes, wedges, saws, augurs, and other hardware. Grant helped keep the books and was often seen bent over the ledgers at night. He made selling trips through Iowa and Wisconsin. Grant attracted little attention in Galena for the eleven months he lived there, but we do have the reminiscence of one man who was curious to see a Mexican War hero:

> I went round to the store [he recalled] it was a sharp winter morning, and there wasn't a sign of a soldier or one that looked like a soldier around the shop. But pretty soon a farmer drove up with a lot of hides on his sleigh, and went inside to dicker, and presently a stoop-shouldered, brownish-bearded fellow, low, with a slouch hat pulled over his eyes, who had been sitting whittling at the stove when I was inside, came out, pulling on an old blue soldier's overcoat. He flung open the doors leading to the cellar, laid hold of the top hide, frozen stiff it was, tugged it loose, towed it over and slung it down the chute. Then one by one, all by himself, he heaved off the rest of them, a ten minutes tough job in that weather, until he had got the last of them down the cellar; then slouched back into the store again, shed the blue coat, got some hot water off the stove and went and washed his hands, using a cake of brown soap, then came back and went to whittling again, and all without a word to anybody.

Each night Grant climbed the two hundred steps, to be met by his son Jesse, who would ask, "Mister, do you want to fight?" "I am a man of peace," Grant would reply, "but I will not be hectored by a person your size." The two would then wrestle into the living room, until Jesse threw his father on the couch.

In December, 1860, a month after Lincoln's election, South Carolina seceded from the Union. In the first two months of 1861 Florida, Alabama, Georgia, Louisiana, and Texas followed. Around potbellied stoves in Galena, men opined that the South was all bluster. Ulysses S. Grant, who knew the quality of Southern officers, offered that there was more than noise to the South's bluster.

Fort Sumter fell on April 15, 1861. Lincoln called for seventy-five thousand volunteers for ninety days' service. On that Monday night, the men of Galena met in the Town Court House. A Democratic lawyer, John Rawlins, later Grant's chief of staff and still later his Secretary of War, brought the men to a crescendo of cheering when he promised to put aside his politics for the one course left. "We will stand by the flag of our country and appeal to the God of battles," he said. On that same night Ulysses S. Grant said, "I had thought I had done with soldiering. I never expected to be in military life again. But I was educated by the Government and if my knowledge and experience can be of any service, I think I ought to offer them."

On Thursday the townsmen met again, this time to form Galena's infantry company for one of the six Illinois regiments. Republican Congressman Elihu Washburne suggested that Captain Grant chair the meeting. In the next two weeks Grant, Washburne, Rawlins, William Rowley, the clerk for the Circuit Court, and Augustus Chetlain, raised the complement of one hundred men. They called themselves the Jo Daviess Guards. The others urged the captaincy of the company on Grant, who demurred. He explained that he had been a captain in the regular army and didn't want to accept a captaincy in the volunteers.

The captaincy went to Chetlain, but Grant remained at hand to provide what help he could. He instructed Chetlain on the manual of arms and undertook all the quartermaster duties to supply the men. When Colonel Dent learned that Grant was enlisting in the Union Army, he roared that his son-in-law was a renegade. Moreover, he hadn't the sense he was born with, for if he joined the Confederates he would be a brigadier within a week.

On April 25, 1861, the countryside for miles around turned out to give the Jo Daviess Guards a sendoff. A parade marched through Galena to the depot, where town officials and ministers took turns delivering patriotic and inspiring speeches. The ladies presented Captain Chetlain with a flag, which Grant had helped them design. Grant was at home, packing. He told Julia and the children that he expected to be gone three months at the most. Then, in his old blue overcoat and slouch hat, he fell into the ranks at the rear of the company, his carpetbag limp and gaunt.

The Jo Daviess Guards from Galena joined an Illinois regiment in Springfield in the late spring of 1861. The thirty-nine-year-old civilian Ulysses S. Grant went into the office of the State

Adjutant General to decipher for other clerks the army forms and explain the difference between a requisition and a demand voucher. He also traveled to small towns helping to muster in newly formed companies.

He was anxious for a command of his own. He wrote Secretary of War Simon Cameron, outlining his army experience and asking respectfully for the command of a volunteer regiment. The letter was never opened. He also went to Cincinnati and spent two days in the anterooms of General George B. McClellan, whom he had known in the old army. McClellan, a major general on the way up, was too busy to see him. Nor did Grant have a response from a request for a command made of a West Point friend, Nathaniel Lyon, commanding the garrison at St. Louis.

After three months there was nothing more to do for the Illinois Adjutant. Grant decided to go home. Governor Richard Yates sent for him the night before he was to leave. Yates had noticed the seedy but efficient old West Pointer. Yates found this quiet man infinitely to be preferred to the constables in his office demanding captaincies and the JPs wanting battalions.

The governor asked Grant to take over the colonelcy of the Seventh District Regiment whose thirty-day enlistments were about to expire. The regiment was ill-disciplined, riotous, had already run off an incompetent commanding officer, and were known as "Governor Yates's Hellions." Grant promised he would make soldiers out of these rough farmboys. Without a uniform, wearing his old felt hat, Grant took command on June 16, 1861. Within three days he convinced the men that if anyone was going to be run off it would be they, not he. They rose for reveille and stood retreat. There were no more unexplained absences. Then Grant mustered them for rousing speeches from two Democratic politicians, John A. McClernand and John A. Logan. The men reenlisted *en masse*, sworn into federal service as the Twenty-first Illinois Volunteers. They awaited a spirited polemic from their colonel. Grant said, "Men, go to your quarters." He was wearing an old tarnished scabbard and saber he had scrounged from an arsenal warehouse.

He received orders to move his regiment by train from

Springfield to Quincy, which was on the Mississippi River. There was a ten-day wait. Grant decided to march his men. The sooner they learned how to march the better.

At Quincy, the Twenty-first Illinois crossed the Mississippi into Missouri and began chasing Confederate guerrillas. Some guerrilla bands robbed hen roosts and some blew up supply trains. Some Union colonels chased guerrillas across Missouri for the whole of the war. Grant was at Mexico, Missouri, in September, guarding the Hannibal and St. Joseph Railway when he read the news that he had been made a brigadier general of volunteers.

As the ranks of the Union swelled with volunteers, Lincoln saw they needed more officers. He asked congressional delegations for recommendations. Illinois sent in four names. Elihu B. Washburne, the congressman from Galena, had forwarded Grant.

The war had not yet shaken down but one thing was obvious to Lincoln and to his war council: one army in one campaign wasn't going to win it. The table of organization had already determined on several commands dividing many armies among them. There was a command in the east, one on the Ohio River, and a command in St. Louis. The commander in St. Louis was General John C. Frémont. He assigned Grant to Cairo, Illinois, where he became the general in charge of southern Illinois and southeastern Missouri.

Cairo, a river port of thirty thousand, was two hundred miles south of St. Louis at the confluence of the Ohio and Mississippi rivers. At the moment Grant took command, Cairo became a geographic configuration. Cairo was *the point*, the staging area from which any attack against the Confederacy in the West would be launched. The Confederacy in 1861 had blocked the Mississippi to Union navigation, an act as hostile and warlike as the firing upon Fort Sumter. In the councils of war in Washington, the presumption was that the Union would fight its way down the river. But from Cairo, Grant saw the truer line into the Confederacy was down Kentucky's Cumberland and Tennessee rivers, which were to the east of the Mississippi. These rivers, which ran north and south, were channels of invasion. Both sides knew this. The Confederacy named battles and the Union named its armies after these rivers.

Across from Cairo was Kentucky, which hoped for neutrality

in the war. Its governor was secessionist but its legislature was Union. If Kentucky opted for the Union, the Confederacy faced disaster. Rather than wait, General Leonidas Polk, formerly an Episcopal bishop, moved troops into the state and established a strong line across its center. As soon as Grant heard that Polk had invaded, he put troops into Paducah, Kentucky, forty miles east of Cairo on the Ohio. Paducah was not far from the loop that connected the Tennessee and Cumberland rivers. Grant sent a message to the Speaker of the State House that the Union had come to protect the fortunes of Kentucky citizens. Frémont congratulated Grant on the move to Paducah but censured him for the political message.

The censure didn't matter because Frémont, neither an efficient administrator nor an innovative strategist, was shortly relieved of his command in St. Louis by Major General Henry Halleck. Halleck shared command with General Don Carlos Buell, whose army was stationed farther east on the Kentucky side of the Ohio River. Halleck and Buell were cautious generals. While they debated when and where to start a campaign, in the process each trying to gain ascendancy over the other, Grant suggested he try to take Fort Henry on the Tennessee. It was a bold and daring proposal and General Halleck said no, it was too bold for his blood.

What Grant proposed was an attack against one of the strategic corners of the Confederacy. The Confederacy was essentially a rectangle—Richmond and Savannah to the east, Vicksburg and Forts Henry and Donelson to the west. Fort Henry and Fort Donelson secured the Confederate line from the Mississippi through Kentucky to Richmond. Fort Henry was on the Tennessee River and was the weaker of the two. Fort Donelson, twelve miles away, was on the Cumberland. It was defended by more than twenty thousand troops. To secure a new nation, the Confederacy had to keep the rectangle inviolate.

On another foray down the Tennessee, Grant divined that the river was about to flood Fort Henry. Undismayed by Halleck's caution, he made another appeal, this time joined by Flag Officer Andrew Foote of the navy, who had command of the small gunboat fleet. Pressed by Washington to do something, wanting to do

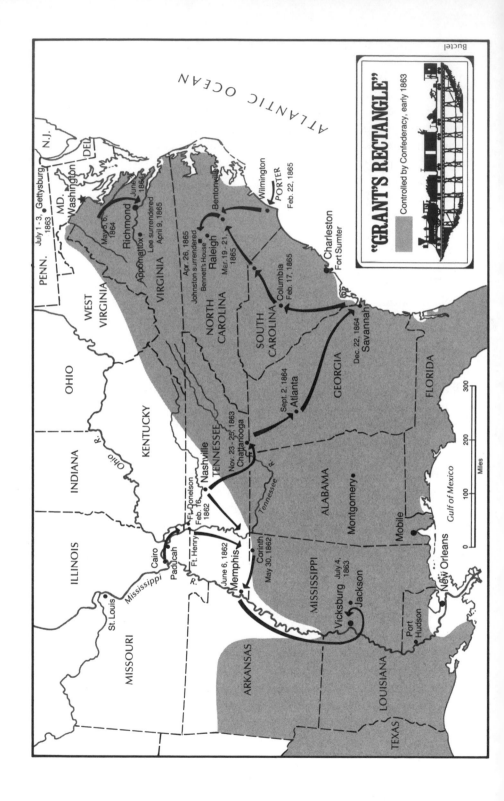

"GRANT'S RECTANGLE"

Controlled by Confederacy, early 1863

PORTER
Feb. 22, 1865

Buctel

ATLANTIC OCEAN

Gettysburg,
July 1 - 3,
1863

N.J.

DEL.

MD.
Washington

PENN.

WEST
VIRGINIA

May 6,
1864

June 3,
1864

Richmond

Appomattox
Lee surrendered
April 9, 1865

VIRGINIA

Apr. 26, 1865
Johnston surrendered
Bennett's House
Raleigh
Mar. 19 - 21,
1865

Bentonville

Wilmington

NORTH
CAROLINA

SOUTH
CAROLINA

Columbia
Feb. 17, 1865

Charleston
Fort Sumter

OHIO

KENTUCKY

INDIANA

Nashville
TENNESSEE
Ft. Donelson
Feb. 16,
1862

Chattanooga
Nov. 23 - 25, 1863

GEORGIA

Savannah
Dec. 22, 1864

Atlanta
Sept. 2, 1864

Ohio R.

Tennessee R.

ILLINOIS

Cairo
Paducah
Ft. Henry

Mississippi R.

St. Louis

Memphis
June 6, 1862

Corinth
May 30, 1862

MISSISSIPPI

Vicksburg
July 4,
1863

Jackson

ALABAMA

Montgomery

Mobile

FLORIDA

Gulf of Mexico

Miles

0   100   200   300

MISSOURI

ARKANSAS

LOUISIANA

New Orleans

Port
Hudson

TEXAS

something before Buell beat him to the punch, this time Halleck said yes.

In February, 1862, Grant loaded fifteen thousand men aboard ferries. One division was commanded by Charles F. Smith, another by John McClernand. Preceded by seven gunboats, four of them wooden, the others ironclad, the invading force set out. When the Confederates spied the gunboats, they immediately abandoned Fort Henry, by now a foot under water, and retreated to Fort Donelson.

On February 6 Grant wired Halleck that Fort Henry was his and that he would push on to take Fort Donelson in three days unless Halleck countermanded the order. This is the oldest trick in the game. By the time the commander realizes he has an option, the subordinate is off and fighting. To say this ploy annoyed Halleck is a grievous understatement.

Grant marched fifteen thousand men in two divisions on Donelson the next day. Sleet and subzero weather slowed him. The Confederates fiercely defended the place. Grant took heavy casualties. He had sent the gunboats under Foote round the loop that connects the Tennessee and the Cumberland. Now he positioned these gunboats behind the fort, which they commenced shelling. He was returning from this positioning when an aide rode up with the urgent message that the Confederates were coming out for a fight. Some had been captured. Their knapsacks were jammed full. Grant said he wanted to see a knapsack. It was filled with rations, and Grant promptly divined the Confederates were not coming out for a fight, but were trying to cut a hole for a retreat. The gunboats had sealed the Confederate rear. Grant ordered Smith and McClernand to move immediately on the fort. They were not to spend time positioning their troops or aligning their artillery, they were to move now, this very minute. The side which can attack today will win. And he was right.

Donelson was commanded by the Virginian John B. Floyd, who had been Buchanan's Secretary of War. Second-in-comand was the Tennessean Gideon J. Pillow, who had fought with Grant in Mexico. Now that Grant's troops had occupied the fort's perimeter defenses, Floyd decided to escape, because he was under federal indictment for transferring armaments into Southern arsenals. Pillow decided to join him because he was frightened.*

This left Simon B. Buckner in command. He had been Grant's classmate and good friend, the officer who had guaranteed Grant's hotel room in New York. Buckner asked for an armistice. Grant sent his famous message demanding unconditional surrender. Buckner had no choice but compliance, though he remarked that if he had been in command, Grant would have had a harder time of it. Grant replied that if Buckner had been in command he would not have tried to take the fort the way he did. Grant knew that Floyd was no soldier and he remembered that, in Mexico, after his men had dug a trench, Pillow ordered them to throw up the embattlements on the wrong side.

Donelson was the first significant Union victory. It cracked one of the corners of the Confederate rectangle and bent the Confederate line. Church bells rang in the North and mayors read proclamations in the town squares. Ulysses S. Grant's name had become magical. It stood for unconditional surrender. Though outnumbered he had captured an entire Confederate army.

The victory earned Halleck supreme command in the West. But he was still nettled by Grant. Halleck complained that he disobeyed orders, was absent from his command, that he drank. Washington replied that if Grant was that unruly, Halleck had better arrest him and have him court-martialed. Considering that Lincoln had just made Grant a major general, this suggestion did not appeal to Halleck.

The fall of Donelson placed Kentucky on the Union side. In their retreat the Confederates also abandoned Nashville and ceded Memphis in June after a gunboat fight. Grant thought that if *all* the Union armies west of the Alleghenies had made a concerted effort to pursue the retreating and demoralized Confederates, the Union could have taken Chattanooga, Corinth, and Vicksburg within a few months. These blows would have encouraged enlistments to provide Union reinforcements. But this did not happen. The Confederacy was allowed not only to strengthen its southern defenses but gained the time to recruit tens of thousands of

---

* For fleeing their posts, Jefferson Davis removed both Floyd and Pillow from the rolls of the Confederate army.

Southern boys who had not yet joined the army. The Confederates regrouped and set up a line anchored in the west at Corinth, Mississippi, a vital rail center just below the Tennessee border in the eastern part of the state.

Halleck ordered Grant to move down the Tennessee toward this objective. Wanting numerical superiority, Halleck sent Buell and his troops from Nashville to join Grant. The two armies, Grant's numbering thirty-seven thousand men and Buell's twenty-five thousand, were to come together at Pittsburg Landing on the Tennessee River just above the Mississippi border. Halleck would then take command and lead this force on to Corinth twenty-five miles south.

Halleck's Confederate counterpart was Albert Sidney Johnston, perhaps the South's ablest commander after Robert E. Lee. He had forty thousand men with which to defend Corinth. He saw that his best chance of success was to defeat Grant and turn him back before Buell joined him. Johnston moved his entire force out of Corinth and marched to a surprise attack.

Johnston fell upon Grant's army on Sunday, April 6, 1862, in a little town called Shiloh, which took its name from a log cabin church. If Johnston could push through Shiloh he would capture Pittsburg Landing.

Facing Johnston on the west bank of the river, Grant had five divisions commanded by Sherman, Prentiss, Hurlburt, W. H. L. Wallace, and McClernand. A sixth division under Lew Wallace was several miles upriver guarding supplies.

The surprise was devastating. Johnston almost threw the Union forces into the river. Thousands of Union soldiers, still raw, broke and fled when three waves of Confederates hit them at 6 A.M. At least five thousand men cowered along the banks of the river during the day, their heads buried in their hands. But Sherman and Prentiss held, though driven back, and their example gave heart to many of the others. One officer later recalled seeing a Union soldier take cover behind a sapling and begin firing. Another soldier stopped his flight to stand directly behind the first, and a third behind the second. In all, six soldiers stood behind the sapling, firing their rifles past each other's ears, virtually deafening the first man. These were new soldiers, untrained, thousands upon thousands of them young boys who had never heard a gun fired in anger. A veteran of Donelson had to walk up and down the firing line at Shiloh showing the recruits how to load and fire their weapons. "It's just like shooting squirrels," he said, "only these squirrels have guns, that's all."

The men also took heart from the presence of Grant. Unperturbed, he rode from one section of the field to another as unmindful of the bullets as though they had been spitballs. Calmly he gave the orders. Stubbornly he insisted the Union men were far from beaten. Sherman had to hold the right. The right guarded the river road and the landing. General Lew Wallace was coming down that road with five thousand men and General Buell would start ferrying his men across the river to the landing late Sunday night.

Prentiss had to hold the center. Directly behind the center, Grant assembled artillery collected from every corner of the battleground. By 5:30 P.M. when Prentiss was finally surrounded and captured, Grant had arranged these fifty guns in a crescent. The cannons began to blunt the Confederate attack.

Johnston had almost swept the field when he was killed leading an attack against Prentiss. General P. G. T. Beauregard took up the Confederate command, his headquarters Shiloh Church. Night fell. A few more hours of daylight and the Confederacy might have won the battle, because Lew Wallace took the wrong road and did not arrive at Shiloh that first day. Grant began to reorganize the thousands of men who had either fled or been pushed back to the river. He got these men into platoons and companies and started sending them to different parts of the field. A drenching rain began to fall.

Sherman found Grant sitting beneath a tree, hat pulled down, coat collar turned up. Sherman had come to ask what line he should follow in retreat. Something about Grant's demeanor made Sherman hold his tongue. Grant had no plans for a retreat. The Union was going to attack in the morning. During the night, Buell's troops began arriving by ferry and Lew Wallace got his five-thousand-man division into position. In the morning, Sherman, Buell, and Wallace began advancing. The firing was heavier than the day before. The Confederates proved as stubborn as the Yankees. But by noon, Beauregard was fighting to keep the road to Corinth from falling into Union hands. By two o'clock Confederate troops began withdrawing along it.

Shiloh was the first bloody battle of the war. Seventy-seven thousand men had met on the first day. Twenty-three thousand men died there. This massive commitment of troops had an impact on the war far above any tactical advantage the fighting secured. The battle revealed that Southern yeomen and plantation squires and Northern farmboys and mechanics could wage war with equal ferocity and valor. Each side showed a willingness to fight and it became clear the war would be a long one.

"New Orleans had never really been glad again after the awful day of Shiloh," wrote Southern novelist George W. Cable. The casualty lists made Northern cities grieve too. Praised as the conqueror of Donelson seven weeks before, Grant was called a bloody butcher now. Yet shrewd military men realized Grant had won a victory. He had not only saved his army when it was near drowning in the Tennessee River, but he had driven back the Rebels, denied them a victory they had to have if they wanted to keep the Mississippi.

After the battle, Halleck assumed field command of the two armies. He assembled one hundred thousand troops for the move on Corinth, which he didn't take until May 30, and then because the Confederates had abandoned the city and fallen back on Tupelo, fifty miles south. Halleck shelved Grant, his second-in-command. Halleck gave him nothing to command nor did he accept his counsel. Having taken Corinth, Halleck began entrenching and fortifying the city rather than moving on to press the enemy. Not only did he fragment a large army, but Halleck again gave the Confederacy breathing space.

Because they had gained breathing space, Robert E. Lee's army crossed the Potomac into Maryland and another Confederate army under Braxton Bragg tried to reclaim Kentucky. Though neither Lee nor Bragg succeeded, their brilliant maneuvers frightened Lincoln and Stanton. They summoned Henry Halleck to Washington and gave him supreme command.

Halleck designated no successor. The command of western Tennessee and as much of Mississippi as he could take and hold thus devolved on Grant, the senior major general. Halleck intended as much. He was not called "Old Brains" for nothing. He knew a capable and efficient soldier when he saw one. Still, it wasn't much of a command. Grant had to dispatch several of his divisions to Buell in Kentucky and he had to use his remaining troops to break up a Confederate attack intended to capture Corinth.

In October he wired Halleck that with some small reinforcements he would move along the railroads down to Jackson, Mississippi, and prepare a campaign to take Vicksburg. Halleck said yes.

Vicksburg, on the Mississippi River in the state of Mississippi, was about halfway between Memphis and New Orleans, both of which the Union had captured by the summer of 1862. But as long as the Confederates held Vicksburg and Port Hudson, two hundred and fifty miles to the south in Louisiana, they denied the Union passage down the river. More than that, the Confederates had a bridge over which flowed critical supplies of grain, livestock, horses, and men from Arkansas, Louisiana, and Texas. Vicksburg stitched these states, called the TransMississippi Confederacy, to the South.

Vicksburg was a tough nut to crack. The city was a fortress situated on high bluffs, its cannons commanding seventeen miles of the river below. The Mississippi flowed past Vicksburg not like an arrow but like a sidewinder rattler, curving back and forth. An amphibious attack against the city was out of the question. Vicksburg was protected to the north by swamps and bayous which the river inundated most of the year. Farther inland a mountain range called the Chickasaw Bluffs formed another escarpment. The best chances for taking Vicksburg lay in an invasion of central Mississippi and an attack launched from there against the city's eastern defenses.

The campaign got under way in December, 1862. Grant drove south hoping to cut Vicksburg off from communications and supplies by taking Jackson. Sherman, starting from Memphis and following the Mississippi, marched on the city from the north. But Confederate cavalry burned Grant's supply depot at Holly Springs, Mississippi, forcing him to come to a halt. The Confederates were able to turn from this danger to Sherman, and coming out of the city, they repulsed his army as it tried to cross the Chickasaw Bluffs.

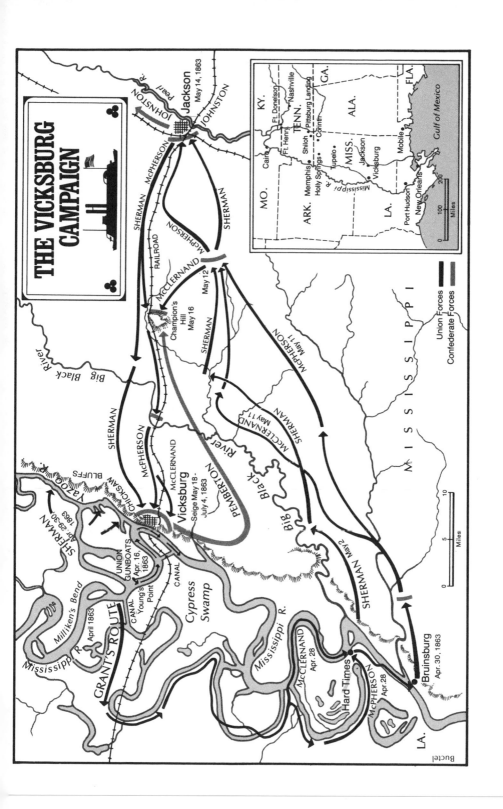

THE VICKSBURG CAMPAIGN

Union Forces
Confederate Forces

Jackson
May 14, 1863

JOHNSTON

JOHNSTON

SHERMAN
McPHERSON
RAILROAD

McCLERNAND

Champion's Hill
May 16

May 12

SHERMAN

McPHERSON
May 11

McCLERNAND
May 11

SHERMAN

Big Black River

Big Black River

SHERMAN

McPHERSON

McCLERNAND

PEMBERTON

Vicksburg
Siege May 18-
July 4, 1863

CHICKASAW BLUFFS

Yazoo R.

SHERMAN
Apr. 29-30, 1863

UNION GUNBOATS
Apr. 16, 1863

Young's Point

CANAL

CANAL

Cypress Swamp

Milliken's Bend
April 1863

GRANT'S ROUTE

Mississippi R.

Mississippi R.

MISSISSIPPI

SHERMAN
May 2

McCLERNAND
Apr. 28

Hard Times

McPHERSON
Apr. 28

Bruinsburg
Apr. 30, 1863

LA.

Buctel

KY.
Cairo
Ft. Donelson
Ft. Henry
Nashville
TENN.
Pittsburg Landing
Shiloh
Corinth
GA.
Memphis
Holly Springs
Tupelo
MISS.
ALA.
FLA.
Gulf of Mexico
MO.
ARK.
Jackson
Vicksburg
Mobile
Mississippi R.
Port Hudson
New Orleans
LA.

100   200
Miles

0   5   10
Miles

Both Grant and Sherman drew their armies upstream to Young's Point. Here they tried to devise another campaign. They set the men to digging canals in the hopes of draining off the river so that they could attack Vicksburg on dry land. This proved futile. They dug other canals and built bridges along the eastern side of the river in the hopes of finding a route over which they could move troops to the northern edges of the city. But in the spring of 1863 the Mississippi, swollen by heavy winter rains, kept dumping caissons and dead mules hundreds of miles to the south. The men along the river mucked their way through a quicksand of mud and swirling waters. It seemed the only way to mount another campaign against Vicksburg was to bring the armies back to Memphis and follow the railroad lines again down into Mississippi. Such a move would have produced widespread demoralization in the North. It would take months to move the troops and more months to outfit them. The only way to take Vicksburg, Grant decided, was from the east. To attack from the east, he would somehow have to get south of the city.

Grant devised his plan. Lincoln cautioned him against it. Sherman begged him to desist. But Grant had made his decision. Stubbornly he implemented it. In April, 1863, he put his armies on the western bank of the Mississippi, on the Louisiana side at Milliken's Bend. Out of sight of the Vicksburg cannoneers, Grant marched through the treacherous swamps and backwaters of Louisiana to Hard Times, a small town twenty miles south of Vicksburg. Sherman remained behind to make a diversionary movement from the north across the Yazoo, as though he were to attempt another debouchment from Chickasaw Bluffs. The feint fooled Confederate General John Pemberton, commanding forty thousand Confederates at Vicksburg. He never looked across the Mississippi.

With his army moving south, Grant brought Rear Admiral David Porter and his small fleet down from Memphis. Porter's gunboats towing empty barges and old transports ran the Vicksburg gauntlet on the night of April 16. Cannons on the bluffs boomed all night. The gunboats sent their salvos toward shore. Houses near the river caught fire. The Mississippi was as bright as day. Shells sank some of the barges and transports, but the rest made it to Hard

Times. Grant had the ferries now to transport his men from the Louisiana side of the Mississippi to Bruinsburg on the eastern bank.

Though outnumbered in the enemy's country, with the Big Black River between him and the stronghold of Vicksburg and with Vicksburg between him and his supplies, Grant said he felt a degree of relief scarcely ever equaled since. He was on dry ground and on the same side of the river as the Confederates. All the labors, hardships, exposures endured since December were for the accomplishment of this one object. Immediately, he sent for Sherman's corps to join him.

At this point, Grant could have moved down the Mississippi. Timing his move with that of General Nathaniel Banks in New Orleans, he could have converged on Port Hudson. But the big prize would remain behind him—Vicksburg, with its defending army. Any delay would make Vicksburg an even tougher nut to crack. For moving across the state with Confederate reinforcements was General Joe Johnston.

No, the main objective was Vicksburg, and Grant decided to go for it. The trick was to get to Johnston before Johnston got to Vicksburg. The problem was that Grant had not yet secured a base of supply. The gunboats couldn't keep running the batteries. So Grant decided to abandon a supply line, to move all his troops from Bruinsburg east to Jackson, where he could prevent Johnston from getting north of him and into Vicksburg. To do this, his army would have to move fast. It would have to live off the country. Grant wired Halleck that unless this plan was countermanded he would proceed at once and promptly he set off. The Union soldiers raided the plantations and small towns for food. They commandeered wagons and carts and buggies and hearses for transport. What they didn't seize they burned. On May 14, Grant beat Johnston to Jackson and drove him off. Now he was between two Confederate armies. By taking Jackson, Grant destroyed the one rail center capable of supplying Vicksburg with men and matériel.

At Vicksburg, Pemberton realized what was up. He came out of the fort with an army determined to cut Grant's supply lines—which he could not find. By the time Pemberton returned to Vicksburg, he realized he was cut off. Grant was moving on his eastern defenses. Joe Johnston ordered Pemberton to leave the city and escape by marching northeast. Jefferson Davis ordered Pemberton to hold out to the last man. Pemberton tried to do both. He left half his army within the Vicksburg perimeter and leading the other half marched to halt Grant.

Grant beat him handily at the battle of Champion's Hill and beat him a day later, on May 19, at the Big Black River. Pemberton withdrew into the city. Grant sent one corps to the south. One corps pressed against the east. A third corps encircled the city to the north. This third corps reached the Mississippi, established a landing, and Grant's problems of supply were over.

Two weeks before, Halleck had countermanded Grant's orders, only to learn that nobody knew where Grant was. Now everybody knew. Grant had a corps on the northern bank of the Mississippi and Halleck began funneling reinforcements, artillery, and supplies to the Army of the Tennessee. Grant tightened his troops around Vicksburg like a vise, trapping within the city the entire Confederate army.

Twice Grant stormed the citadel. Twice the Confederates repulsed him. Daily, the Union army, however, dug its entrenchments ever nearer the city. By July 1 there was food neither for the civilian population of fifty thousand nor for the almost equally large Confederate army. When he ran out of ball ammunition, Pemberton came to surrender his army. He and Grant discussed surrender terms over an old oak stump which later, said Grant, furnished more cords of wood in the shape of trophies than the True Cross. The date was July 4, 1863. Vicksburg never celebrated Independence Day again until 1945.

The fall of Vicksburg capped the crucial forty-eight hours of the Civil War. The day before, on July 3, Pickett's charge was repulsed at Gettysburg, and Lee retreated from Pennsylvania with a beaten army. Gettysburg was the climactic battle of the Civil War. But it was not disparate from the Union victory at Vicksburg. Lee moved into Pennsylvania hoping to relieve Virginia from the constant battering of the Army of the Potomac; he hoped also that by winning a battle in the North he would take the heart out of the Union and perhaps also win recognition from England; and lastly Lee hoped that by moving north, he would panic the Union to draw off troops from Grant for the defense of Washington, which the Confederacy momentarily imperiled.

Abraham Lincoln sent Grant a personal message confessing he had been wrong and Grant had been right and celebrated the victory with the announcement to the Congress that once more the "Father of the waters rolls unvex'd to the sea." Lincoln also sent Charles Dana, Assistant Secretary of War, to Vicksburg, ostensibly to determine if Grant was drinking. The gossip always pursued Grant. The regular officers of the old army were as busy with gossip as the ladies of a New England quilting bee. Covertly, Dana was to determine if Grant had political ambitions for 1864. Grant wanted only to win the war. Lincoln decided to let Grant win it, and win it in his own way.

With Vicksburg secured, Grant's hope was to march his army through the Deep South to Mobile, seizing munitions, destroying factories, burning warehouses, closing ports. He saw no way the demoralized Confederacy could stop him. But Halleck again ordered Grant to entrench and give up plans for attack. Again Halleck began to deplete Grant's army to reinforce other positions.

Halleck was annoyed too that Grant had paroled the thirty-seven thousand Confederates who surrendered at Vicksburg and later at Port Hudson. Grant explained that moving these prisoners of war to northern prison camps would tie up Union transportation along the Mississippi for weeks. These Confederates had been recruited in Alabama, Mississippi, Arkansas, Missouri, and Louisiana. Once paroled, they would go home to their farms and small towns. But officers who did not go by the book worried Halleck. Halleck thought Grant's strategy superfluous because General William Rosecrans, who had relieved Don Carlos Buell, was outmaneuvering Braxton Bragg. Rosecrans had occupied Chattanooga and was chasing Bragg through northern Georgia.

What Halleck didn't know was that Bragg had been reinforced by "Pete" Longstreet's infantry corps, which had moved down from Virginia. Bragg turned suddenly on Rosecrans, broke his lines, and almost decimated the entire Army of the Cumberland. But George H. Thomas, a Virginian who had opted for the Union, helped blunt the ferocious Confederate attacks at the sluggish Chickamauga

River outside Chattanooga. The little river foamed with the blood of brave men. Thomas, the "Rock of Chickamauga," had bought an afternoon's time for Union troops to find refuge in the city. Bragg laid siege.

Chattanooga was an unfortunate place for an army to withstand a siege. The rugged Tennessee mountains oppress the city from the north. Located on the southern bank of the Tennessee River, Chattanooga is even more tightly girdled by Raccoon Mountain to the west, Lookout Mountain to the south, and Missionary Ridge to the east. Bragg seized these heights and fortified them. He waited for Rosecrans's army to starve. Complicating matters was the fact that Burnside had taken a smaller Union force east to Knoxville. With Chattanooga cut off, Burnside was also without supplies.

Thoroughly alarmed over the situation, Secretary of War Stanton summoned Grant to Indianapolis. He and Lincoln wanted Grant to relieve Chattanooga. To accomplish this end, they gave Grant supreme command in the West. He was in charge of everything from the Alleghenies to the Mississippi.

Grant removed Rosecrans from command of the Army of the Cumberland and made Thomas its head. He ordered Sherman to forget mending railroads in Mississippi and hurry into Tennessee. Grant asked for and received two corps commanded by General Joe Hooker from the Army of the Potomac. Elements of his own Army of the Tennessee came on. But to get these forces into the city and then from the city out against the rebels meant securing a supply line. The Tennessee River at Chattanooga is no more tractable than the Mississippi at Vicksburg. The river flows past the city here like a bullwhip about to crack. Grant had to open a route from Bridgeport, Alabama, fifty miles away through the Raccoon Mountains and twice cross the twisting Tennessee to bring supply wagons and soldiers and cannon into Chattanooga. This involved laying 102 miles of rails and building 182 bridges. The engineering, transport, and supply problems were of a magnitude never before attempted, but Grant's solution fit the picture he imagined.

Grant saw his chance in November when Bragg dispatched Longstreet's superb soldiers to attack Burnside one hundred miles upriver. On November 23, General Thomas's men, after moving

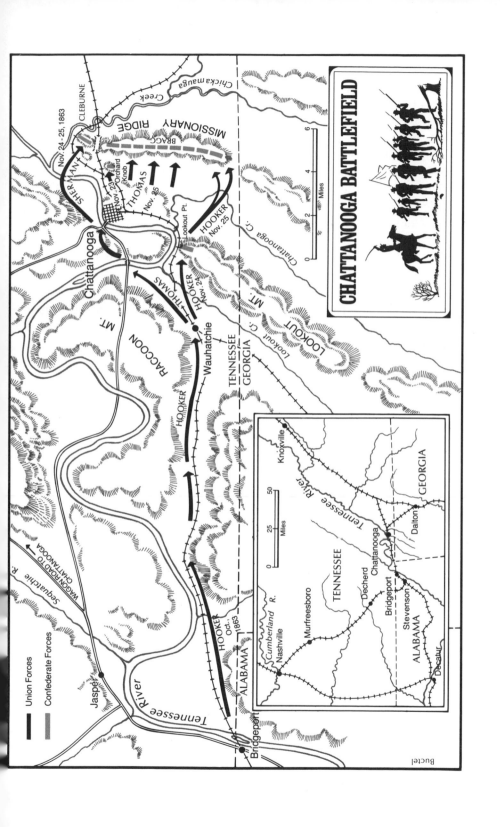

CHATTANOOGA BATTLEFIELD

Miles
0 2 4 6

Union Forces
Confederate Forces

MISSIONARY RIDGE
BRAGG
CLEBURNE
Chickamauga Creek
SHERMAN Nov. 24 - 25, 1863
Nov. 23 Orchard Knob
THOMAS Nov. 25
Chattanooga
Lookout Pt.
HOOKER Nov. 25
HOOKER Nov. 24
THOMAS
RACCOON MT.
Wauhatchie
HOOKER
LOOKOUT MT.
Lookout C.
Chattanooga C.
TENNESSEE
GEORGIA
HOOKER Oct., 1863
ALABAMA
Tennessee River
Jasper
Sequatchie R.
WAGON ROAD TO CHATTANOOGA
Bridgeport

Miles
0 25 50

Knoxville
TENNESSEE
GEORGIA
Tennessee River
Dalton
Decherd
Chattanooga
Bridgeport
Stevenson
ALABAMA
Decatur
Cumberland R.
Nashville
Murfreesboro

Buctel

out of the city, took the rifle pits at Orchard Knob, a small elevation on the plain from which an attack could be launched against the slopes of the four-mile-long entrenchments on Missionary Ridge.

On the next day, Joe Hooker's corps stormed Lookout Mountain on the right. Their passage up the mountain was by a series of rocky ledges which the Confederates defended ledge by ledge. A heavy mist shrouded the mountain. Hooker's men forced the Confederates into the mist and up past it. From their position at Orchard Knob all Grant and his generals could see were the gun flashes "like swarms of fireflies" as Hooker's men pushed upward. Finally, the Union soldiers emerged from the mist to seize the crest of Lookout Mountain in what has become known as the Battle Above the Clouds. But the Confederates withdrew in orderly rank and file to Missionary Ridge, burning the bridges behind them. This made it difficult for Hooker to attack Bragg's western flank. The key Union movement, however, took place on the left. Sherman sneaked an army upstream on the northern bank of the Tennessee, crossed the river on the night of the twenty-fourth and on the twenty-fifth began an all-out attack on the eastern tip of Missionary Ridge, Bragg's other flank. But working up Missionary Ridge was murderous going. The ridge first of all was not a continuous slope but a series of precipitous hills humping up to the crest. The Confederate cannons could not depress low enough to hit the advancing forces but the Rebels rolled charged shells down upon the Yankees. Sherman was also contending against Pat Cleburne, the best division commander in Bragg's army. Cleburne made Sherman pay for each hill. Cleburne even launched a surprise counterattack in the afternoon. For eight hours Sherman and Cleburne fought while Hooker tried to bring his men across from Lookout Mountain. By 3 P.M. Sherman could push his troops no farther. The attack was stalled.

In the hopes of relieving Sherman, Grant ordered the center at Orchard Knob to make a diversionary attack against the line of rifle pits at the base of Missionary Ridge. These were Thomas's men, men of the Army of the Cumberland, who three months before had fled into Chattanooga like hounded rabbits. Now the cooks, the blacksmiths, the clerks grabbed guns, and at 3:30 P.M.

charged out of Orchard Knob toward the blazing Confederate pits. Shouting "Chickamauga! Chickamauga!" they overran the pits. A withering fire raked them from above. Without a halt, these Cumberland men continued on up the ridge, dislodging Confederate batteries, charging past trenches.

"Come on, boys," shouted a Union sergeant, "grab a gun and see 'em run." There was no formation, just triangles of blue scrambling up a steep hill. When the color bearer fell, another picked up the flag and kept going until he, too, fell and then a third seized the banner to lead up.

Pressed hard on his flanks, Bragg could not rally his center. The Confederates streamed southward from Missionary Ridge in a rout. The boys from the Cumberland stood on the ridge laughing at Hooker's tough Gettysburg corps and Sherman's hardened Vicksburg veterans.

Grant had been lucky. The truth was he had helped make his own luck. "It is decisiveness and energy in action that always accomplishes grand results, and strikes terror to the heart of the foe. It is this and not the conception of great schemes that makes military genius," wrote John Rawlins, Grant's dependable aide.

The victory at Chattanooga inspired the Congress to revive the grade of lieutenant general. Lincoln nominated Grant in late February, 1864, and asked him to come to Washington to become general-in-chief of the Union armies. Grant appeared unannounced at a White House reception on the evening of March 8. Lincoln, the tallest man in the room, spied his new general, the shortest, and said, "Why, here is General Grant." People surged around Grant, pressing, eager to meet this unknown hero. It was, in the words of one witness, "the most coat-tearing button-bursting jam" ever to transpire in the White House. Lincoln and Secretary of State Seward persuaded Grant to stand upon a sofa so that he might more easily shake hands with those who wanted to meet him.

As the Union's commanding general, Grant saw clearly that as long as the Confederacy remained an integral unit its military forces and matériel could be shifted easily and quickly wherever they were needed. And he saw that occupying localities was fruitless, that the end of the Confederacy could come only from the destruction of its armies. Consequently, he determined to cut the Confederacy into fragments, to engage all its armies at the same time, and to destroy these armies by following them no matter where they might go, warring with them relentlessly, pounding them to pieces.

The Civil War was about union. The cost of union was sacrifice. Grant became Lincoln's general, not only because he had the will, determination, and tenacity to carry out military decisions that entailed sacrifice, but also because he knew intuitively that the Union soldiers would pay this terrible price.

Grant would much more have preferred to lead the Army of the Tennessee and the Army of the Cumberland from Chattanooga through the heretofore untrammeled states of the Confederacy. He knew the war would be won in the South. But he gave this task to Sherman, whom he named Commander-in-the-West. He himself rode with the Army of the Potomac and made his headquarters in the field. The Army of the Potomac needed leadership. Lee had bloodied this army and for three years sent it northward in humiliating retreat after humiliating retreat. The Army of the Potomac knew how to fight. It proved that at Gettysburg. Now it was going to learn how to win.

When Sherman left Chattanooga for Atlanta in May, 1864, Grant crossed the Rapidan River heading for Richmond. Grant's purpose as general-in-chief was to take neither of these cities but rather make the Confederate armies fight for them. He knew the Union would win the war by beating armies, not by taking cities. The strategy of Joe Johnston in Georgia and Robert E. Lee in Virginia was to prolong the war in the hopes the North would quit in despair of ever clearly winning it.

With four thousand wagons in its train, the Army of the Potomac penetrated the Wilderness, a miles-wide thicket between the Rapidan and Spotsylvania Court House, a key road juncture. The Wilderness was a thick and tangled place of second-growth trees and vines, heavily thicketed with underbrush, with few roads and fewer clearings. It was cut by ravines and small streams. Only a compass gave a man direction. Soldiers saw no more than twenty yards ahead of them. Grant's army plunged into it like an arrow.

On May 7, Lee hit this arrow at right angles with three corps.

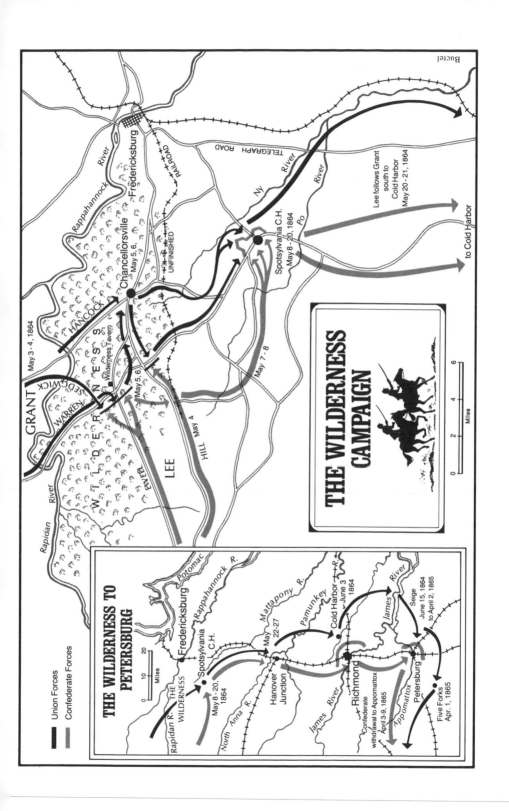

Buctel

THE WILDERNESS CAMPAIGN

0   2   4   6
Miles

Lee follows Grant
south to
Cold Harbor
May 20 - 21, 1864

to Cold Harbor

Spotsylvania C.H.
May 8 - 20, 1864

TELEGRAPH ROAD

Ny River

Po River

May 7 - 8

Fredericksburg

Rappahannock River

RAILROAD

UNFINISHED

Chancellorsville
May 5, 6,

Wilderness Tavern

May 5, 6,

HANCOCK

GRANT
May 3 - 4, 1864

SEDGWICK

WARREN

WILDERNESS

EWELL

HILL May 4

LEE

May 4

Rapidan River

THE WILDERNESS TO
PETERSBURG

Union Forces

Confederate Forces

0   10   20
Miles

Potomac R.

Fredericksburg

Rappahannock R.

Spotsylvania
C.H.

May 8 - 20,
1864

THE
WILDERNESS

Rapidan R.

North Anna R.

Hanover
Junction

May
22 - 27

Mattapony R.

Pamunkey R.

Cold Harbor
June 3
1864

James River

Richmond

James River

Confederate
withdrawal to Appomattox
April 3 - 9, 1865

Appomattox

Petersburg

Seige
June 15, 1864
to April 2, 1865

Five Forks
Apr. 1, 1865

Troops could not make out their own lines, let alone the enemy's position. An artillery commander moved his cannons from the rear to the front and fired dead ahead down a narrow road. But if Lee meant battle, Grant would give it to him here. He moved up his divisions and sent them as fast as he could into the blind undergrowth. "Feeding a fight" he called it. The rifle fire reached such intensity that the Wilderness was set ablaze, and Union and Confederate troops fought amid raging forest fires. Wounded men burned to death. Clubbed muskets shattered skulls and bayonets thrust between the logs of the parapets drew blood.

The Wilderness was no place for traditional strategic concepts. When Sedgwick was outflanked during the battle a general warned Grant, "This is a crisis. I know Lee's methods. He will throw his whole army between us and the Rapidan and cut us off completely." The General removed his cigar and replied, "I am tired of hearing what Lee is going to do. Some of you always think he will suddenly turn a somersault and land in our rear and on both our flanks. Go back to your command, and try to think what *we* are going to do instead of what Lee is going to do."

Demoniacal men screamed above the raging wind and a hell-sent storm failed to halt the fight. Coolly Grant awaited the reports of his generals. While he waited, he whittled.

For two days the Wilderness was a blinding, choking fog of fire, a crescendo of shouted commands and the shrill moaning of the wounded. On May 7, the battle broke off. Far from beating Lee, the Army of the Potomac had barely saved itself. The battle had claimed seventeen thousand Union men. There were so many amputees they were packed sidewise like spoons in the horse-drawn ambulances for the tortuous trip to the hospitals at Fredricksburg.

Despite these losses, the Army of the Potomac was inspirited by Grant's command. Instead of retreating across the Rapidan when the indecisive fighting slackened, Grant went for Lee's right flank, hoping to get between the Army of Northern Virginia and Richmond. On the night of May 7, men who would never see another dusk cheered when Grant and his retinue rode through their ranks to lead the columns south. Grant instinctively understood one truth about fighting, that men who will fight will give their lives to beat the enemy.

Lee was not flanked at Spotsylvania. But this time it was Lee who barely saved his army in another ferocious battle. Grant kept pressing and forced Lee back toward Richmond. By early June, Lee succeeded in entrenching at Cold Harbor. There, a few miles from Richmond, Grant stormed the Confederate position in the bloodiest battle of the Civil War. Lee was a pioneer in trench warfare and in less than four hours the Union lost eight thousand men. The campaign from the Wilderness to the temporary stalemate at Cold Harbor cost the Union sixty thousand men and the Confederacy twenty thousand. The Union could better bear the loss. Longstreet had warned Lee that Grant was a general who would fight every day and every hour until the end of the war.

The overland route to Richmond by frontal assault was too expensive. Grant slipped his army south across the James River and the troops began a long siege against Petersburg, the supply depot for Richmond. They skirmished whenever the Confederates offered themselves. They raided when they could. They blew up mines under Confederate embattlements. They also dug trenches ever closer around Petersburg. Pick and shovel during the fall of 1864 were more effective than rifle and mortar. By the beginning of the winter, Grant's lines looked like a sickle. The handle lay against Richmond in the north and the blade almost encircled Petersburg twenty miles to the south. The more the sickle threatened to thrash Petersburg, the more Lee had to stretch his lines to ward off the cut.

Men died from dysentery and exposure. Others fell from snipers and were blasted to bits by the random cannonading. A general said to Grant that the war had come to resemble the fight between the Kilkenny cats that devoured each other. Grant said, "Our cat has a longer tail."

As troops glowered from fortified trenches, the tenor of the war changed. What had been a bloody war marked with romantic cavalry charges and courageous hand-to-hand combat became a bloody, grim, and malevolent war. Grant dispatched Sheridan and the cavalry into the Shenandoah Valley, the granary of Virginia. Behind him Sheridan left scorched fields and burning plantations. Troops slaughtered cattle on the hills and reduced warehouses to rubble.

In September, Sherman took Atlanta and set out for the sea

leaving a blackened swath of destruction twenty-five miles wide in his wake.

In November, Abraham Lincoln was reelected. In the same month, the Confederate cabinet voted to make soldiers out of slaves, thus ending slavery, the cause for which the South fought. The same cabinet also voted to melt down locomotive engines for cannon.

In January, Grant sent out an expedition under Admiral Porter and General A. H. Terry to take Wilmington, North Carolina. With the city's capture, the Confederacy lost its last remaining port.

In February, Sherman left Savannah and began marching north across the Carolinas. Joe Johnston's decimated army of thirty thousand had no choice but to keep backing away.

At City Point in Virginia, Grant began the buildup for the spring offensive. Union supplies were not only in profusion, they were extravagant. In Petersburg and Richmond, Confederates maintained their morale on ashcakes and water.

The Appomattox campaign got going on March 29. In the muck and slime, Union troops began moving out of their trenches to build corduroy roads for the transport of artillery. Sheridan's cavalry circled round and hit at Five Forks, which was west of Petersburg on Lee's extreme right. To lose Five Forks meant to lose the last avenue of escape for the Army of Northern Virginia. Lee pulled troops from the center and sent them to George Pickett, who was trying to hold off Sheridan. Now the Confederate lines were stretched beyond endurance. The Union charged. The lines in front of Petersburg broke.

Lee had one last chance—to get his army out of Richmond and make his way south to Johnston's army in North Carolina. But Sheridan had taken Five Forks, which meant that, to get south, Lee had first to proceed west. On April 3, Grant took Petersburg and Richmond and began racing his troops westward to catch Lee before he could turn south. While Lee waited for supplies at Amelia Court House, Sheridan cut the Danville Road at Jetersville. Lee tried to push farther west toward Lynchburg. But Grant's infantry beat him to Appomattox Court House. "There is nothing left for me to do," Lee said to Longstreet, "but go and see General Grant, and I would rather die a thousand deaths."

Grant and Lee discussed surrender in the red brick home of Wilmer McLean, formerly a Confederate major. McLean once inhabited a beautiful plantation house at Manassas Junction in Virginia. It was riddled with bullets during the battle of Bull Run in 1861. During second Bull Run the house was again devastated, when it served as a Confederate hospital. Wanting safety for his family, McLean moved them to the small, out-of-the-way village of Appomattox Court House. Wilmer McLean knew something about the hounds of war because they followed him right into his parlor.

After he signed the surrender, Lee strode to the porch. Grant saw him slam one gauntleted fist into the other. Quickly Lee mounted his horse Traveller and rode off. Union troops started firing a salute of one hundred guns in honor of victory. Grant ordered the cannonading stopped. "The Confederates are now our prisoners," he said, "and we do not want to exult over their downfall."

After Appomattox, Grant remained the general-in-chief with headquarters in Washington. He also served eight months as interim Secretary of War for the beleaguered Andrew Johnson. Congress authorized the grade of four-star general for him. He was the embodiment of victory and the nation elevated him to the presidency in 1868.

When he became President, he brought to the White House a quartermaster from the old army and installed him as chef. Daily the pot roasts grew bigger, the stews meatier, and the chowders more like puddings, until Julia Grant remarked that the French ambassador seemed to tire of apple pie. Then the quartermaster went back to the army and Julia introduced to the White House an Italian chef who was a graduate of the Cordon Bleu. The ennui of the French ambassador noticeably abated.

Grant thought he deserved the presidency in the same way and for the same reasons he deserved the fourth star. Yet he imperfectly understood the constitutional process. He once told his Secretary of State he was sure Congress would ratify a proposed treaty and

Hamilton Fish had to point out that only the Senate ratified treaties.

Grant tried to run the executive branch as he had run the army. But where a general-in-chief can shift a disputatious general to another command to lessen the conflict between them, it is impossible to shift a disputatious senator. Grant wanted to annex Santo Domingo, hoping to establish there a republic for recently freed blacks much as the American Colonization Society had set up a black republic years before in Liberia. The way for him to have succeeded was to have confided the project to Charles Sumner, chairman of the Senate Foreign Relations Committee. But Grant was not politic. He disliked Sumner. He called him a "narrowhead" and said, "His eyes are so close together he can peep through a gimlet hole without blinking." Sumner, no friend of Grant, defeated the projected annexation handily.

Grant had known early poverty in a crude background. That background sometimes demeaned him, as it demeaned Andrew Johnson, but elevated Lincoln. Grant never overcame it as President. It made him reticent, doubtful of his superior ability, and encouraged his distrust of men with sophisticated talents and learning. He refused an appointment to the brilliant John L. Motley because, "He parts his hair in the middle and carries a single eyeglass."

Grant had entered the White House as President of the whole country and left it as a partisan boss representative of the country's more reactionary interests. He failed to see the central issue of post-Civil-War America. The old issue had been whether the United States "is" or the United States "are." For over eighty years the three sections of the country, North, South, and West, agreed the United States "is," but each section wanted to control the administration and lawmaking for the others. The war broke the intensity of this sectional rivalry, yet hardly had Lee surrendered when the North, now an industrial giant, compelled the other sections to endorse a policy of protection against foreign competition. To Westerners, the protective tariff was a menace as evil as slavery. Grant championed Eastern interests, those of the manufacturer, banker, and railroad magnate. As President, he remained deaf to the pleas of the farmer, who always had to sell his wheat in a falling market, and the cotton grower, whose cotton brought so little he burned it for heat in the winter.

Grant is the only American President to have escaped from a dismal administration with any of his reputation intact. He is also one of the only two Republican Presidents to have served two full terms.*

He was loyal, often an unfortunate trait in Presidents. He did not demand loyalty, he expected it; and he often confused criticism with disloyalty. He wanted loyalty and he rewarded it. All of Grant's appointments to West Point or Annapolis were the sons of army and navy men. Too many of his appointments in government were incompetent old-army men.

The nation slackened after the war and Grant slackened with it. The Lincolnian vision belonged to the ages and not to the present. It wasn't long before wise heads in Washington realized that, not only was Grant not the greatest President since Washington, he was not the greatest since Lincoln.

It was also Grant's misfortune to preside over the vindictive Reconstruction. The Radical Republicans divided the South into five units governed by a military administration. The North succeeded in doing what Lincoln had started the war to prevent— making two nations out of one, one nation the conqueror, the other the vanquished. To secure a perpetual hegemony for their party in these provinces, the Radical Republicans enfranchised the entire black population. The votes of these newly freed slaves were shamefully and brutally manipulated by carpetbaggers and scalawags. This was neither Lincoln's hope for reunion nor the Northern constituency's, nor was it Grant's. He knew that the Republicans were engendering a race problem that even another Civil War could not solve. What doomed Reconstruction finally was its own corruption, a corruption made visible and magnified by the widespread corruption and fraud in the federal government, a corruption over which a naïve and eventually powerless Ulysses S. Grant presided.

Grant was President only a few months when Jim Fisk, Jr., and Jay Gould, Wall Street speculators, saw a chance to use him to

* The other is Dwight D. Eisenhower, another West Pointer.

[93]

corner the gold market. It was said of Jim Fisk that he was "first in war, first in peace, and first in the pockets of his countrymen." Jay Gould was described succinctly as "the meanest man born since the beginning of the Christian era." Together Fisk and Gould had looted the Erie Railroad. This wasn't big enough for them. Now they determined to loot the country.

During the summer of 1869 gold sold at $135: that is, 135 greenbacks purchased $100 worth of gold, of which there was $15 million in circulation. Fisk and Gould hoped to buy up this gold and set their own price. They thought $270 would do for a start. This posed a prospective catastrophe. While the country did not operate on the gold standard, banks, shipping combines, and brokerages often promised to pay debts in gold specie. If the price of gold doubled, it halved the greenback assets of a corporation, it drove down stock prices that had been purchased on margin, and it left hundreds of banking and financial institutions with a weakened currency.

To guard against such a catastrophe, the President of the United States was enabled to sell off government gold reserves to stabilize the price. If Ulysses S. Grant did not sell gold promptly, Fisk and Gould had every chance of success. They had to persuade Grant that their buying up gold was in the best interests of the country.

To gain the President's confidence, Fisk and Gould enlisted the services of Abel Rathbone Corbin, who had married Grant's spinster sister, Virginia. Corbin was a sixty-seven-year-old "lobby jobber," an agent employed by special interests to influence legislation, a profession at which he had proved a has-been for the last fifteen years.

Corbin gave them entrée. Fisk and Gould invited President and Mrs. Grant for a night cruise to Providence aboard Fisk's yacht. Each stateroom on this floating palace contained a canary named after one of Fisk's friends. There were canaries named John D. Rockefeller, J. P. Morgan, Leland Stanford, and one named General Grant. But entertaining Grant proved fruitless. He would not divulge his policy on gold.

So Corbin persuaded Grant to appoint dapper General Daniel Butterfield as the head of the New York sub-Treasury, upon whose collusion Fisk and Gould could depend. It was the duty of the New York sub-Treasurer to warn the government of a precipitate rise in gold. For $1 million in gold purchased on a $10,000 margin, Butterfield joined the Gold Bugs, as Horace Greeley later called them. Grant innocently made the appointment, happy to do so because Butterfield had once headed the subscription that purchased Mrs. Grant's Washington property.

When Corbin learned that Grant was distant from a telegraph office on September 23, the conspirators struck. Fisk and Gould began buying gold. There was no warning from Butterfield. The price soared to $161 before noon. September 24 is still known as Wall Street's Black Friday. Small brokerages closed. Shaky banks defaulted. Commodities offered for export could not be sold. Imports could not be unloaded. Credit ceased.

Visiting a cousin in Pennsylvania, Grant finally divined the plot and telegraphed Secretary of the Treasury George Boutwell to sell government gold reserves. This action defeated the corner and ended the panic. Later a congressional committee discovered there was no law against cornering gold or pressuring a President. Fisk told the committee, "Why, damn it! Old Corbin married into Grant's family for the purpose of working the thing in that direction." Because of Corbin, the Gold Bugs had not only put the stamp of venality on the new administration but had laid the scandal on the President's threshold.

Another brother-in-law, James F. Casey, was guilty of misconduct as Collector of Customs in New Orleans. Despite the published report of Casey's malfeasance, Grant appointed him to a second four-year term. Still a third brother-in-law, the Reverend M. J. Cramer, used to sell political favors without telling either Grant or the party they had been sold. Cramer also harangued the General and Mrs. Grant with lengthy disquisitions on the nature of God.

If his brothers-in-law were rascals, his friends were unconscionable. Because General W. W. Belknap had marched to the sea with Sherman, Grant appointed him Secretary of War in October, 1869. Belknap, a Princeton man with a pretty wife and no money to indulge her, quickly discovered that post traderships in the Indian Territory were exceedingly profitable. The traders enjoyed a monopoly as merchants in the military encampments and settlements. Traderships were so profitable, in fact, that Belknap succeeded in selling several of them, including one for $40,000 to a man named Marsh who already owned it.

A House Committee exposed these extortions as Belknap hurried over to the White House. By accepting Belknap's resignation, Grant effectively forestalled the Secretary's impeachment and punishment. He explained that he had accepted Belknap's resignation because he did not in the least comprehend what the Secretary was talking about and he had no idea that accepting resignations wasn't a matter of course.*

Toward the end of his first term another scandal of unprecedented proportions sadly diminished the remnants of any moral effectiveness left in his administration. This was the Credit Mobilier scandal which implicated Vice President Schuyler Colfax, Speaker of the House James G. Blaine, Senator Roscoe Conkling, Representatives Oakes Ames and James A. Garfield, among others.

The scandal had its inception during the Civil War when the government determined to build a railroad across the continent. The Union Pacific was formed for this purpose. Congress put the national treasury behind the undertaking. It gave the Union Pacific 12 million acres of government land for a transcontinental right-of-way and lent the company $27 million in United States bonds. The government did not insist on a property lien against this loan. Instead it let the company issue an additional $27 million in first-mortage bonds which took precedence over the government's claims. The promoters now had the land free and clear, a government loan they need never repay, and $27 million in cash. It seemed silly to turn these assets over to the Union Pacific Company when they could keep them themselves.

Consequently, the promoters acquired the ownership of a small construction company in Pennsylvania named Credit Mobilier. Credit Mobilier then contracted with the Union Pacific to build the railroad at three times the amount it would ordinarily have cost. To keep what they had and to make even more money, the promoters began to bribe members of Congress. They did it crudely. They sold

* The Senate went ahead and impeached him anyway, though the proceedings failed, 37 for conviction, 25 against. Of the 25 nays, 23 voted "not guilty" because they thought they could not impeach a man who had already resigned.

them stock in Credit Mobilier. The guaranteed dividends were of such enormity that not a representative or senator was out of pocket for his purchase. As often as the Union Pacific needed money, it went back to Congress, proved that it was broke, and won the appropriation, which was quickly assigned to the Credit Mobilier. Credit Mobilier in turn greased a dozen or so palms here and there with dividends that returned $3,000 for a $100 share.

About the time the Union Pacific reached Promontory Point, Utah, Oakes Ames, the representative from Massachusetts and a promoter of the Union Pacific, had a family quarrel with the directors of Credit Mobilier. Angrily, Ames wrote some indiscreet letters. Two years later, Charles Dana of the *New York Sun* got hold of these and printed them. Congress conducted two simultaneous investigations in the course of which the political lives of several elected officials were ruined and the reputations of others forever tarnished. Schuyler Colfax would have been impeached had he not shortly been succeeded by Henry Wilson. James G. Blaine was subsequently known as "the Continental liar from the State of Maine" for his part in the venture.

The Credit Mobilier scandal got its start before Grant was elected President. His administration had in no way lent itself to these peculations. But the scandal surfaced during an election year after other scandals had been exposed. Though he had neither known about the conspiracy nor profited from it, Grant was tarred by its brush. By the time of his second inaugural, "Grantism" was the linguistic convenience denoting fraud and corruption.

He seemed incapable of saving his administration from the depredations of the corrupt and the fraudulent. He was incapable because of an unwillingness, almost an inability, to suspect friends of wrongdoing. And when it was clear friends had betrayed him, he could not be pitiless.

The President's private secretary was Orville Babcock, who had served on his wartime staff. Babcock was the Union colonel who talked to Robert E. Lee in McLean's parlor while Phil Sheridan rode to summon Grant. Babcock was the principal instrument by which the Whiskey Ring defrauded the United States Treasury of millions of dollars. It was said of Babcock that he fished for gold in every stinking cesspool.

The Whiskey Ring was bribery on the grand scale, an operation that drew into its net hundreds of lower-echelon government employees on the take as well as White House and Treasury officials. Since the Civil War, the government had levied heavy taxes on bottled (as opposed to barreled) whiskey. Depending upon congressional action, the taxes on liquor were double, triple, sometimes quadruple the price of the whiskey itself. To collect the taxes, the Treasury Department established "rectifying houses" inside the sixteen large distilleries, which were located in Chicago, Milwaukee, and the majority in St. Louis. The rectifiers kept track of the bottles capped in each distillery and affixed a tax stamp on each. The distiller paid the tax upon shipment and passed the cost along.

Here and there it had occurred to a distiller to bribe a rectifier and thus keep subsequent taxes collected for himself. Here and there a distiller succeeded, but not on any large scale because the government also kept records on the quantity of whiskey shipped by steamer and rail. Any significant discrepancy summoned surprise government inspections. Sitting in the White House, Orville Babcock saw that a network of informers would subtract the risk of discovery from a large-scale operation. A day's warning was sufficient for a distiller to doctor manifests and books for government inspection. Seeing eye to eye with Babcock was John A. McDonald, formerly a general of volunteers, bluff, hearty, gregarious, and totally illiterate. McDonald had won his post as the Internal Revenue Supervisor in St. Louis on Babcock's recommendation. They became a formidable entente in 1870 when McDonald, at Babcock's suggestion, began soliciting political contributions from distillers.

The ring used duplicate serial numbers on forged internal revenue stamps affixed by rectifiers who were bribed. Clerks faked bills of lading and shipping manifests. Higher officials certified these as genuine. A network of informers in the Treasury and rectifying houses kept distillers on the alert. Babcock distributed the payoffs. By 1874, the ring was profiting to the amount of $3 million a year.

There were often rumors of a ring bottling "crooked whiskey." But no Treasury official had obtained hard evidence of its existence.

No Treasury official during Grant's administration had spurred a serious investigation because the President had come to think of reformers as political enemies.

But a newly appointed Secretary of the Treasury, Benjamin Bristow, entertained presidential aspirations for himself.* Bristow found the circumstantial evidence he needed in the St. Louis newspapers. St. Louis was preparing for a fair and the newspapers constantly celebrated the city's increasing industry, often pointing out that St. Louis was the whiskey center of the United States. The paper published the number of cases shipped each month, a figure far higher than the one the Treasury received. Bristow confided his suspicions in Attorney General Edwards Pierrepont.

Then he and Pierrepont assembled a team of incorruptible agents who simultaneously conducted surprise raids on the sixteen distilleries on May 10, 1875. These agents sealed books and records and seized counterfeit stamps for the Bristow-Pierrepont inspection. Wholesale arrests shortly followed. One of the men arrested was John McDonald. At his trial, in which the government proved he was the kingpin, McDonald implicated Babcock.

What disgraced Grant was that he had accepted McDonald's hospitality while visiting the St. Louis Fair. In fact, McDonald had picked up a $3,000 hotel tab for the presidential entourage. Grant also insisted Orville Babcock was innocent.

Babcock was separately indicted and tried in St. Louis. Grant became the first and, so far, the last President to testify for the defense in a criminal proceeding instituted by the government. His deposition was read to Babcock's jurors. The jurors acquitted. To have convicted Babcock would have seriously compromised the President of the United States either by complicity or invincible stupidity.

Grant trusted such men as Corbin, Belknap, Babcock, and many others principally because he hungered for admiration, comradeship, and loyalty. He had grown up in a home not so much mean as it was affectionless, and the poverty and failure of his bleak years had taught him that confidence is often inspired by admiration, comradeship, and loyalty.

* Grant made twenty-four cabinet appointments for the seven posts during his two administrations. One Secretary of State lasted a little longer than a week.

He toyed with the idea of a third nomination in 1876. But the Republicans lost badly in the elections of 1874. When the Pennsylvania Republicans convened in May, 1875, for the purpose of electing delegates to the national convention, Grant wrote a letter to the chairman repudiating any desire for a third term. "I did not want the first nomination," he wrote, "and I do not want a third any more than I did the first."

His two administrations were not without their accomplishments. After the war, it took great work, energy, and imagination to bring the nation back to a stable economic footing. Grant was also the first President to insist on a humane policy for the American Indian, not an easy position when it is remembered that Sitting Bull ambushed Custer at Little Big Horn in 1876. And Grant's administration under the astute guidance of Secretary of State Hamilton Fish established for the first time in history the principle of international arbitration. In Geneva the United States and Britain adjudicated territorial disputes in the Northwest and Britain agreed to pay indemnities for serious breaches of neutrality during the Civil War.

At the end of his second administration, Grant was faced with a grave constitutional crisis which he resolved if not with equity at least with grace.

One of the dirtiest campaigns ever waged occurred in the election of 1876. It was in this election that John Mosby, the Confederate guerrilla turned Republican ambassador, coined the expression "the Solid South." With eleven Southern states firmly in its column, the Democratic Party seriously challenged the Republican monopoly. For their presidential candidate, the Democrats chose Samuel J. Tilden, governor of New York. Tilden had an impressive record of incorruptibility, having helped convict members of the Tammany Hall Tweed Ring. He had also amassed a large private fortune as a railroad corporation lawyer, and he must have earned every penny for he had ulcers so severe his health was a campaign issue.

As their candidate the Republicans chose Rutherford B. Hayes, a graduate of Kenyon College in Gambier, Ohio. By no means a brilliant man, Hayes had a reputation for stability. He had practiced law, served as a general in the Civil War, been elected to

Congress, and won three terms as Ohio's governor. He was conservative yet flexible, honest and only occasionally astute.

On the morning after the election Tilden had a plurality of 286,000 votes and, so the Democrats thought, a plurality of 18 votes in the electoral college. But there were three states with inconclusive returns: Florida, South Carolina, and Louisiana. By challenging these returns, the Republicans held up the convention of the electoral college. In the House and the Senate, filibusters, investigations, and parliamentary anarchy brought about an impasse. To break the impasse, Ulysses S. Grant first devised, then appointed an electoral commission to certify the winner. This electoral commission was composed of five senators, five representatives, and five Supreme Court justices. The commission gave the election to Hayes by dividing along party lines, eight Republicans for Hayes, seven Democrats for Tilden, though it did not decide in Hayes's favor until March 2, 1877, three days before Grant left office. On March 3, Grant invited Hayes to dinner at the White House. Among the guests was Chief Justice Morrison Waite of the Supreme Court. During the evening, Grant sent his son Buck for a Bible and then, beckoning to the President-elect, persuaded Hayes quietly to go through with a secret oath-taking ceremony in the Red Room of the White House.

In May of 1877, a little more than two months after he left the presidency, the General and Mrs. Grant boarded the steamer *Indiana* in Philadelphia. They embarked on a round-the-world trip which would not bring them to San Francisco until September, 1879, two years and four months later. Without question, the trip was one of the most thrilling experiences ever to befall an ex-President of the United States. Everywhere kings and workingmen cheered Grant as the embodiment of the American ideal.

In Scotland, Clan Grant received him as one of its distinguished sons. In England the Grants dined with Queen Victoria. He said, "The Queen was *too* anxious to put me at my ease." In Rome the Pope received him, and in Belgium King Leopold called informally at his hotel. The Greeks lit the Parthenon at night for him. In Palestine the American consul saw to it that the General entered Jerusalem with more fanfare and a greater throng than had attended Jesus. Sultan Abdul-Hamid II of Turkey gave Grant four Arabian horses, and the British raj made him a guest of honor in India. The General enjoyed the saltless, butterless, and breadless cuisine of the Japanese royal court. He advised the Mikado never to borrow from Europe and to forestall war in China.

The General informed American reporters on his return that he had met the four great men in the world: Lord Beaconsfield (Benjamin Disraeli); Léon Gambetta, the French premier; Prince Otto von Bismarck, with whom the General shared one of the most revelatory and remarkable *tête-à-têtes* ever recorded; and Li Hung-chang, the noted statesman of the Celestial Empire of China.

He had financed the trip on $25,000 that he realized on a lucky mining investment. He resolved to go as far as the money would carry him—which was Vienna. But the Grants were able to continue eastward because Buck Grant, who was managing the General's money, had realized substantial profits on advice supplied by one Ferdinand Ward, known as the Young Napoleon of Wall Street.

After a triumphal zigzagging tour of the United States and Mexico, the General and Mrs. Grant returned home to Galena, Illinois. Confidently the General awaited nomination for a third term in 1880, which the Republican Stalwarts, the Old Guard, assured him was his.

"Grant does not care to be President again. He wants employment. He needs money," wrote the insightful William Tecumseh Sherman to his brother, John, the senator who later gave his name to the Anti-Trust Act.

Grant did not win the nomination. On the thirty-sixth ballot dark horse James A. Garfield did. The defeat mortified the General. "My friends," he said, "have not been honest with me. I could not afford to be defeated. They should not have placed my name in nomination unless they felt perfectly sure of my success."

With this failure, life in Galena paled. Grant wrote to friends, "One thing is certain: I must do something to supplement my income or continue to live in Galena or on a farm. I have not got the means to live in the city." It was at this moment that Ferdinand Ward proposed that he and General Grant establish a banking house of their own. No sooner had the General agreed than George

Jones and George Childs successfully raised the two subscriptions that made the move to New York both feasible and comfortable.

By April, 1884, Ulysses S. Grant was so firmly established in New York City that he undertook to raise a special subscription on his own for a project dear to his heart: he pledged $5,000 toward the construction of the pedestal for the Statue of Liberty. He asked nineteen millionaire friends to do the same.

By the end of May, he and Julia Grant were living on borrowed money with barely enough of that to see them through a Spartan summer at Long Branch.

PART III

HE BECOMES A WRITER

He did not really earn a living, because like so many men, that is people, it is hard to earn a living. Everybody knows that in a kind of way it is hard if not almost impossible to earn their living. Grant did this and knew this.

Gertrude Stein
Four in America

NO MATTER WHAT MISFORTUNES BEFELL HIM, ULYSSES S. GRANT WAS Long Branch's first citizen and he would always be its first citizen. He had done more for Long Branch by his presence than for any other place he ever lived. But then, he more enjoyed himself there than anyplace else.

Long Branch, which takes its name from its location on the longer branch of the Shrewsbury River, was one of the country's leading summer resorts in the second half of the nineteenth century. Midway on the New Jersey coastline, equidistant from New York and Philadelphia, Long Branch began attracting visitors for its salubrious climate as early as 1820. Mary Lincoln was at Long Branch in 1861, during the Battle of Bull Run, and General Winfield Scott regularly summered there. The actors Edwin Booth and Edwin Forrest came there with their friends and their girls. Long Branch was characterized by *Harper's Magazine* as "the great marine suburb of the great metropolis."

But Long Branch never really challenged Saratoga and Newport. Its egalitarian popularity kept it from being as exclusive. Its brass bands, refreshment tents, and shooting galleries gave it a Coney Island air. The *Long Branch Record* was fond of boasting that, on Sundays in the 1800s, the combined wealth of the congregation worshipping at St. James Chapel on Ocean Avenue was $120 million. But Long Branch attracted the nouveau riche millionaire. Solomon Guggenheim chose it as the site of his multi-million-dollar Moorish-style summer home, Aladdin's Palace, unrivaled for sheer vulgar exhibitionism and bad taste.

Besides its climate, what made Long Branch popular was its

gambling casinos and its racetrack. The gamblers began to put up purses to attract the best trotters, and the best trotters attracted everyone, even ladies. The *Record* boasted that Long Branch was America's Epsom Downs, but it lacked the gentility and the festive picnic air that attend the steeplechase. On the other hand, the word "hop" originated in Long Branch. The hops were informal nightly balls. The Grants attended these, and once the General took a turn with a lady. He was a disaster.

George Childs first invited the General to Long Branch in 1869 when he was sweltering in the White House, beleaguered by office seekers in the first summer of his presidency. Childs, who published the *Philadelphia Ledger*, had become one of Grant's closest friends and warmest admirers. It was in Childs's *Ledger* building that the General became a member of the Grand Army of the Republic, George C. Meade Post No. 1 of Philadelphia. Childs had become a heavy investor in Long Branch's growth. He was no doubt pleased that Grant delighted in the gaiety of the place and found ease in its healthful pleasures that summer. In fact, he, George Pullman, and Moses Taylor bought a cottage in Elberon, a beachside neighborhood on Ocean Avenue, which the Grants were invited to use for the rest of their lives.

The "cottage" was a three-story structure with seven dormers, an encircling balcony, and an octagonal porch. The house had twenty-eight rooms, into which the General stuffed secretaries and heads of agencies busily conducting government business. There was always a safari of office seekers and petitioners swelling the local population; and reporters referred to Long Branch as the "Summer capital."

Grant's arrival in Long Branch charged the atmosphere. When he donned a white plug hat and linen duster and stepped into his carriage, teeth clenching a lighted cigar, he galvanized a social complex that began rotating on an axis all its own. Long Branch became more than popular, it became spectacular.*

* The General set a precedent. Subsequent Presidents summered at the resort. Rutherford B. Hayes, Grant's successor, owned a summer cottage at Elberon. Mrs. Hayes was called "Lemonade Lucy" because she banned spiritous drinks wherever she lived. President James A. Garfield died in Long Branch in September, 1881, from wounds inflicted by his assassin, Charles Guiteau, on June 5. To move

The Grants particularly liked sitting side by side on the porch in the morning. Julia wore a sunbonnet and he wore a broadcloth coat and a top hat, which he never tired of tipping in deference to the passing grande dames. In the afternoons he liked riding behind his team of trotters, and he knew the countryside for miles around. His political enemies magnified this harmless diversion into a scandalous indulgence, and ridiculed it as vulgar display. But it gratified a basic feeling in Grant, one that had led him to say during the war that he would like to close his days breeding fine horses. The trotters also gave him something to talk about to politicians who wanted to talk about patronage.

He loved the racetrack at Long Branch, and when he took a box everyone followed. In 1882, Oscar Wilde, who was visiting the General at the cottage, turned down an invitation to the track with the remark that he had long ago come to the conclusion that one horse was capable of running faster than the others. In the evenings, Grant often liked to swap stories with Len Van Dyke, the special policeman who patrolled Ocean Avenue, and Henry Van Brunt, who owned the nearby bathing pavilion.

The friends in Long Branch were longtime friends. That summer of 1884 Grant still played poker on Friday nights with his friend General Henry Van Vliet, who lived in nearby Shrewsbury. The local newspapers still reported the guests who came and went from the cottage. But the General and Julia no longer took Thursday excursions into New York, and they lived without any indulgences. Julia managed the house and did all the cooking. Except for the shouts of Fred's children playing on the swings, the cottage was a depressed place.

Julia was deeply outraged by the debacle. Along with his other crimes, Ward had persuaded her to invest the small hoard of twenty-dollar gold pieces she kept in a vase on the mantelpiece. The General had received these as remuneration for the many

Garfield from the White House to the Charles Francklyn cottage on the grounds of the Elberon Hotel, two thousand men worked round the clock to lay a railway spur five-eighths of a mile long in twenty-four hours. The most fashionable hotel in Long Branch was named the Garfield-Grant. Benjamin Harrison and William McKinley rode up and down Ocean Avenue in electric cars. In 1916, Woodrow Wilson accepted renomination as his party's candidate for President from the home of J. B. Greenhunt in nearby Shadow Lawn.

[109]

board meetings he attended. When he gave them to her, one-by-one as he received them, there was a sentiment behind the gift that only two people who have successfully weathered a long spell of rough seas could understand. That Ward conned those gold pieces from her was evidence that he was not only shallow, stupid, and criminal, but depraved, as well. She had neither liked nor trusted Ward, and tolerated him only because of Buck. The General was convinced that his boy was a financial genius whose insight into people could not be wrong. Julia knew her children better than the General did, but she had gone along with him, much to her sorrow.

The General spent most of the early weeks in June staring wordlessly at the sea. That was always his way. His spirits were lifted by an invitation to address a convention of army chaplains held at nearby Ocean Grove. He went principally to pay his respects to fellow veterans. Dr. A. J. Palmer, who introduced Grant to the audience of two thousand, concluded: "No combination of Wall Street sharpers shall tarnish the lustre of my old Commander's fame for me."

Like a wave, the chaplains rose in their place. Their tumultuous cheering, sustained for several minutes, so overcame the General that he could not control his feelings. The ovation lent him a certain security about his good name.

He always made solitary plans, and was never one to confide. He had not even confided the names of his cabinet members to Julia. The nominees themselves did not learn of their appointments until he sent their names into the Senate.

Grant was not lost or bewildered in his pain. He was considering ways to scrape together enough money for another start, so he could repay some of those whose trust in him had led to their ruin. And he had a means for making money at hand. An offer had come in from *The Century* magazine for a series of articles describing his battles. It was not the first such offer he had been tendered, but before this he had always refused.

For one thing, he was innately modest. Friends noted that he rarely used "I" in describing battles and campaigns. Additionally, he had urged friends to write about him. Adam Badeau, his wartime secretary, had published the *Military History of General Grant*, in three volumes, in 1868, and John Russell Young brought out

Around the World with General Grant, in two volumes, in 1879. Grant felt that a book under his own authorship would diminish the sales and popularity of these. Also, he had never needed the money.

There was still another reason, idiosyncratic perhaps, but compelling nevertheless. He dreaded retracing his steps. He had developed this peculiarity as a boy and it stayed with him all his life. Once he started to go anywhere or do anything, he would not turn back or stop until he had accomplished the thing intended. In later years he explained, "I have frequently started to go places where I had never been and to which I did not know the way, depending upon making inquiries on the road, and if I got past the place without knowing it, instead of turning back I would go on until a road was found turning in the right direction, take that, and come in by the other side." He carried this superstition to obsessional lengths. One night in Virginia while fighting Lee, Grant and his retinue lost their way. Grant steadfastly refused to return to his headquarters by the way he had come. Finally, in exasperation, one of his aides pointed out they were about to run into the Confederate picket lines. The General also amazed several friends in New York when he would not reenter his 66th Street house to reclaim an umbrella he had forgotten. With no servant in sight, Grant insisted on walking around the block before going back in. This fear had kept him from describing his personal military history. Recapturing the past is retracing one's steps. Now he had a reason for writing—his desperate need of money—more compelling than any reason for not writing. Like a soldier who does not relish his orders, he began planning what help he would have to recruit in order to charge over the ground again.

The Century was about to embark upon one of the most ambitious and successful ventures in American publishing history. The year before, the magazine had published a two-part description, from opposing viewpoints, of John Brown's raid on Harpers Ferry. One of the younger editors, Clarence Buell, suggested to his colleague, Robert Underwood Johnson, a series of articles on the great battles of the Civil War, written by the generals who opposed each other. Johnson agreed it would be an admirable series and convinced managing editor Richard Watson Gilder of its merit.

The series, which ran for three years, earned *The Century* over

$1 million. The articles, written by Grant, Sherman, McClellan, Pope, Rosecrans, Franklin, and others on the Union side, and Longstreet, Hill, Wheeler, Law, Beauregard, and Joe Johnston of the Confederacy, were eventually turned into the 3,000-page *Battles and Leaders of the Civil War*. The articles created a sensation because they fueled the controversy and speculation that surrounded almost every battle of the Civil War. Controversy and speculation still attend these conflicts, and did so from the very moments they were fought.

In the post-Civil-War era magazines became the popular interpreters of national and moral issues. Unlike newspapers, they had been able to thrive for many years without running advertisements in their pages. But after the panic of 1873, magazines actively began to solicit advertising. And if they wanted to increase their advertising revenue, they had constantly to increase readership. A series of popular articles on a controversial subject virtually assured a magazine of a jump in circulation. *The Century*, for example, increased its circulation with the Civil War articles from 120,000 in 1885 to 225,000 in 1888.*

The lynchpin of its Civil War series was obviously Ulysses S. Grant. The military history of the war was largely the story of two great generals, Grant and Robert E. Lee. Lee had died in 1870, leaving behind no memoirs, notes, or personal accounts of battles. He was a soldier in the classic mold. Grant was as intrepid a fighter and more: where Grant commanded, momentous and dramatic events transpired; where he did not, the war was often a fiasco.

Robert Underwood Johnson understood this, and first approached Grant in January, 1884, when the series was in its initial stage. Grant's reply was discouraging. "It is all in Badeau," he said. Johnson tried again in the spring, this time with his chief, Richard Watson Gilder. They approached Grant at the Union League Club. Gilder asked Grant if *The Century* might have an article from

* It was probably the preeminent magazine of its age, an age in which *The Nation*, *Atlantic Monthly*, *Harper's*, *North American Review*, *The Galaxy*, *Lippincott's*, *The Outlook*, *Publishers' Weekly*, and *The Delineator* were but a few of its competitors. *The Century* had published Jack London and William Dean Howells, Rudyard Kipling and Mark Twain, Frank Stockton's "The Lady or the Tiger?" and Alice Hegan Rice's *Mrs. Wiggs of the Cabbage Patch*. It was the best-printed magazine in the world.

him in the form of an interview. He suggested that the interviewer be E. V. Smalley, who had already been engaged to do the interview with Sherman.

"Which Smalley is it?" asked Grant. "I know two Smalleys— one that looks like Garfield and the other an anti-American in London."

"Our Smalley looks like Garfield," said Gilder quickly.

The Garfield Smalley was to no avail. Grant said no. "His declination was so decided," wrote Johnson in his memoirs, *Remembered Yesterdays*, "that it left us without hope."

In mid-May the General was elected president of the Society of the Army of the Potomac. Gilder and the persistent Johnson tried again, hoping that the honor had rekindled Grant's interest in military matters. Johnson wrote that the country looked with such regret on the General's recent misfortune, everyone would take heart at the news he was going to write a piece about his military career. That career, concluded Johnson, did honor to all Americans. This time the General replied that if *The Century* still wanted him to write for the series he would be glad to talk to one of their representatives.

Johnson, who was spending the summer at Point Pleasant, New Jersey, immediately called on the General. They spent a morning talking on the veranda. Though it was mid-June, Grant wore a white silk scarf and a heavy, dark cape, because of a sore throat. He began the discussion by describing to Johnson the distressing situation caused by the failure of Grant and Ward. Covering all the details directly and simply, he talked without restraint and, as Johnson noted, with deep feeling and bitterness.

Johnson had no idea of the extent of the family's ruin. He assured the General that the country still had the highest confidence in his integrity. "He gave me the impression," wrote Johnson, "of a wounded lion. He had been hurt to the quick in his proud name and in his honor, and the man, we had been told, was stolid and reserved showed himself to me as a person of the most sensitive nature and the most human expression of feeling."

At last, the General broke off and asked Johnson what *The Century* expected of him. Johnson replied that the magazine would use as many articles as the General chose to write. But for the moment, the editors thought, articles on Shiloh, Vicksburg, Chatta-nooga, and the Wilderness campaign would cover the ground. For each of these *The Century* would be glad to pay him $500. It was a fair, even generous offer. In the 1880s one could live on $2,000 a year, but to earn that much a writer would have to contribute an article a week. The prospect and the money were agreeable to Grant. He promised to start writing on Shiloh immediately.

The General had no trouble in re-creating this battle. He described the fighting and his role in it in four brief, hardly discursive pages, and sent it off to Johnson within a week. It represented no more than he had submitted to Washington as his official report. Johnson, Gilder, and Buell knew it would not do. It was decisive and soldierly, but nothing more.

So Johnson returned to Long Branch several times to coach the General in what was wanted. A man of tact and subtlety, Johnson made no comment on the article. Instead, he engaged the General in a leisurely dialogue about the battle. He asked why the General hadn't entrenched against the Confederates, to which Grant answered that, at that stage in the war, neither side had learned how. Johnson asked if the situation had been saved by the arrival of Buell and the Army of the Ohio. Grant replied, "No commander regrets to see reinforcements. But we were by no means whipped or demoralized and were ready for a forward movement in the morning." Johnson discovered that the General was not a "silent" man, rigid, without the urge or courage to give vent to his feelings. Rather, he was a hero, capable of sorrow and sympathy, who revealed modesty and honesty as well as greatness and deep sensitivity. The General recalled how, in the pouring rain that followed Sunday's battle, he had sought shelter in an improvised military hospital. "But I couldn't stand the amputations," he said, "and had to go out in the rain and sit for most of the night against a tree."

The General also made Johnson laugh with his comments about different generals. He told a story about Braxton Bragg, a Confederate and West Pointer, who was a litigious and argumenta-tive man. Before the war, while he was serving as a company commander, Bragg was also detailed as supply officer. As company commander he ordered his troops equipped with new rifles. As supply officer he denied the request, because these munitions and arms were not immediately procurable. Then, with his endorsement on one side of the paper and his cancellation on the other, Bragg proceeded to his colonel and asked for a resolution of the matter.

"My God," said the colonel, "you have quarreled with every officer in the army, Bragg, and now you are quarreling with yourself."

Quick to realize his moment, Johnson interrupted the General to tell him it was precisely such anecdotes and precisely such feelings that professional publication required. What the General had told him this morning, Johnson went on, depicted the battle.

"I told him that what was desirable for the success of the paper was to approximate such talk as he would make to friends after dinner, some of whom should know all about the battle and some nothing at all, and that the public . . . was particularly interested in his point of view, in everything that concerned him, in what he planned, saw, said, and did."

The General accepted the advice and urgings impassively. He promised he would try again. Within another week, Johnson had a much longer manuscript in which, among other things, Grant described how ". . . a ball had struck the metal scabbard of my sword, just below the hilt and broken it nearly off: before the battle was over it had broken off entirely."

The Century series was off to an auspicious start, and Johnson continued his visits to Long Branch, counseling and advising the General on subsequent articles. He accepted the title as Grant's "literary tutor" with the remark that no teacher ever had a student more apt. But Grant had one gift that a writer cannot be taught: clarity. As President, he had written all his policy papers, and though not always politic, they were always clear. And biographer Bruce Catton has noted that it is always possible to pick out Grant's wartime reports, communiqués, and orders because of their clarity and simplicity.

There is a forceful directness to Grant's best-known Civil War statements. At least two of them have a ringing permanence: "No terms except unconditional and immediate surrender can be accepted. I propose to move immediately upon your works," and "I propose to fight it out on this line if it takes all summer." The phrase with which he was identified in his lifetime, "Let us have peace," was struck off in sudden inspiration at the end of his speech accepting the nomination in 1868. It is inscribed on his tomb.

The battles of Shiloh, Vicksburg, Chattanooga, and the Wilderness, one way or another, engaged the energies of a million men. They were to Grant's generation what D-Day and Iwo Jima were to another generation almost a century later. They helped determine the outcome of the Civil War. The strategies and tactics for these battles were the work of one general, Ulysses S. Grant.

Until now generals had rarely availed themselves of the chance to tell their stories. There had not been the available magazines and newspapers, or publishers anxious to bring the story to a waiting public. Nor had the generals been democratically educated men whose war was supported by a democratic constituency.

In the back of Grant's mind was the idea that what he was about to do would result in more than four military articles by an old soldier. He began to realize that he could make a significant statement. Lincoln had made a statement in the Gettysburg Address about *why* the war was fought. Grant could make a statement about *how* the war was fought, and why it was fought the way it was.

But it was hard. Getting straight the names of narrow country roads and little creeks, the dates and times when events transpired, the skirmishes incidental to the campaigns but affecting them, the names of generals by the score, was tedious, time-consuming work. And it was hard because Grant was still trying to crawl from a chasm. Memories are one of the ways men preserve identity in calamity. Memories also flood men as they begin to count the time left and the limitation fading appetites and weakening organs place on the time left.

The General had help at hand. Good men always gravitated to him. He always received more from them than loyalty, often because he would use what else they offered. His chief aide in the coming months would be Fred Grant, a six-footer, as big as his grandfather, Jesse. At thirteen, Fred had accompanied his father in the field during the Vicksburg campaign, where he sustained a leg wound. Julia had entrusted the boy to the General without tears.

She said Alexander the Great was no older when he went with Phillip of Macedon. Fred had been graduated from West Point in 1871, had served with the Fourth Infantry in the West, and had, in fact, written a book about the Yellowstone Expedition. In 1874, he married Ida Honore, a beauty whose sister, Mrs. Potter Palmer, almost single-handedly created Chicago society.

The General had labored, sweated, and persevered for the family. He was about to discover that none of the work, the sweat, or the stamina was vainly expended. "Never had a father a more devoted son," wrote Johnson of the relationship between Fred and the General. "Indeed, if I may venture to say so, the whole family gave him a respect and tender care that were conspicuous and beautiful."

The General also asked Adam Badeau to visit him at Long Branch. Badeau had been a drama critic for several upstate newspapers before going off to the Civil War. In 1863, while serving as a secretary on Sherman's staff, he was badly wounded. After convalescence, he was assigned as Grant's military secretary. Grant relied heavily on Badeau's sphinxlike discretion, as well as his modest literary facility. He eventually made Badeau a general by brevet.

The friendship that ripened between the two men dictated the course of Badeau's life. He attached himself to the person and fortunes of Ulysses S. Grant, remaining with the General until his inauguration as President. He served as the secretary of the American legation in London, and later accompanied Grant on some of his travels. Besides the *Military History*, a definitive but uninspired work, Badeau had already published several novels and travel books. When Grant summoned him in 1884 he had been consul general in Havana for two years. But he had just resigned because the Arthur administration refused to investigate frauds he had exposed. *The Century* had made one of its offers to Grant through Badeau, who was preparing for them an article on Grant's presidency and a novel about Cuba.

Badeau had an intelligence and a point of view remarkable enough to engage the attention of Henry Adams. Adams re-created their conversations in his chapter on Grant in *The Education of Henry Adams*. "Badeau," wrote Adams, "was stout; his face was red and his habits regularly irregular; but he was very intelligent, a good newspaperman, and an excellent military historian."

Badeau hastened to Long Branch, and the General showed him the four-page Shiloh article. Badeau said it wouldn't do, and proceeded to tell the General what would do. In his subsequent biography, *Grant in Peace*, Badeau was to make the same claims as Robert Underwood Johnson, that he had coaxed from Grant literary excellence.

Later in the summer Badeau came to Long Branch for a ten-day stay. The two men worked on the Vicksburg article and planned the narrative for Chattanooga and the Wilderness. At this time the General confided to Badeau that he was going to write his memoirs that winter, and suggested that his friend help him with the project. Badeau had spent seventeen years of his life in the study and exposition of the General's campaigns. He knew the details of the General's battles better than the General did.

Badeau demurred, explaining that he was working night and day on his novel about Cuba. He wanted to see it published before Chester A. Arthur left office. The General insisted.

"The proposition was a great blow to me," wrote Badeau, "for I had looked forward to going into history as his mouthpiece and spokesman, and, of course, if he wrote a new work himself my special authority would be superseded. But he was my chief and my friend and in trouble, and the work at least would distract him from his misery. We both considered his memoirs might yield from $30,000 to $50,000. I consented to aid him."

Shortly thereafter the General wrote Badeau, ". . . There will be a room for you (at East 66th Street) all the time you want to spend with us. There is room also for you to work on your own book. I have taken a room in the front—the small one at the head of the stairs for my own work and converted the boudoir into a bedroom. Where I am now there is a table to write upon, and a large desk." The General also promised Badeau $5,000 out of the first $20,000 that the book earned, and another $5,000 out of the next $10,000. If the book did not earn $20,000, Badeau would receive nothing. Grant was a bankrupt, he confessed, and could offer no more.

The General also insisted that their agreement be kept secret, principally because he was a secretive man. It was a mistake, of course. But there is ample evidence that the General was capable of monumental mistakes in business dealings. Badeau was reconciled to receiving nothing if the book did not earn $20,000. But he was by no means reconciled to receiving only $10,000 if the book met with a huge popular success.

Their working arrangement made Badeau less than a collaborator, but more than a secretary. Robert Underwood Johnson, however, said of the Shiloh article: "A duplicate was sent General Badeau, who made a few single word corrections of no importance such as 'received' for 'got'—by no means an improvement on the General's Saxon style." But Johnson had his own reasons for downgrading Badeau's role.*

The idea growing in Grant's mind grew simultaneously in the minds of *The Century* editors, particularly Richard Watson Gilder, the editor-in-chief. Gilder enjoyed an immense and well-earned reputation in publishing. He had an unerring instinct for what people wanted to read, and he had discrimination, but he was also genteel. Gilder was not above editing Mark Twain's *Huckleberry Finn*, when sections appeared in the magazine. He deleted references to nakedness, blasphemy, smells, and dead cats, and changed "in a sweat" to "worrying."

The prospect of publishing a book by General Ulysses S. Grant galvanized him. Gilder had enlisted in a Pennsylvania artillery regiment at nineteen, and spent his first week in the army trailing about the countryside trying to locate booming cannons off in the distance. His regiment never found the fight, and Gilder spent the rest of the war on garrison duty in Philadelphia. When he discovered that the battle he had not caught up with was Gettysburg, he put a GAR pin in his lapel and never took it out. He was prouder of the pin than of the honorary degrees colleges bestowed upon him. Bringing Grant into the house would make up for missing Gettysburg.

Gilder came near doing it. Grant was discovering that writing

* In *The Captain Departs*, a thoroughgoing and detailed account of the General's last year, Thomas M. Pitkin comments, "The evidence is overwhelming that nearly everyone who had a long and intimate association with General Grant became devoted to him. It did not follow they became devoted to each other."

agreed with him. He had long been in awe of generals who could write their own books; now he found that he too had this facility. The General worked in an upstairs room on a white pine table usurped from the kitchen, his materials spread before him. Julia came often and sat in a wicker chair to watch him pore over maps with the old intensity.

When he began to describe Vicksburg from an omnipotent viewpoint, as though he weren't there, Julia, Fred, and Ida all reminded him that "Grant" and "Vicksburg" were synonymous. He wrote with incredible speed, which suggests an omnivorous concentration. He was halfway through a first draft of the Vicksburg campaign when Johnson, at Gilder's behest, asked if the General had considered extending the articles into a book, after they were published in the magazine. Grant replied that George Childs had been urging such efforts on him for several years. He also told Johnson he was working four hours a day, sometimes seven, Saturdays and Sundays not excepted.

Gilder passed this information along to his boss, Roswell Smith, president of the Century Company. Smith thought a book on the war by Ulysses S. Grant was a capital idea. He would have liked to have the rights secured at once, but made no effort to secure them until the end of the summer. Then he and Johnson went to Long Branch together and lunched with the General at George Childs's house. Later in the afternoon, the three walked slowly across the lawn to Grant's veranda, and took their ease in rockers around a wicker table.

The General finally asked, "Do you really think anyone would be interested in a book by me?"

"General," replied Roswell Smith, "do you not think the public would read with avidity Napoleon's personal account of his battles?"

This was not exactly an answer to Grant's question. But the General let it pass. He was often compared to Napoleon, a parallel he thought anachronistic and pointless.

Smith did not secure the book then and there because he was a gentleman publisher, which is to say he was a cautious business-man. He doted on luncheons and praise and abhorred advances until a manuscript was firmly in hand; even then he thought advances bad policy. Still, he had elaborate plans for the book. He intended to issue it simultaneously in England, France, and Germany; give it a handsome manufacture; and, above all, play fair with the General. "Ever since the war," he stated, "every one who has had to do with Grant has been trying to make something at his expense. I do not intend that the reputation of the Century Company shall be compromised by even the appearance of sordidness. We shall publish the volume on terms entirely satisfactory to him." But he had not considered that Grant was still an eminent public figure visited by reporters. To these reporters Grant hinted about a book.

Gilder, Johnson, and Buell guessed that sooner or later other publishers would compete for it. "Evidently the firm that pays down is going to get the book," warned Buell. Johnson reported that Grant was marching double quick through the four articles. Gilder noted that even if the book were not a resounding financial success, it would greatly advertise the house that published it. This was an important consideration for the Century Company, which had only recently begun to issue books. But Smith replied by correspondence, "We do not want Grant's book unless he wants us to have it nor unless terms are equitable."

Gilder, Johnson, and Buell were not the first nor the last editors to tear their hair over a publisher's good manners. They were sure Grant was going to write a book. They were not sure who was going to publish it. Smith remained confident that when the General was ready, he would bring the book to them. But Grant, who wrote to Badeau that, in his opinion, Century would make the best publisher, added, "I will make no committal until time for publication."

To the end, Roswell Smith remained a gentleman. When he saw what Grant's Shiloh article did for *The Century*'s circulation, he doubled the payments the magazine had originally offered, from $2,000 to $4,000, some of which Grant used to repay Mathias Romero.

Other publishers did, indeed, approach Grant. However, unlike Smith, they all proposed to sell the book on the "subscription plan." Subscription distribution offered publishers a guaranteed return for their books, but, in turn, it demanded a large initial investment. This method of selling books, popular in the nineteenth century, has largely gone out of favor, and is associated today with encyclopedias. Sixteen general agents divided the country into markets, and hired the canvassers who sold the book door-to-door. While subscribers were not obligated to make payment until delivery, the majority, having signed a contract, paid the money then and there. Thus many of the publisher's costs were met before the book went to press. Subscription publishing, however, had resulted in an infamous literature. For their money, the subscribers usually wanted bulk rather than quality, and the publishers obliged them. They sold them 1,000-page tomes of *Lives of the Vice-Presidents* and plagiarized accounts of *Great Battles of the World.*

When Smith mentioned this method, Grant said he hoped his publisher wouldn't pay a scalawag canvasser $6 for selling a $12 book not worth half the price to begin with. Smith assured the General they would distribute the book "through the trade," that is, through bookstores. Unfortunately there were not many bookstores in the country. Most of them, in fact, were adjuncts of the publishing houses.

Apparently only the General and Roswell Smith were trepidatious about the probable sales. Adam Badeau had been part of the literary world long enough to realize that a book on the Civil War by Ulysses S. Grant was an event. And certainly Johnson, Gilder, and Buell realized as much. In fact, to the misfortune of the Century Company, there were all too many who realized just what a coup it would be to publish Grant's memoirs. Among them was a colorful figure, who—second only to Ulysses S. Grant—was the most famous living American of the day.

"In time I came to know that Union colonel whose coming frightened me out of the war and crippled the Southern cause to that extent—General Grant. I came within a few hours of seeing him when he was as unknown as myself; at a time when anybody could have said, 'Grant?—Ulysses S. Grant? I do not remember hearing the name before.' It seems difficult to realize there once was a time when such a remark could be rationally made; but there *was,* and I was within a few miles of the place and the occasion, too, though proceeding in the other direction."

[122]

So wrote Mark Twain in "The Private History of a Campaign That Failed," published in *The Century* Civil War series in December, 1885. Twain, an "irregular Confederate," as he characterized himself, had enlisted in the Marion Rangers as a lieutenant in the late spring of 1861. He spent two weeks in this guerrilla band, in the rain, retreating, hiding at night in corncribs. Finally, near Florida, Missouri, they were in danger of being flushed by the Twenty-first Illinois Volunteers, Grant's first independent command. By his account, Twain saw enough shooting to convince him war was intended for men, while he was intended for "a child's nurse." He deserted and lit out for the territories. "I could have become a soldier myself if I waited," he concluded. "I had got part of it learned. I knew more about retreating than the man who invented retreating."

The inspiration for the story came to Twain in Grant's library on East 66th Street. The General had been recalling the early days of the war, when he was trying to clear Confederates out of Missouri. Twain shared many a cigar and many a talk with Grant. Both were men who could tell a story. As often as he came to New York, Twain stopped at the house. He was a Grant-intoxicated man.

Having missed surrendering to Grant, Twain didn't meet him until 1870. By that time he had established himself as a humorist of wide appeal. He had also married Olivia Langdon, daughter of a wealthy Elmira coal dealer. On behalf of his father-in-law, Twain went to Washington to lobby for a judicial redistricting bill that affected the Langdon holdings in Memphis. An old friend, Senator William Stewart of Nevada, took Twain in to see the President.

Grant was signing bills in a duster spattered with ink. After the introduction, there was a lengthy pause. Grant was morose with strangers. Finally, Twain said, "Mr. President, I am embarrassed. Are you?" The General gave him a smile that would have done no discredit to a cast-iron statue. Under the smoke of his volley, Twain said, he made his escape.

They became close friends in 1879, at the GAR reunion in Chicago. The convention was welcoming the General home after his round-the-world trip (during which Grant read *Innocents Abroad*). Twain, now the most sought after lecturer in America, was invited to Chicago as an honored guest of the Army of the Tennessee. He was scheduled to speak at a banquet honoring Grant at the Palmer House on November 13.

"I wanted to see the General again and renew the acquaintance," Twain wrote to William Dean Howells. "He would remember me because I was the person who did not ask for an office."

On the flag-draped balcony of the Palmer House, which was to serve as a reviewing stand, Mayor Carter Harrison reintroduced the two men to each other. Twain started to move to the rear of the stand, and Grant asked him where he was going. Twain replied that he was making room for the General, because he didn't want to interfere with his speech.

"I'm not going to make any," Grant replied. "Stay where you are—I'll get you to make it for me." Then they turned to the sight of Lieutenant General Phil Sheridan, in a plumed hat and cape, mounted on a giant black horse amid his cannons, leading a procession miles long. Three thousand veterans crowded into the Haverly Theater that night to pay homage to the General. Twain sat beside Grant on the stage, along with Sherman, Sheridan, Logan, Pope, and Schofield. He described the scene to Howells:

> Imagine what it was like to see a bullet-shredded old battle flag reverently unfolded to the gaze of thousands of middle aged soldiers, most of whom hadn't seen it since they saw it advancing over victorious fields when they were in their prime. And imagine what it was like when Grant, their first commander, stepped into view while they were still going mad over the flag, and then right in the midst of it all, somebody struck up "When We Were Marching Through Georgia."

What amazed and stunned Twain was the control and iron rigidity of his new hero. Grant sat through the demonstration and the laudatory speeches, right leg crossed over left, arm reposing on his chair, never nervous, never moving, never responsive to the praise. The General may only have been steeling himself against the music, but Twain couldn't know that. He himself courted and reveled in adulation. Grant rose only when Sherman whispered to him that the cheering wouldn't halt until he acknowledged it. Then, with his rising, the cheers welled into a hurricane.

The climax of this celebration, its triumphal apogee, one of the golden moments in Twain's life, was the Palmer House reception.

Six hundred old soldiers crowded into a banquet at which they were served oysters, filet of beef and buffalo steaks, washed down with claret, champagne, and rum punch. Then, with whiskeys and cigars, they settled back for six hours of speeches.

In his response to the toast to the Army of the Tennessee, Colonel Robert Ingersoll declaimed: "They fought that a mother might own her child. Blood was water, money was leaves, and life was only common air until one flag floated over the Republic without a master and a slave."

Scheduled as the last speaker in order to hold the audience, Twain responded to a toast of his own devising: "To the babies—as they comfort us in our sorrow let us not forget them in our festivities." Magically and masterfully he played his audience. "And now in his cradle, somewhere under the flag, the future illustrious commander-in-chief of the American armies is so little burdened with his approaching grandeur and responsibilities as to be giving his whole strategic mind, at this moment, to trying to find out some way to get his own big toe into his mouth, an achievement which, meaning no disrespect, the illustrious guest of this evening also turned his attention to some fifty-six years ago. And if the child is but father of the man, there are mighty few who doubt that he succeeded." *

Twain finished to a tornado of applause and turned to see Grant with tears of laughter rolling down his bearded cheek. "I fetched him," Twain wrote to Howells. "I broke him up utterly. The audience saw that for once in his life he had been knocked out of his iron serenity. I shook him up like dynamite. My truths had wracked all the bones of his body apart. He laughed until his bones ached. Grand times, my boy, grand times."

He had made the iron man laugh with all the others and he saw himself as the hero of the banquet. So did the audience. So did Sherman, Logan, and Ingersoll. Twain was in such euphoria over

* "The reader of today," remarks Albert Bigelow Paine in his definitive biography of Mark Twain, "may find it hard to understand the flame of response it kindled so long ago. But that was another day—and another nation—and Mark Twain, like Robert Ingersoll, knew always his period and his people." Amen.

his accomplishment he went to bed without his usual toddy, some whiskey in a little water.

Grant, and the worship of Grant, which enlarged from this time on, wrought a change in Twain's life and in his career. In his penetrating psychological study *Mister Clemens & Mark Twain*, Justin Kaplan writes, "He worshipped Grant, he identified himself with Grant. Their lives, it now seems, became interlocked: when Grant died in 1885 Mark Twain started on the long downhill toward ruin. But as a former Confederate who comes to terms—of intimate friendship, it developed—with the Union commander, he combats in subtle and symbolic ways Grant's tremendous authority, competes with him, even seems to want to destroy him . . . (for) he thought of his humor as something violent and painful that he did to someone else."

In one sense it was a curious fixation, in another not. Twain was a reconstructed Southerner with a more profound sympathy for and understanding of blacks than any abolitionist. But he was not much interested in the Civil War. The subject that perpetuates his genius is the quality of life along the Mississippi in the 1830s and '40s. Nor was Twain a jingoist. He had virtually nothing to say about the Spanish-American War except that it was an imperialistic adventure. Yet Grant fascinated him, an unprepossessing man who had, in the crunch, the powers of a giant, and who could not explain these powers any more than Twain could explain his. This deep-seated profound reverence explains much about Twain—but even more about Grant, once the reverence is related to the total, global concept Twain was trying to construct in his best works. These works are *Life on the Mississippi, Tom Sawyer,* and *The Adventures of Huckleberry Finn.* By 1879, Twain had published the first two and was deep into the third. What Mark Twain saw in Ulysses S. Grant was Tom Sawyer grown up.

While Twain idolized the General, he never fawned, nor was he obsequious. It became a working friendship, not a friendship for amusement. Grant came to Hartford in the fall of 1880, campaigning for James A. Garfield. Twain stumped with him, then sponsored a Republican gala for the General, the invitations concluding, "No ceremony. Wear the same shirt you always wear."

In 1881, Twain and his friend William Dean Howells, the

editor of the *North American Review*, paid an emergency call on the General in his Wall Street offices. Garfield had died the month before, and President Chester A. Arthur was widely regarded as "an excellent gentleman with a weakness for friends." Several of these friends were importuning him for appointment as the American consul in Toronto. The post was presently held by Howells, Sr., a man in his seventies, who was dependent upon it for his livelihood.

The General and President Arthur were then on good terms. Twain asked if the General would write a word on a card that Howells could carry to Washington to help preserve his father's modest sinecure. Grant did better than that. He took up the matter with the President himself, when they dined together later in the week, and Howells *père* stayed on in Toronto.

The General insisted that Howells and Twain have luncheon with him in a small private room behind his office. The three dined on bacon, baked beans, and coffee sent in from a nearby restaurant. In his soft Ohio River accents, Grant reminisced about the war. That afternoon he was plutarchian. "It was but baked beans, but how he sits and towers," remarked Howells, paraphrasing Dante.

When Grant finished his recitation, Twain tried to persuade him to put it all down, to prepare his memoirs for publication. To which the General said determinedly he had no wish to place himself under scrutiny as an author. He doubted he could write well and doubted the book could sell well. He was at an age in life, he explained, where it was important to avoid humiliations. He intended to make copious notes before he died, from which his children, if they chose, could fashion a book. "Of course," wrote Twain later, "he could not foresee he was camping on a volcano, that as Ward's partner he was ruined even then."

Three years later the subject came up again. Twain had concluded a lecture tour with a reading at New York's Chickering Hall on November 18. Leaving with his wife, Livy, Twain saw through the mist of the rainy night two dim figures, one of whom said to the other, "Did you know General Grant has actually determined to write his memoirs and publish them? He said so today, in so many words."

The articulating "dim figure" turned out to be Richard Watson Gilder. The editor invited Twain back to his home on East

15th Street for a late supper, where he confirmed that the Century Company had been seriously negotiating with Grant for his memoirs since the summer. He described how the Century had gladdened the General's heart by handing him his first check.

"The thing which astounded me," wrote Twain, "was that, admirable man as Gilder certainly is, and with a heart which is in the right place, it had never seemed to occur to him that to offer General Grant five hundred dollars for a magazine article was not only the monumental injustice of the nineteenth century, but of all centuries." Twain knew whereof he spoke. He was advertising his books in *The Century.* During the run of the Civil War series his rates went from $700 to $1,800 for one fifth of a page.

Twain had a gold-rush mentality. He was constantly investing in business ventures, underwriting clumsy inventions, and trying to distribute games nobody wanted to play. Recently he had set up his own publishing house, Charles L. Webster & Company—Webster, his nephew-in-law, being the manager and Twain the company—through which he intended to distribute his own books. Now Twain was pierced by the arrow of American business morality. He could make a lot of money with Grant's memoirs, while administering a sacrament in the form of high royalties to his friend and hero.

In the morning Twain made straightaway for the General's East 66th Street house. He arrived, according to his own recollections, at the moment Grant was about to affix his signature to the Century Company's contract. Twain stayed that hand and persuaded Fred Grant to read the contract to him.

He snorted at the royalty figure of 10 percent. Ten percent, he explained, was the royalty for a Comanche Indian whose books wouldn't sell 3,000 copies. Fifteen percent was more usual for a book with a guaranteed sale of 35,000 copies, 20 percent for a book bound to sell 80,000 copies. He advised Fred and the General to strike out the 10 percent and put 20 percent in its place; better still, he urged, strike out the 20 percent and write in 75 percent of the net returns.

The General demurred. He felt that he had walked too far with the Century Company to turn back. But Twain persevered. He pointed out that the contract proposed to deduct from Grant's 10 percent the author's share for clerk hire, office rent, and advertising, stipulations against which even the Comanche would mutiny. It was unbusinesslike, he insisted, a phrase calculated to turn the General around 180 degrees. Twain concluded by saying there wasn't a reputable publisher in America who wouldn't pay the General the terms he had suggested.

"The idea distressed General Grant," Twain wrote twenty years later. "He thought it placed him in the attitude of a robber—robber of a publisher. I said if he regarded that as a crime it was because his education was limited. I said it was not a crime and was always rewarded in heaven with two halos. Would be, if it ever happened."

Fred urged his father to put the pen aside and think the matter over strictly as a business proposition. Grant was still reluctant. He said he thought he owed the Century Company something, they had come to him first.

Twain played his trump. "In that case," he said, "I'm to be the publisher because I came to you first. I came to you in the company of William Dean Howells three years ago." He boasted that his firm was presently selling *Huckleberry Finn* by the thousands, and within a short time he expected the Charles L. Webster house to have the best-equipped subscription establishment in the country. Under subscription distribution, the memoirs could not sell less than 100,000. He was so sure of it, he would make an offer now: $10,000 against a 20 percent royalty or 70 percent of the profits. Before they left the library, Fred had agreed to see what more advantageous offers they could find.

The three men withdrew to the living room, where the General had a visitor, Lew Wallace, who had fought with him at Shiloh. General Wallace had gone on to become a territorial governor, and had just finished a four-year stint as the American minister to Turkey. His famous novel, *Ben-Hur: A Tale of the Christ*, was already one of the most popular novels ever published in America. Grant had read the book in one thirty-hour sitting.

Julia remarked, "There's many a woman in this land would like to be in my place and tell her children that she once stood elbow to elbow between two such great authors as Mark Twain and General Wallace."

"Don't look so cowed, General," said Twain to Grant. "You

have written a book, too, and when it is published you can hold up your head and let on to be a person of consequence yourself."

Three months later, Wallace was begging Robert Underwood Johnson to ask Grant to reconsider the facts about Shiloh. Grant reported that Wallace had come late into the battle. Wallace succeeded in demonstrating that the fault was not his, that the verbal order had been misunderstood, and that his division had followed the safer but longer road. The General willingly accorded Wallace his due, and the text and the faulty map were altered for *Battles and Leaders.*

"I wanted the General's book, and I wanted it very much," Twain recalled in his autobiography, "but I had very little expectation of getting it." He supposed that once the General and Fred laid the suggested new terms before the Century people, they would accept. They did not. When Roswell Smith, "with the glad air of a man who has stuck a nail in his foot," congratulated Twain on securing the rights, he said Grant had asked if the Century would guarantee him what Scribner's had paid Sherman for his memoirs, $25,000. "I would not risk such a guaranty on any book ever published," said Smith.*

One of the reasons Twain got the book was that other publishers weighed in with offers similar to his. Several asked Grant to tell them his best offer and they would better it.

The General went to George Childs for advice. Childs sent competent legal and actuarial investigators to several publishers. Because Charles L. Webster & Company was sufficiently capitalized and expert in subscription publishing, Childs tendered the advice that the General should follow his inclination and give the book to Mark Twain.

Robert Underwood Johnson commented: "The General, who knew nothing of the customs or etiquette of the publishing business, had been won over by the humorist. It was not time for a contest, nor was it a book to be contended for in the customary fashion, and Mr. Roswell Smith, pocketing his disappointment, wrote a polite and generous letter to the General conveying our regrets that we

* Within a few years he was to invest over $1 million in a new dictionary, and sell hundreds of thousands of copies in a market already thought to be saturated.

were not to be associated with so distinguished an enterprise and our cordial wishes for its success."

When the contract was being drawn, Twain asked whether Grant wanted the 20 percent royalty or 70 percent of the profits. He suggested, however, that the former was the best deal all around for the General. It was the surest, easiest, and simplest way of accounting, and he would be certain of some income.

The General said that, while he was sure to make some money on the 20 percent plan, the publisher might not, and would stand to lose money. Therefore, he would opt for 70 percent of the profits, since if there were profits the publisher would be sure of a share. He did not want to prosper at Twain's risk.

Twain put aside a $10,000 advance for the General's use, if he needed the money before publication, but Grant never applied for it. Appended to the contract, however, was the transfer of the book to Julia Grant, and from Julia to the firm, for the consideration of $1,000 "in hand paid." This would prevent the General's creditors from seizing the profits of the book. Charles L. Webster, who presided over the contract signing, presumed that the transfer was a mere formality. But Grant's lawyer, Clarence Seward, the son of Lincoln's Secretary of State, insisted that the contract meant what it said, "in hand paid." He told Webster that the General and his family were waiting at this moment with lively anxiety for the money. Reciting this incident, Twain concluded, "It was a shameful thing that a man who had saved his country and its government from destruction should still be in a position where so small a sum—$1,000 could be looked upon as a godsend."

In times of stress, Grant and William Tecumseh Sherman gravitated toward each other. Theirs was a lifelong friendship, and it was unclouded by sentimental disguises. They knew each other's worth to the last dram. In their coming together, one of them always found release from binding trouble.

After Bull Run, the first major battle of the Civil War, Sherman suffered a nervous breakdown, a loss of nerve. He became dependent, and his superiors relieved him. But he managed to pull himself together, and Henry Halleck gave him command of a division in the West. Early in 1862, as Grant moved against Fort

Donelson, Sherman, who was his superior, commanded reinforcements to the rear. He offered to send these men forward, waiving his rank so that Grant's attack could proceed as planned. It was a generous offer that Grant never forgot.

Sometime later, Halleck, jealous of Grant's success, took personal command of the Army of the Tennessee. He not only threatened Grant with a court-martial, but worse, saw to it that he had nothing to do. Grant, brooding in his tent like Achilles, determined to resign from the army. Sherman came to Grant unbidden and warned that such a decision would take him out of the war. There would come a time, he said, when the men would need Grant.

Sherman was an imposing six-footer, as handsome as an actor, with fierce eyes and impulsive gestures. Like Grant, he was an Ohio boy. Orphaned at nine, he had been raised by Thomas Ewing, a prominent politician, whose daughter he later married. Where Grant was guarded and prudent, Sherman was outspoken and careless. He was a man who found exultation in battle. "To be at the head of a strong column of troops in the execution of some task that requires brain is the highest pleasure of war," he wrote, "a grim one and terrible but which leaves on the mind and memory the strongest mark." Grant was the general who would turn in his saddle to stare sadly and wordlessly at some dead soldier as he and his aides rode to the front.

But they had this in common: they were soldiers who saw that their first duty was to command and obey, to wage war with one consideration—victory. Grant once stated that the Union generals did not believe in the war at the start; they fought without the complete assurance in success that marks a good general; their vision of the war was clouded by views about slavery, property, and states' rights that affected their judgment. Grant and Sherman changed this. Grant reduced war to four words: "When in doubt, fight." Sherman told his troops, "War is cruelty and you cannot refine it."

They were neither self-serving generals nor manipulative for their own ends. Both were apolitical, although they seem to be the only two Union generals who understood exactly what Lincoln wanted from the peace they would secure. Where Grant let Lee's men keep their horses, mules, and sidearms, Sherman promised Joe Johnston's men their state legislatures. This so outraged Secretary of War Stanton that he called Sherman a traitor. Grant had to go secretly to Raleigh, North Carolina, to inform Sherman that the administration policy had changed since Lincoln's assassination. Sherman, he explained, was empowered only to accept the surrender of Johnston's army. Though Grant had been ordered by Stanton to supersede Sherman, and could have arranged the surrender himself, he refused to do this and left as quietly and as inconspicuously as he had come. Sherman never spoke to Stanton again. He came to despise politicians so that, when he was general-in-chief, he established army headquarters in St. Louis, to be away from Washington and the chicanery and deceit of elected officials.

Both were considered has-beens before they were forty. Sherman, bankrupted by a California panic in the 1850s, left the army to seek marginal employment as a lawyer, then as manager of his father-in-law's salt works, finally as superintendent of a military academy in Louisiana. Yet, by the time they were fifty, both had trod Mt. Olympus, wielding influence and power enough to satisfy the most grandiose appetites.

Sherman was the only officer in whom Grant ever confided his plans for a campaign. Grant did not even suggest the nature of his Virginia campaign to Lincoln; but he confided in detail to Sherman how he proposed to take Vicksburg. Sherman begged him to desist. "The campaign of Vicksburg," wrote Sherman in his memoirs, "in its conception and execution belonged exclusively to General Grant, not only in the great whole but in the thousands of details."

He had a wit as sharp as Grant's. When his wife, Ellen, told him, "You knew I was a Catholic when you married me," he said, "I did not know you were going to get worse every year." He had a lively imagination and a gift for language. The flair for narrative he displays in his memoirs is so pronounced he could easily have been a professional writer. When President Polk read the announcement of the discovery of gold at Sutter's Mill, the words were those of Lieutenant "Cump" Sherman. His phrases have passed into the language. "Vox populi, vox humbug" was his comment on the democratic process. Late in the war he wrote, "I can make that march and I can make Georgia howl!" In 1879 he told the graduating class at Michigan Military Academy, "War is hell," perhaps the most quoted remark ever made by an American. And in the summer of 1884, six months after he had retired as general-in-chief, he wired James G. Blaine at the Chicago Republican Convention, "I will not accept if nominated and will not serve if elected." He had refused to endorse Grant for President in 1868, a refusal Grant understood. If Grant had ever asked him about it, Sherman would have replied that generals make poor Presidents. He was anything but tactful. Because he had attended reputable prep schools, he used to boast to Grant that he was the better educated of the two by virtue of his ability to speak and understand French. The General used to blink at this and look for another cigar.

As a general, Sherman was always anxious and ready for command and responsibility, but never for rank. On one occasion Sherman tried to persuade Grant that the two of them should turn down promotions. When Sherman was promoted, it was to a rank Grant had vacated. Sherman became the commander of the Army of the Tennessee when Grant became the commander in the West; when Grant became general-in-chief, Sherman became the commander in the West; and when Grant was elected President, Sherman became the general-in-chief. Sherman wanted to succeed to a certain point but no further. To succeed further would be to overtake Grant.

These two soldiers were involved in a psychological romance. Sherman called it an *entente cordiale*. Sherman venerated authority, saw in it something mystical. Coming out of the psychotic episode that had seized him after Bull Run, Sherman symbolically saw in Grant the authoritative figure, the father he lost as a boy, the man who will put things right, who knows always what he is doing and who demands not obedience, but manliness.

For Grant, Sherman was the perfect general. Grant was clear about perfect generals. He knew who they were, and named them: James Birdseye McPherson, who was killed by skirmishers near Atlanta; Phil Sheridan, the Irishman, the perfect vision of a fighting man; and "Cump" Sherman, who, along with him, was one of the most innovative generals any war has ever produced.

Before he came east in December, 1884, Sherman had no idea of how the swindle had devastated the Grant family. While he himself had no interest in the acquisition of money for its own sake, he was sensible about it and tightfisted. He was always complaining to his family they had to keep expenses down or drive him to the poorhouse. Back in St. Louis, Sherman knew that Grant had lost money, but did not realize the financial mess his old comrade had gotten into.

When Sherman arrived in New York, just before Christmas, Grant's plight disturbed him. He told a reporter who interviewed him that he would volunteer half his pension—he had retired with the full pay of a lieutenant general—to relieve the Grant family's distress. One has to believe him. He never volunteered for dramatic effect. He spent a good deal of money every year traveling to *every* GAR gathering, and in lending small sums to old veterans. He would doubtless have sacrificed these expenses for Grant.

An impulsive man, though an inspired one, he set about convening millionaires to raise a subscription for Grant's relief. Among these men who met on December 28 were Cyrus Field, George Childs, and Anthony J. Drexel. They pledged another subscription of $150,000. Sherman, at first, did not describe this plan to Grant. Perhaps he should have, because the General was having none of it.

During the first week in January, Phineas T. Barnum offered the General $100,000 to let him exhibit the trophies now being readied for shipment to the Smithsonian Institution. The offer was repellent to Grant. He wasn't going to make himself one of Barnum's circus attractions. He had no money; but, now that he had an alliance with Mark Twain, he was not ready to be counted down and out. He wasn't fair game for display, and never would be. Rudely he told Barnum that he wasn't interested. The impresario dusted off the refusal and said that whenever the General was ready, P. T. Barnum was, too.

This offer was not the only one he turned down. He wrote a letter to Childs, which made its way into the *Tribune* on January 8: "Through the press and otherwise I learn that you, with a few other friends of mine, are engaged in raising a subscription for my benefit. I appreciate both the motive and the friendship which have dictated this course on your part but, on mature reflection, I regard it as due myself and my family to decline this proffered generosity. I regret I did not make this known earlier."

The millionaires did not disband in defeat. Sherman spurred them to a much more sensible effort—to have the Congress restore Grant to his rank as lieutenant general and thus qualify him for his pension. Before the General's inauguration in 1868, James G. Blaine, then the Speaker of the House, formally suggested that the Congress pass a special bill enabling Grant to take a leave of absence, so that at the end of his term in office he could resume his four-star rank as general-in-chief, a rank created especially for him. Grant refused, saying he could not sleep at night if he kept Sherman, Sheridan, Meade, and other general officers junior to him from promotions they deservedly merited. He said they had won their promotions as rightfully as he had won his, and to qualify them for their advancement he was resigning from the service. He did so on the day he became President, and appointed Sherman general-in-chief the day after.

Grant was always cavalier about employment. The Illinois legislature wanted to elect him senator in 1876, when his second term ended. Grant turned them down on the grounds that he didn't want to displace John A. Logan, who had always supported him.

The General had penalized himself for the morale of the army, and Sherman asked the millionaires if there was any reason why Congress should perpetuate the penalty. Knowing there were men among them who could dictate votes at will, Sherman advised them to get to lobbying.

Sherman's visit gave Grant the chance to confide that he was writing his memoirs. It was no secret, but it was not yet general knowledge. The General had not confided these efforts to Hamilton Fish, a good friend and neighbor, or even to Phil Sheridan.

Sherman had an interest at stake in Grant's memoirs. He had conceived of the March to the Sea and would want his due from his former commander. Ten years before, Sherman had published his own memoirs, and many of Grant's friends complained at the time that the General had been slighted. George Childs had observed,

"General, you won't find much of yourself in Sherman's book. He doesn't seem to think you were in the war."

Grant had different thoughts. He said, "It has done me more than justice. It has given me more credit than I deserve. Any criticism I might make would be that I think he has not done justice to Logan, Blair, and other volunteer generals whom he calls political generals. These men did their duty faithfully and I never believe in imputing motives to people."

Certainly Sherman wanted as much from the General. Both of them were well aware of the changes they had introduced to warfare. Authorities as diverse as Earl Schenck Miers and B. H. Liddell-Hart have argued that Grant invented and Sherman developed the blitzkrieg. To secure mobility, these two generals saw that they must free themselves from dependence on a fixed line of supply and communications. Troops must be self-contained, carrying everything they needed with them in initial and sustained attacks. Once Grant had dared this, both saw they could hasten victory by demoralizing the civilian population. A man will fight for his home and his country, but his loyalty to his country is loosened when his home is threatened in his absence. With the March to the Sea, Sherman spread widespread demoralization in Confederate armies. He was attacking not the rear of an army, but the rear of a whole people, weakening the will to fight.

On New Year's Day, 1885, Sherman expressed his enthusiasm about the memoirs, and told Grant he was doing what he should have done years before.

The General anticipated Sherman's enthusiasm and encouragement, but he had a more compelling subconscious motive for his confiding. What Sherman couldn't know was that Grant not only needed enthusiasm and encouragement, but needed them made articulate. For Grant was about to retrace his steps, an act he dreaded and which made him anxious. To ready himself for his ordeal, Grant was symbolically enlisting the best general he knew.

At last the General could see where he was moving, and he had his forces in perfect line. But he also knew there was an ominous implacable foe ahead, one he couldn't flank or outmaneuver, one he would have to meet head on. This knowledge had come to him unsought, a few months before, from his doctors.

Second Lieutenant "Sam" Grant, before the Mexican War. This is the picture that Grant's sister gave to Twain for the frontispiece of Volume One of the *Personal Memoirs. Courtesy Library of Congress*

Hannah and Jesse Grant. She was cold and an unresponsive mother. He was a bullying braggart, but a doting father. *Courtesy Library of Congress*

Hardscrabble, the home Grant built for Julia and himself. *Courtesy Library of Congress*

Grant's rented home in Galena. After the war the citizens of Galena bought him a more luxurious home. *Courtesy N.Y. Public Library*

Grant as Lincoln's commanding general. The strain of war is clearly
visible. *Courtesy Library of Congress*

Julia Dent Grant and her two youngest children, Jesse and Nellie, during the Civil War.

Julia Grant as First Lady. She disliked posing for pictures because of her squint. *Courtesy Library of Congress*

Grant at City Point, in the last days of the war. He weighed 147 pounds. *Courtesy Library of Congress*

President Grant in his first term. The presidency appears to agree with him, although as usual he is unsmiling. *Courtesy N.Y. Public Library*

The Grants at the Pyramids on their world tour. He loved travel, but it appears this once to have gotten the better of him. *Courtesy Library of Congress*

President and Mrs. Grant (right) and a party of friends. The other man is Orville Babcock, Grant's official secretary. At Babcock's trial, Grant became the only President to testify for the defense in a federally instituted case. *Courtesy N.Y. Public Library*

A drawing of Grant and Ferdinand Ward, of whom there are virtually no pictures extant, and an unidentified man in the background.

The "cottage" at Long Branch, which reporters called the "summer capitol." *Courtesy N.Y. Public Library*

The Grant home at No. 3 East 66th Street shortly before its demolition in 1936. It was originally one of a row of similar houses (see next picture).

Reporters outside the Grant house during the newspaper "death watch." *Courtesy N.Y. Public Library*

Dr. Fordyce Barker.

Dr. John Hancock Douglas.

Dr. George Frederick Shrady.
Courtesy N.Y. Public Library

Adam Badeau, Grant's onetime secretary and friend, who later sued Grant's estate.

Reverend J. P. Newman, who made a career of being "Grant's Pastor," though Mark Twain and Grant's doctors considered him a complete nuisance. *Courtesy Library of Congress*

Colonel Frederick Dent Grant, the General's oldest son, who worked with his father on the *Personal Memoirs.*

Robert Underwood Johnson, the editor who first approached Grant about his memoirs. *Courtesy Library of Congress*

General William Tecumseh Sherman, one of Grant's closest friends. His military and psychological relationship with Grant is reflected in the *Personal Memoirs. Courtesy Library of Congress.*

General Simon Bolivar Buckner, another close friend, photographed late in life. When he died in 1914, he was the last remaining Confederate general. *Courtesy Archives USMA Library*

Mark Twain. He was a Grant-intoxicated man who undertook to publish the *Personal Memoirs. Courtesy Library of Congress*

Dr. I ask you not to show this to any
one, unless physicians you consult
with, until the end. Particularly
I want it kept from my family. If
known to one man the reporters will
get it and they will get it. It
would only distress them almost
beyond endurance to know it, and
by reflex, would distress me.

I have not changed my
mind materially since I
wrote you before in the same
strain. Occasionally I know
that I gain in strength
some days, but when I do go
back it is beyond where I started
to improve. I think the
chances are very decidedly
in favor of your being able
to keep me alive until the
change of weather towards

First page of a handwritten note from Grant to Dr. Douglas.

Mount McGregor. To the right is the Balmoral Hotel; to the left is Eastern Lookout. Barely discernible between them is the cottage occupied by the Grants. *Courtesy N.Y. Public Library*

The cottage at Mount McGregor. *Courtesy Library of Congress*

A weekend family gathering at Mount McGregor. On the porch, from the left, Julia, daughter Nellie, the General, Fred, and Jesse. On the steps, from the left, Buck, Fred's daughter Julia, son Ulysses S. III, and wife, Ida, Jesse's daughter, Nellie, and wife, Elizabeth. *Courtesy Library of Congress*

On the porch; Grant, Julia, Nellie, and Ida. Faithful Harrison (left) peeps cautiously at the camera.

The last picture taken of Ulysses S. Grant. *Courtesy Library of Congress*

At work on the *Personal Memoirs. Courtesy Library of Congress*

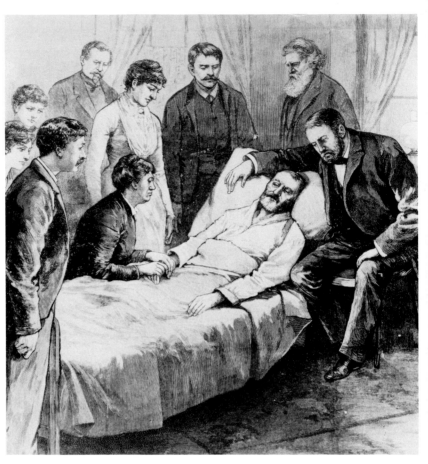

The death scene as rendered by an artist for *Frank Leslie's Illustrated Newspaper. The Granger Collection, New York*

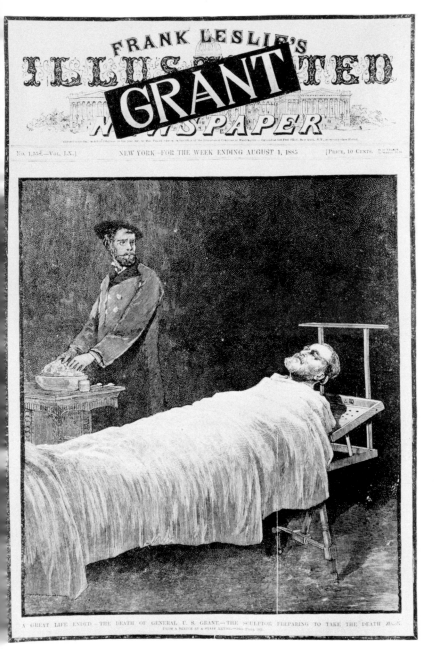

FRANK LESLIE'S ILLUSTRATED GRANT NEWSPAPER

No. 1,558.—Vol. LX.]   NEW YORK—FOR THE WEEK ENDING AUGUST 1, 1885   [Price, 10 Cents.

A GREAT LIFE ENDED—THE DEATH OF GENERAL U. S. GRANT.—THE SCULPTOR PREPARING TO TAKE THE DEATH MASK.
FROM A SKETCH BY A STAFF ARTIST.—SEE PAGE 395.

A Leslie artist depicts sculptor Karl Gerhardt preparing to take the death mask. *The Granger Collection, New York*

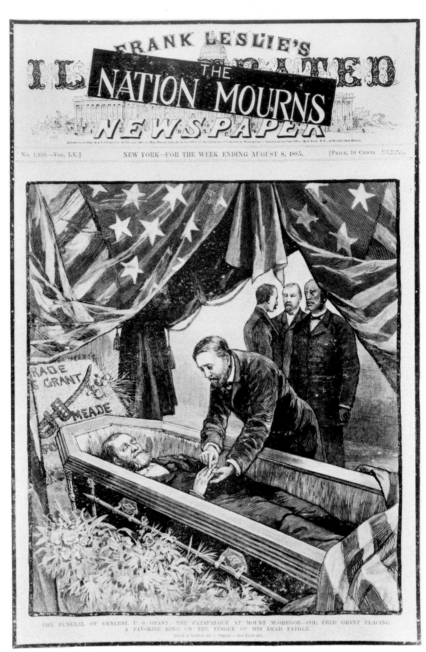

The nation mourns. *The Granger Collection, New York*

The funeral train leaves Mount McGregor.

The funeral procession passes City Hall and continues up Broadway. *The Granger Collection, New York*

The funeral procession at 13th Street and Broadway. *Courtesy Library of Congress*

The procession arrives at the Claremont area, what is now Riverside Drive and 122nd Street. *Courtesy N.Y. Public Library*

The pallbearers prepare to lay the coffin in the temporary vault. *The Granger Collection, New York*

The temporary vault, which was built within ten days of the General's death.
Courtesy Library of Congress

President Benjamin Harrison laying the cornerstone of Grant's Tomb in 1892. *Courtesy N.Y. Public Library*

West Point cadets pass in review at the dedication of the Tomb in 1897. *The Granger Collection, New York*

The fleet salutes Grant's Tomb. The second ship in the line is the battleship *Maine*. Less than a year later it blew up in Havana harbor. The flagship, *New York* (foreground) would avenge the *Maine* in the Spanish-American War. *Courtesy N.Y. Public Library*

A bare-headed President William McKinley dedicates Grant's Tomb, April 27, 1897. Beside him is New York City Mayor William L. Strong. *The Granger Collection, New York*

Grant's Tomb. *Courtesy N.Y. Public Library*

PART IV

THE NEWSPAPER WATCH

. . . in all thy walks with kings,
Those prairie sovereigns of the West,
     Kansas, Missouri, Illinois,
Ohio's, Indiana's millions, comrades, farmers,
     soldiers, all to the front,
Invisibly with thee walking with kings
     with even pace the round world's promenade,
Were all so justified.

                    Walt Whitman
                    "What Best I See in Thee:
                    to U. S. G. return'd
                    from his World's Tour"

HAUTE CUISINE REMAINED AS MUCH A MYSTERY TO GRANT DURING HIS lifetime as had his course in French at West Point. The General ate beef as often as it was served, but barely tolerated mutton. He usually ate a pork chop and an egg for breakfast. He liked pork and beans, corn, tomatoes, cucumbers, and buckwheat cakes. Above all, he loved fruit: oranges, apples, grapes, cherries, and melons. He particularly relished peaches.

Biting into a peach at the close of his big midday meal on June 2, suddenly the General leaped up from the table in distress. Julia thought he had been stung by an insect in the peach. But, when the moment passed, Grant said an almost unbearable pain had flashed through his mouth. It quickly subsided. During the next few weeks at Long Branch, however, the General found he could not eat a peach without feeling pain. Oranges also bothered him, and he felt a curious dryness in his throat. He passed off this discomfort as a minor annoyance, but its persistence finally led him to mention it to his neighbor, Childs.

Childs said he had invited the Philadelphia surgeon Jacob Mendez Da Costa to Long Branch for a week's stay. The doctor would be glad to look at the General's throat. So Da Costa walked over to the Grant cottage and, informally settling the General in the sunlight on the porch, asked him to open his mouth.

He saw something. What it was Da Costa didn't know, it was too minute to tell. But Da Costa knew it was no ordinary inflammation. He wrote the General a prescription and advised that he see his family physician at once for a thorough examination.

Grant's family physician, Fordyce Barker, was in Europe, a

fact the General neglected to reveal to Da Costa. Besides, the prescription helped. Occasionally, a tomato or stewed rhubarb would remind him that something was wrong. Later in the summer, the General asked Childs for Da Costa's Philadelphia address. He said he would pay Da Costa a visit the day after next. But the following morning he felt better. Going back to his *Century* articles, Grant put his discomfort out of mind. The pain remained quiescent in September, but from time to time he was aware of the irritation in the back of his mouth.

In October, after the Long Branch season, when the family settled again at East 66th Street, the pain came back. This time it did not subside after a momentary flare. It kept him awake nights. He began coughing frequently, and soon his mouth throbbed all day. Now he could not ignore the pain. It drove him to Barker, one of the most fashionable and competent doctors in the city.

Barker wore sideburns that looked like spinnakers, traveled extensively through Europe, and was the first doctor in America to use a hypodermic needle. He and the General were old acquaintances and good friends. He saw more than Da Costa had seen—enough to alarm him. The General visited him on October 22, and that very day Barker sent Grant to John H. Douglas, the foremost throat specialist on the eastern seaboard.

Douglas, a tall imposing man with a mane of white hair and a full beard, looked like the poet Longfellow. The General knew him even better than he knew Barker. During the war, Douglas had served in the field with the United States Sanitary Commission. He had met and admired Grant marching to Fort Donelson. The admiration strengthened into devotion. Douglas served at Shiloh, Fredericksburg, Gettysburg, and the Wilderness, setting up and supervising the field hospitals—requisitioning, demanding, sometimes expropriating the bandages, medicines, scalpels, and bedding these hospitals needed. He had also discovered two easily obtained remedies and preventatives for scurvy—sauerkraut and pickles. By the end of the war Douglas was as devoted to sauerkraut and pickles as he was to Grant.

When Grant came to see him, Douglas noted there was a halt in his step, as though one leg were shorter than the other. He knew that the General suffered from severe neuralgia. Grant told him that, aside from his lameness and his headaches, he was having trouble swallowing certain foods. Douglas asked the General to sit down and, adjusting one of the newly invented reflecting mirrors, looked into his throat.

The trouble wasn't in the throat at all. It was at the root of the tongue, which was rigid on the base of the right side. The soft palate was inflamed in a deep, dark, congestive hue, scaly and swollen. When Douglas stepped back and removed the mirror, the General could see the verdict in the doctor's face.

"Is it cancer?"

As a matter of fact, Douglas never answered Grant's question directly. "The question having been asked," reported Douglas in his diary, "I could give no uncertain, hesitating reply. I gave him that which I believed—qualified by hope. I realized that if he once found that I had deceived him, I could never reinstate myself in his good opinion." Douglas said, "General, the disease is serious, epithelial in character, and sometimes capable of being cured."

What Douglas saw was the beginning of an epithelial carcinoma at the base of the tongue, the epithelium being the tissue that lines membraneous surfaces. The gland on the right side of Grant's tongue was enlarged and was the chief source of pain. There was a slight ulceration in the right tonsil and also an irritated area on the roof of the mouth where the hard joins the soft palate. Here, like stalactites, three cancerous warts less than one eighth of an inch in length threatened.

A malignant cancer—beginning as a cell or cells that invade and bite into healthy cells while they themselves multiply without limit—can be controlled by excision in its earliest stages. If it was a malignant cancer, Grant was past that. The crab had begun to spread two claws left and right into the neck of its victim. But Douglas wasn't clinically sure that it was malignant. But he said later that in his heart he knew.

He applied muriate of cocaine to the diseased area, which brought the General immediate relief. Lodoform, a derivative of chloroform that also disinfected, helped heal the ulcerated tonsil. Swabbing removed the mucous and the discharge from the wound. Repeated treatment cleared up the congestion in the General's throat and eased the pain, so that sleep again came easily.

Grant submitted to these ministrations twice a day. Douglas's urgency and his own common sense convinced the General of the gravity of his affliction. Because he knew how grave it was, he did not confide in Julia or Fred. But he couldn't hide from them the fact of his visits. He left the house twice a day, taking the streetcar to Douglas's office, two miles away, to save cab fare. Julia and Fred paid Douglas a visit. He told them the General had a complaint with a cancerous tendency, and took the opportunity to instruct them on how to help the General perform his daily prophylaxis. This was important to keep the affliction from smelling offensively as it grew. He also warned them away from irritating solutions for swabbing. Douglas told them it was crucial for the General to follow the regimen Fordyce Barker would prescribe. Grant's whole system needed a healthy tone to enable him to resist the ravages of the disease. Lastly, Douglas explained that the disease would have a long course, and that during it the General would alternate between despair and hope. By understanding this prospect, they could be of inestimable help.

Cancer patients invariably do exactly what their doctors advise. The General visited his dentist for the extraction of a tooth that was proving a minor obstacle to Douglas. When the dentist suggested pulling two adjacent teeth that were in bad shape, the General characteristically ordered him to do it right away. It was fortunate that Harrison Tyrell, Grant's manservant, accompanied him on this trip, because he was spilling blood from his mouth and staggering when he left the office. The General collapsed as soon as he was inside his front door. He convinced Julia that it was nothing, that anyone would collapse after several bad extractions. But Fred knew better.

"During all of General Grant's illness," wrote Badeau, ". . . Mrs. Grant never could bring herself to believe she was about to lose him. A woman with many of those singular premonitions and presentiments that amount almost to superstition but which yet affect some of the strongest minds, and from which General Grant himself was certainly not entirely free, she declared always, even at the moment which everyone else thought would prove his last, that she could not realize the imminence of the end. Her behaviour was a mystery and a wonder to those who knew the depth of the tenderness and the abundance of the affection that she lavished on her great husband. Her calmness and self-control almost seemed coldness, only we knew that this was impossible."

Julia was exhibiting the psychological phenomenon of denial, the apprehension of a catastrophe of such magnitude that it cannot be assimilated by the mind. Denial was operative, too, in the General. Without denial it would prove virtually impossible for a physician to treat a cancer patient or one with a terminal illness. But intimations of impending catastrophe encroach on the patient's consciousness often enough. Grant could ignore, but he could not deny the pain.

His family insisted that he take a carriage to Douglas's office, instead of the streetcar. The General argued with them, and Badeau, listening at the breakfast table, sided with Fred and Julia. Grant proved obstinate, and Badeau rose from the table in agitation saying that he would rather the General stuck a knife in him than go again by streetcar. Grant made no reply, but that afternoon he ordered a carriage.

When he had narrowed the ulceration until it was present only at the base of the tongue, Douglas suggested a further examination by other specialists. He consulted with Fordyce Barker and Drs. Henry B. Sands and T. M. Markoe. After their examination, Douglas sprayed the General's throat with a 4 percent solution of hydrochlorate of cocaine. From the ulcerated edge he removed a small piece of tissue about the size of a pea. Then, hardening the tissue in alcohol, Douglas submitted it to Dr. George R. Elliott for microscopic inspection.

Elliott performed the biopsy and asked Dr. George Frederick Shrady to confirm his findings. Douglas had suggested Shrady because he was not only a microbiologist, but a pioneer in plastic surgery. If an operation was possible, Shrady would perform the surgery. Without knowing from whom the tissue came, Shrady said to Elliott, "This specimen comes from the throat and base of the tongue and is affected with cancer."

"Are you sure?" asked Elliott.

"Perfectly sure," said Shrady. "This patient has a lingual epithalioma—cancer of the tongue."

"This patient is General Grant."

[145]

"Then General Grant is doomed," answered Shrady slowly.

Douglas and Barker consulted Shrady about the advisability of operating. Shrady said the tissue revealed developing cell growth; the growth had already led to a rupture of the capillary blood channels and escaped into the surrounding tissues. The cancer had perforated the anterior border of the tonsular cavity. An operation was futile. In any other part of the body, surgery might halt this cancer. Not in the mouth.

The other doctors agreed. "The wisdom of such a decision," Shrady later wrote, "was manifested in sparing him unnecessary mutilation and allowing him to pass the remainder of his days in comparative comfort. Relatively, however, it meant suffering for him until the end."

The only difference expressed by the doctors concerned how long it would take the cancer to kill the General. Markoe and Sands thought two years was an optimal expectation; Shrady and Douglas thought one.

At the General's request, Shrady attached himself to the case. "It would hardly have been possible to recognize Grant from any striking resemblance to his well-known portraits," he later wrote of their first meeting. "It was not until he bared his head and showed his broad, square forehead and the characteristic double-curved browlock that his actual presence could be realized. The difference in this respect between the lower and upper part of his face was to me most striking and distinctive. There was the broad and square lower jaw, the close-cropped full beard, the down-curved corners of the firmly closed mouth, the small straight nose with the gradual droop at its tip, the heavily browed and penetrating deep blue eyes and withal the head itself, which crowned the actual Grant with dignity and force."

A noted medical writer, Shrady was the founder of the *Medical Record*, a journal that crusaded against charlatanism in the profession. He had been called in to attend the assassinated James A. Garfield, and was also consulted on the illness of Frederick III of Germany. His "Surgical and Pathological Reflections on President Garfield's Wound" and "The Surgical and Pathological Aspects of General Grant's Case" are the only clinical reports that explain the cause of death for both men.

In ministering to Grant, a stolid and reticent man, both Shrady and Douglas took pains to honor his disposition by studiously avoiding familiarity. They did not want to fatigue him with unnecessary conversation or tire him by the exercise of strained courtesy. Even so, a genuine friendship ripened between Grant and these two doctors. This friendship encouraged the General in the short length of time remaining to him, and impressed and influenced the doctors for the rest of their lives. They both left written memoirs of the relationship—Douglas in his diary, which his nephew, Horace Green, incorporated into *General Grant's Last Stand*, published in 1936; and Shrady in a posthumously published memoir, "General Grant's Last Days," which appeared in three installments in *The Century* in 1908.

Toward the end, when Grant's voice failed, he had to communicate by written notes. Douglas saved one hundred and twenty of these, which are now in the Library of Congress. Grant observed that every time he wrote Douglas a note, the doctor stuffed it in his pocket. He cautioned him against saving any of them: "Some day they will be coming up against my English." These notes were not solely restricted to his medical condition. "Did you know that colored people have no regular time for sleeping?" Grant asked Douglas in writing. "They are social and visit other servants when the families are asleep and catch their rest during the day every moment when they are not at work. I venture that you will never find a colored person in their beds."

Shrady, who was no hero worshiper, found casual conversation with the General exciting. Grant was perfectly willing, often eager, to talk about himself. During the war he had been called a relentless butcher, but he told Shrady the carnage was a positive horror to him. His conscience tolerated it because of necessity. "It was always the idea to do it with the least suffering," he said, "on the same principle as the performance of a severe and necessary surgical operation." He said he made such amends to the wounded as he could by seeing to it they had prompt and tender care. And he always took into account the casualties each engagement would cost, but felt a quick and decisive battle saved subsequent and useless slaughter.

They talked of historical topics too. The General said Cromwell was an able general and a good statesman and, although a fanatic, admirably suited to the conditions of his time. Wellington was lucky, he thought, but the good general takes advantage of luck. While he considered Napoleon a military genius, Grant felt that his motives were grasping, arbitrary, and selfish. The man worked for himself, not for France. Besides, there was no excuse for the way Napoleon treated Josephine. "That treatment will be a blot on his character for all time," the General concluded.

The doctors told him to give up cigars; smoking irritated the anterior of his mouth. If he had to smoke, he must restrict himself to three cigars a day. Cigars were as much a part of Ulysses S. Grant as the grizzled beard. He had smoked them from the moment he first became a popular hero.

When he took Fort Donelson one of the reporters described Grant, an occasional pipe smoker, as a cigar-clenching general. Cigars of all varieties promptly innundated his headquarters. Cuban manufacturers sent him a wagonload of boxes. It was impossible to give away the cigars stacked outside his tent like a breastwork. Grant began smoking some of them, and after awhile was rarely seen without a cigar. The General said he was never better prepared for calm deliberation than when enveloped by heavy smoke. One of his most treasured objets d'art was a briarwood cigar case. A Union soldier who had carved it with a penknife gave it to Grant after the victory at Chattanooga.

Some people wondered if the cigars had caused his illness. His doctors replied that a variety of causes contributed to his affliction, including distress over the failure of Grant and Ward. The cigars, however, were certainly doing his condition no good.

In November, the General visited Alden Goldsmith, a wealthy horse fancier, at his stock farm at Goshen, New York, where the famous Hambletonian trotting race was run yearly on the Good Time Track. Grant liked to look over Goldsmith's corral and discuss horseflesh. C. B. Meade, a native of Goshen and a nephew of General George C. Meade, joined Grant and Goldsmith at the stables. As the three men chatted, Meade offered the General some chestnuts he had collected. Grant reminisced about how he had roasted chestnuts at midnight in his room at West Point, and how his men had roasted them after the Battle of the Wilderness. But now, he said, he couldn't swallow them, because of his throat. Goldsmith offered to boil the chestnuts until they were as soft as mashed potatoes, and Grant accepted, saying, "All right, Goldsmith, you be the doctor."

Then he removed a solitary cigar from his pocket, lit it, and said, "Gentlemen, this is the last cigar I will ever smoke. The doctors tell me I will never finish my work if I do not stop." Then as the General smoked slowly, the three men looked over the stubbled fields to the winding Wallkill River. The foliage, radiating from the sun, lent the day an ambience of gold and vermilion. A tumult of birds filled the sky. It was one of the last good moments the General ever knew.

Soon after, when Childs invited Grant to Philadelphia for a few days, he declined, writing: "The doctor will not allow me to leave until the weather gets warmer. I am now quite well in every way, except a swelling in the tongue above the root, and the same thing in the tonsils just over it. It is very difficult for me to swallow enough to maintain my strength and nothing gives me so much pain as to swallow water. If you can imagine what molten lead would be going down your throat, that is what I feel when swallowing." Shrady, who called the General "an example of Christian fortitude the like of which has seldom been recorded," noticed that he would write stubbornly for hours and sometimes the whole day without water, rather than submit to the intense pain that swallowing occasioned.

His suffering was noticeable at the dinner table. By December he had to depend upon milk and cold soups for nourishment. He steeled himself to gulp the contents of a bowl at a single swallow, to get it down before pain made his throat contract. Mealtimes had always been, and still were, the important part of the day for the family. Julia, Fred and Ida and their children, and often Buck and his wife and Badeau assembled around the table, as well as some afternoon visitor, who was always invited to join them. The General still sat at the head of the table and bowed his head for grace, but he no longer carved or helped serve. Often he would leave before the meal was over, to pace in the hall or in the adjoining living room until his throat spasm relaxed.

The General's departure was a sign that he was in pain, and

his silence about it only convinced Julia that the pain was intense. Silence, to her, meant suffering. She confided her distress to Sherman during the Christmas season. Sherman reminded her that silence was the General's way. He asked her to remember the times he or Sheridan or Meade had stormed up and down the length of the headquarters tent shouting, cursing, slamming the field maps, while Grant sat at a makeshift table, silent, wreathed with cigar smoke, waiting for their passion and excitement to dissipate.

The General lost weight steadily. But he disguised his condition to visitors. He was always dressed when he received his friends, and he always covered his lap with a shawl. With his bearded, broad, full face it was hard to determine that he was wasting away.

Surcease from the pain of swallowing and the need for rest became constant preoccupations, draining Grant of strength and vitality. Pain and coughing kept him fretful all through the night, until sheer exhaustion closed his eyes. He remarked to Julia how easily and quickly he had fallen asleep during the Battle of the Wilderness, and how terribly hard it was to fall asleep now.

In a letter to General Edward F. Beale, a Washington friend, Grant revealed how poor his health was, and Beale realized the seriousness of the complaint when Fred revealed to him that the General was confined to his rooms by weakness and that his condition alarmed the family. Through Beale, the first hint of the General's worsening state appeared in a Philadelphia newspaper in January, 1885. When reporters queried Grant's doctors, they replied that he was sick, but they had every expectation he would get better.

"My tears blind me," Julia wrote to Mrs. William S. Hillyer, the wife of a former officer. "General Grant is very ill. I cannot write how ill."

Anodynes administered to bring sleep often proved disappointing. One evening Grant was so desperate for sleep he sent for Shrady at dusk. Shrady observed his patient's heightening anxiety over another restless night. Not wanting him to yield to fear, Shrady persuaded him that changing his position in bed would bring sleep. The doctor turned the pillow to the cooler side and told Grant to pretend he was a boy again.

"Curl up your legs," Shrady instructed, "lie over on your side and bend your neck while I tuck the covers around your shoulders."

The idea appealed to the General. Shrady placed Grant's hand under the pillow and said, "Now go to sleep like a good boy."

In a few minutes the General fell asleep. He was resting, thought Shrady, as he must have rested as a boy. The doctor turned to Julia and apologized for the process. He hoped the General wouldn't think it inconsistent with dignity.

"There is not the slightest danger of that," said Julia. "He is the most simple-mannered and reasonable person in the world, and he likes to have persons whom he knows treat him without ceremony."

On several subsequent occasions Shrady coaxed the General to sleep in this way. Grant said he had not slept with his arm under the pillow and his feet curled up since he left Georgetown for West Point, forty-five years before.

Sleep was often disturbed by bad dreams. Fred saw the General clutch his throat one night and shout, "The cannon did it!" On another occasion, Fred heard him bark, "I am detailed from four to six." Some dreams had symbolic content. He told Douglas, "It seemed to me as though I had been traveling in a foreign country. I had only a single satchel and I was only partially clad. I found to my surprise that I was without any money and separated from my friends. While I was traveling I came to a fence. There was a stepping stile but it led up to only one side. I climbed over, however, and then found I had left my satchel on the other side. Then I thought I would go back home and borrow the money from Mrs. Grant. I asked her for it, but she said she had only seventeen dollars and that was not enough; at which I woke." The dream was terrifying because he had to retrace his steps.

Worse than the dreams, worse even than the pain of swallowing, was the sensation of choking that overwhelmed Grant when he was lying down. Choking will inspire panic in even the most restrained and self-contained person. When the General lay back he could not breathe. He was afraid he would choke to death in his sleep. The doctors assured him this could not happen. A disautonomic tensing of his muscles shut off air while he was conscious. But if he denied himself oxygen, he would faint. The muscles would relax. Then he would breathe again. It was not a comforting assurance, and the General would have none of it. From the winter on, he slept sitting up on two large leather armchairs placed together facing each other.

In this middle stage of the disease, emaciation and exhaustion made savage inroads on the General's morale. He confessed to Fred and Badeau that he had no desire to live if he was not going to recover. He preferred death to a hopeless affliction that was strangling and starving him.

Badeau thought he lost not courage, but some of his hope, his grip on life. He stopped writing with the advent of winter, a depressing, gray season in the city, the sludge and the cold and the wet clamping down on the streets. And he stopped talking, too. He sat for hours in his easy chair, propped by a pillow, his back to the window, staring at a blank corner of his library. Instead of street clothes, he wore a dressing gown and a loose scarf. For the General to give up all physical and mental effort appalled Badeau. It made him think of a man staring into his open grave.

Whenever Julia entered the library, she smoothed out the General's frown with her tiny hands. She tried to laugh with him, but his responses were slower. Laughter hurt. The perceptive Shrady knew from experience that to accommodate oneself to the burden of sickness requires time and patience. It is hard for anyone to submit to the inevitable, but the wise doctor knew that a brave man will manage it.

So it was with Grant. Staring at his wall, the General realized that he was under heavy marching orders, that what was required of him now was no more than what he had required of others. He must brave death; soldiers transcend themselves by braving death. He went back to work, back to fighting. Finishing the memoirs was a race with time and an hourly struggle with pain.

Bravery to a soldier like Grant is often a matter of priorities. On Christmas day, the General came to the festive table and insisted that Julia seat all the grandchildren near him. He let them monopolize the conversation, though their mothers tried to shush them. The General said Christmas day belonged to the children. He was proud of his progeny. And children always charmed him.

When Dr. Titus Munson Coan, a navy surgeon, called on the General, he left his six-year-old son, Philip, in the reception room below. Grant said he wanted to meet the little boy. Sick as he was, he rose from his chair and walked halfway across the room to shake hands with the child. "I am glad to see you, my little man," he said. The boy thanked Grant and stared at the face bent over him. "What are you going to be when you grow up," asked the General, "a sailor or a doctor?"

The boy offered no answer and Grant, understanding the bashfulness of children, smoothed his hair with his hand and bade him call again. He had an intuitive consideration for young people. When Shrady's little girl, Minnie, asked if she could meet the General, Grant told the doctor not to hesitate. But before Shrady ushered his daughter into the library, Grant changed from his bed jacket into a frock coat.

It was in large measure on behalf of his own and his children's children that he reapplied himself to his writing. He began using the library on the second floor. Two bay windows fronted on 66th Street. They stretched from ceiling to floor and admitted into the farthest recesses of the room a generous light. Behind the library was his bedroom, with Julia's beyond that, the two rooms separated by folding doors. The bedrooms were filled with flowers, because Childs sent them two and sometimes three days a week.

On the General's desk were several neatly categorized piles of notes. Beside the desk was a folding card table on which the General kept his maps, marking his position and the position of the Confederates in bold crayon. He began work at ten o'clock, dictating to N. E. Dawson, a stenographer provided by Mark Twain. Using his notes, the General dictated in consecutive paragraphs and pages. Dawson transcribed the session by hand and distributed copies to Fred and Badeau.

Fred filled in the fine details—birthdates of the generals, biographical background, the identity of every regiment, and a description of the terrain. One of the later editions of the *Personal Memoirs* includes all of Fred's marginal notes. Badeau made editorial comments. He asked for clarity, or for deletions and additions. He checked the General's descriptions against the official reports and other accounts.

In the afternoon, the General composed his notes for the next morning's dictation. He could write with ordinary rapidity, but often paused in concentration for long periods to make clear something that was complicated. When the General read over his notes he appeared to weigh every word carefully. Often he kept his place in the line with his index finger. He would look away, as if to fix more firmly in his mind the idea conveyed. The only reference the General used at these times was Sherman's memoirs, although Fred and Badeau kept extensive libraries in their working quarters.

If the General hit upon a felicitous phrase, he would call in Julia or one of the doctors, or whoever was handy, to read it aloud with the embarrassed pride of a schoolboy who has surprised himself by arriving at the right answer. As he wrote he sat sideways, so he could cross his legs, his favorite position. His calligraphy was abrupt, nervous, jerky, and sometimes illegible. He did not dot his "i's" or cross his "t's"; he made capital "S's" like inverted "V's," and his spelling was still imaginative. He used pencil, because he did not want to interrupt his thoughts by constantly dipping a pen into an inkwell.

He wore a knitted skating cap whose crown fell across his shoulder to ward off the cold. Drafts caused him severe neuralgic headaches. He wore large spectacles with hard rubber rims. Faithful Harrison waited quietly on a chair in one of the corners of the room. Whenever the General paused, Harrison rose to readjust the shawl that covered his legs.

In the evening, in a small sitting room on the second floor, the General, Julia, Fred, and Ida gathered for family chatter. Often Ida read aloud other books about the Civil War, from which the General took notes. While he had established a writer's regimen, there were fitful interruptions when his health broke down. He went for an afternoon ride with his friend Romero, and caught cold, which caused him to halt work. Some mornings he was simply too weak to walk from his armchairs to his desk; and sometimes, when Harrison walked him there, he was in too much agony to work.

Any change in his routine taxed him. In early March, Nellie Grant Sartoris arrived in New York from England to join her father for the spring and summer. Grant had written her simply that he wasn't well, but that he was busy writing his memoirs, so that she could know "what sort of a man your father was before you knew him." But Nellie knew the situation because Fred wrote her that their father was dying. The boys were the General's strength, but Nellie was his treasure.

Called the "Daughter of the Nation," Nellie was the first girl ever married in the White House. In 1874, at eighteen, she had wed Algernon Charles Francis Sartoris, the scion of a wealthy English family. At the time, the Grants thought Nellie was too young. The Sartorises thought Algy, though an Oxford man, too immature. Nellie married him anyway and bore him two children. Unfortunately, the Sartorises knew their own child. Algy proved a mountebank, a rake, and a philanderer. The Sartorises sided with Nellie, and Algy became that special creation of the English ruling classes, a remittance man, paid a monthly stipend on the condition that he never come home. Like her father, and like the English, Nellie was uncomplaining and uncommunicative about her bad luck. However, Algy died of his dissipations in 1890, leaving her a wealthy widow.

The General insisted on going twice to the steamship pier, once to inquire about Nellie's crossing and again to meet her. She was now a handsome English matron, but still adored her frontier father. The excitement of her arrival, the embraces and the tears, weakened the General. Within a few days the joy of Nellie's homecoming was suppressed by the morbid apprehension of the household.

At the end of March, Grant insisted on testifying at the trial of James D. Fish. He had already volunteered his testimony to Attorney General Elihu Root. Though he was held guiltless in the defalcations, the General wanted this last opportunity to dispel any lingering doubts about his personal honesty. Mark Twain was present one day when Fred argued with his father that he was too sick to testify, and that his testimony, if delivered, would only prompt more ridicule. Fred looked at Twain and said, "Father is letting you see that the Grant family is a pack of fools."

The General replied that nobody would call the president of the Erie Railroad a fool, yet Ward cheated him out of $800,000. Ward tricked another man into buying one of Senator Chaffee's silver mines, a property that was not for sale and that Ward had no authority to sell. Yet he got $300,000 out of that man, without producing a single piece of evidence to show that the sale had been made. Grant mentioned several other titans of the financial world whom Ward and Fish had bilked. They were all out of pocket, but they chose not to testify in order to preserve face. That was their business. But now Grant had the chance to swear it was he who had been swindled, and not he who swindled others.

Too weak to appear in court, Grant testified in his library. Root listened to the testimony for the government. C. B. Clark and Edwin Smith undertook cross-examination for the defense. Grant was counseled by his attorney, Clarence Seward. Talking produced extreme fatigue. Grant had to clear his throat as his voice grew husky. Clearing his throat brought on pain. He spent more than two hours answering questions, and the effort cost him several days of work. But his testimony helped convict Fish.

When he got back to his writing, he took pains to leave no other business unfinished. He went over his will again; he performed small favors he had promised to do for old veterans; and he informed his sons about the gifts he wanted each of them to have from his personal belongings. He began to do things on the spur of the moment, so that nothing might be left undone. He autographed a picture of himself that an army publication had requested.* At this point, Shrady suggested that he sign a photograph for each member of the medical staff. Cheerfully the General obliged. Fred spread the pictures on the table to let the ink dry and then quietly said, "Father, I would like you to sign this also." He produced a letter which Grant read and promptly signed:

> To the President of the United States:
> May I ask you to favor the appointment of Ulysses S. Grant (the son of my son, Frederick Grant) as a cadet at West Point upon his application. In doing so, you will gratify the wishes of
>
> Ulysses S. Grant

The letter, preserved in the Library of Congress, later bore the endorsement of William Tecumseh Sherman and a final endorsement by President William McKinley directing the appointment to be made in 1898. The pathos of the moment suffused all those in the room. Fred Grant carefully folded the signed letter and slipped it

---

* The photograph he preferred was the one made by William E. Marshall.

into an envelope. Everyone was aware that in a matter of months, perhaps weeks, the hand that had affixed the signature would never sign another letter. Ulysses S. Grant, III, was then three years old, and Shrady thought no young soldier would ever have a worthier benediction.

Mark Twain returned to New York in February from one of his popular lecture tours, the last he was ever to make through America. Before he left on tour he knew that the General had been bothered by a sore throat and had given up cigars to remedy the annoyance. On the day of his return he read a report in the *Tribune* issued by Grant's doctors. The rumors about the General's bad health were unfounded, the doctors said, and he had been responding satisfactorily to treatment. When Twain was shown into the library at East 66th Street, he greeted the General with a sally about the good news of his improving health.

Grant smiled and said, "Yes—if only it had been true."

Twain was surprised and dismayed to find the General thinner and obviously weaker than he had been in November. Dr. Douglas was in the room and he startled Twain by volunteering that the General's condition was anything but encouraging. He and Barker had issued the report to the newspaper because they could not think of what else to say when the reporter cornered them. The General was seriously sick, said Douglas, but, of course, his doctors still had hopes.

To the unasked question that must have registered on Twain's face, Grant said, "I mean you shall have the book." The notes and the manuscript were ready for Twain's inspection if he chose. As Twain was leaving the house, Fred Grant stunned him by confiding that the doctors were trying to conceal from the General the gravity of his illness. The doctors considered him under a death sentence. The General could be dead within three weeks, or at any moment after that.

Twain had some hard thinking to do on the front stoop. The formal contract between Charles L. Webster & Company and General Grant was finally ready for signatures. In fact, this was precisely why Twain had returned to New York. But now there was a distinct possibility that Grant would not live long enough to finish his memoirs. Backing off now would save Twain money he could never recoup. The General was three or four chapters from finishing volume one—three or four lengthy and important chapters, because they described the siege and surrender of Vicksburg. There could be no volume one without Vicksburg, and no volume two without Appomattox.

Mark Twain was never noted for business acuity. A saner publisher would have held back on his commitments until he had the manuscript in hand. But Twain was not a sane businessman. He was always committed to an "excess of enterprise," as Howells characterized it. When he did realize profits it was because he was reckless and bold. Two considerations made him plunge ahead: he adored the General and the General could draw a map that would lead Twain to a pot of gold.

In Twain's pocket was a letter from his partner, Charley Webster: "There's big money for both of us in that book and in the terms indicated in my note to the General we can make it pay *big*." This was not idle enthusiasm on the part of either Twain or Webster. Charles L. Webster & Company, which had published *The Adventures of Huckleberry Finn* in December, was already assured of selling out the first printing of fifty thousand copies. Within months, Twain would earn from it a royalty check of $55,500. To follow this unqualified success with Ulysses S. Grant's memoirs would establish Charles L. Webster & Company as one of the premier publishing houses in the world. The prospect was dazzling. It was more than dazzling; it was compelling. There was a force in Mark Twain that always inspired him to subvert his own work for some temporary allurement, to ignore his own writing for the pursuit of a fabled business grail.

Certainly he had a moral commitment to the General. And certainly he was a moral man. Grant had told him, "I mean you shall have the book," and to Twain that was a promise. Grant was promising not just to sign the contract, but to finish the memoirs. Twain had a bet to make and that bet was on General Grant. He thought it was a good bet.

Upstairs in the library, in what was now transformed into the General's sickroom, there was a difference of opinion. There had been muted arguments and whispers about the book. Drs. Douglas and Shrady and Fred Grant thought the book was keeping the General alive. Dr. Barker and Julia felt that the General's anxiety over finishing it sapped his energy and strength. They thought the book was killing him. But, of course, no opinion, no matter how well articulated or how well motivated, ever exercised the slightest influence over the General.

When Grant signed the contract with Charles L. Webster & Company on February 27, Twain issued a publicity release that his firm was publishing the book. This was news. Grant and Twain were the two most newsworthy celebrities of their time. That they had combined to publish what promised to be the most significant memoirs of the Civil War excited the public. "No publishing enterprise of such vast moment," wrote Twain's biographer Albert Bigelow Paine, "had ever been undertaken, and no publishing event, before or since, ever received the amount of newspaper comment."

Not all the comment was laudatory. Among others, the *New York World* and the *Boston Herald* charged that Twain, through guile, had taken unfair advantage of the Century Company. Century had considered the book its property, inasmuch as the terms of publication were mutually agreed upon when Twain put in his meddling appearance. Now, the papers reported, there was a chilling coolness between Grant and the Century Company, which had decided not to publish the Grant articles despite their widespread advertisement.

Twain addressed himself to exposing this canard. In a news release he noted that there was no estrangement between Grant and *The Century*, which would print the articles for which it had contracted. In fact, the General insisted on revising his articles for the magazine before essaying his history for Twain.

The statement was brief, concise, and inoffensive. Yet it never appeared in any newspaper. Twain had given it to the Associated Press, an entity different from the present-day AP, which advised him that, although his release was news of universal interest, it was also more or less an advertisement for the forthcoming book. It was not their policy to indulge free advertising. But he could get it printed, suggested one of the telegraphers, if Twain wanted to offer a bribe. Twain was so shocked by this knavery that he fell into uncharacteristic silence.

The New York Times also got the story wrong. The *Times* told its readers that General Grant had long ago finished his articles for *The Century*, and that his *History of the Rebellion* was practically completed. The General had aggravated his illness by his compulsion to hurry. Even if he did not live to finish the remainder, it could easily be finished by his son.

This was interpretive reporting. Gilder and Johnson had only two of the articles in their office. They had made several inquiries as to the General's progress, and on occasion had importuned him to work faster. Their impatience and nervousness annoyed Fred Grant. He chided them to their faces for their rudeness and remarked behind their backs on their general inhumanity.

Having made the decision to go ahead meant more to Twain than moral commitment or quick riches, it meant frenzy. The "best seller" did not become a publishing concept until after the turn of the century, but a best seller was what Twain and Webster had on their hands. They would have to let contracts to numerous presses and binderies, buy tons of paper and gallons of ink, and ready a phalanx of canvassers. Charles L. Webster & Company had harpooned the Leviathan itself, and everyone would soon be working night and day to bring it in.

There was an unequal division of duties between Twain and his partner. Charley Webster, as a matter of fact, was only a nominal partner. The company was financed wholly by Twain out of his royalties and lecture fees. Webster received a salary of $2,500 a year plus 10 percent of the profits which, however, remained on deposit with the firm. So did Twain's profits—except when he needed them. Webster had agreed to take charge of all technical and business matters connected with publishing the books, from printing through advertising and distribution. But he was also detailed on occasion to travel from New York to Hartford to supervise the installation of a new furnace in the Twain home on Farmington Avenue, or to traipse the streets of New York hunting up a mustachioed peddler who sold make-believe watches, to replace the one broken by Twain's youngest daughter.

When Webster moved the firm's offices to more spacious quarters on 14th Street, Twain grumbled. When he hired two clerks to help with the production of the book, Twain made the air blue with his swearing. Twain even complained about Webster's purchase of a better stock of stationery. But he calmed down long enough to propose that the new letterhead should read: "Charles L. Webster & Company, publishers of Mark Twain's books and the forthcoming *Personal Memoirs of General Grant*." Twain specified that the italicized words be printed in larger type and red ink.

Virtually all of Twain's money was tied up in the venture. In addition, he borrowed $200,000 to finance publication and he canceled what promised to be a profitable lecture tour through England and Australia. He wanted to be close at hand while the General's book was passing through the presses and into the hands of the distributors. He wanted nothing overlooked or neglected. He rushed two and three times a day between his publishing offices and the General's home, constantly filled with ideas and suggestions. "Clemens was boiling over with plans for distribution," wrote Paine. "Webster was half wild with the tumult of the great campaign."

Webster announced that the firm would accept applications from canvassing agencies and agents. Applications inundated the office. Webster summoned the most responsible applicants to New York, among them James H. McGraw, who later went on to found the firm of McGraw-Hill. Webster laid out the publishing schedule, told the agents he wanted nothing tentative in their approach and nothing questionable in their distribution. Twain also rose to exhort them. He wanted them to "keep pouring hot shot" until the customer signed a contract. Webster and Twain were inspiring. When the agents left the 14th Street headquarters, they had pledged 250,000 sets of the Grant book.

The bet was paying off. Grant finished the account of Vicksburg for *The Century* in late March. He had worked in fits and starts, but there were days when he wrote 10,000 words. "It kills me these days to write half of that," said Twain. Twain saw the finished manuscript of Vicksburg on Grant's working table one morning, picked it up, and began to read it. Counting three hundred words on the first page, Twain guessed conservatively that the article ran from 18,000 to 20,000 words. There was matter enough in this one chapter for three or four ordinary magazine articles. He turned to the General and said as much. If that were true, remarked the General stolidly, then it satisfied him that he had fulfilled his obligation to *The Century*. Twain said he meant that the General was entitled to four times as much as he had agreed to accept. "But the General's modesty in money matters was indestructible," said Twain.

Twain determined to bring the matter of its parsimony to *The Century*'s attention. He was also suddenly and painfully aware that there was no written agreement between Grant and *The Century* that returned to the General the rights to his material once the magazine had printed it. Accompanied by Charley Webster and Clarence Seward, Twain paid a call on Roswell Smith.

Smith agreed immediately that the magazine would return the rights to the General for his own use as soon as the articles appeared in print. Having won this point so easily, Twain proceeded to shame Smith for the niggardly payments to Grant for such detailed and lengthy articles. Twain reminded Smith that not only did he intend to print these articles in the magazine, but to incorporate them later in *Battles and Leaders*.* Smith, who may have had enough of Twain at this point, produced a receipt signed by the General assigning the Century Company the permission to print the articles in the magazine and in a subsequent book.

"It was easily demonstrable they were buying ten-dollar gold pieces from General Grant at twenty-five cents a piece, and I think it was as easily demonstrable that they did not know there was anything unfair about it," wrote Twain in his *Autobiography*.**

The first volume of Grant's memoirs went promptly to the typesetters. In addition to the problems of printing, distribution,

* The Century Company published its series of articles in two volumes in 1887 under the title *Battles and Leaders of the Civil War*.
** Twain was also a mark, second only to Grant. Like most marks he was unusually canny about protecting the interests of friends. When *The Century* later consented to cut the Vicksburg article from twenty-two galleys down to nine, Twain gracefully remarked, "Those people could be as fair and liberal as anybody if they had the right schooling." Meanwhile the accountant of Charles L. Webster & Company was doctoring the books, just as Ferdinand Ward had doctored Grant and Ward's books, and embezzling thousands of dollars.

rights, the assigning of territory to canvassing agents, and the struggle to keep costs within measure, Twain and Webster had to guard constantly against Canadian pirates. These were unscrupulous publishers who would steal proofs from the printers or from the copyreaders, flee to Canada, where they would have the proofs reset in Montreal, and then start distributing the book in America before Twain could secure his copyright (for only printed matter can be copyrighted). As the proofs of the first volume came from the presses, Webster kept them locked in the company's safe. In fact, Charles L. Webster & Company guaranteed $6,000 to the printers and the binders if they could account for every proof sheet. Twain even took out an insurance policy against theft and loss of these proofs.

Twain was cool-headed in this regard. There was no international copyright protection for writers in the 1880s. The Canadian pirates smuggled out of the United States and printed as many books as they could lay their hands on. Dickens, Sir Walter Scott, Gilbert and Sullivan, and Twain had all had their work pirated.*

Twain himself checked proofs for the first volume, something he never did for any other author. "My marks will not be seriously important," he told Webster, "since they will concern grammar and punctuation only." While Twain corrected and read the proofs, he made no editorial comments. This omission began to trouble Grant. He had come to learn that writing was hard work, and had done enough of it to sense some excellence in his book, to feel its quality. Grant longed to know whether his own judgment was right.

Fred mentioned this to Mark Twain, who wrote in his diary that it never occurred to him that the General would have any use for anybody's assistance or encouragement in anything he chose to do. "I was much surprised," wrote Twain, "as Columbus's cook would have been to learn that Columbus wanted his opinion as to how Columbus was doing the navigating." Twain seems to have forgotten that he was a famous author and that for most writers the paramount criterion of excellence is the judgment of another member of the profession.

* "Mark Twain was a leader in copyright reforms, both national and international," wrote Samuel Clemens Webster in *Mark Twain: Business Man.* He even had the name Mark Twain registered as a trademark so that it could never again be used as a name.

[163]

Thus Twain discussed with the General the quality of his prose. He compared the *Personal Memoirs* to Caesar's *Commentaries.* Like Caesar, said Twain, Grant was direct and unmartial. Grant's book belonged with "the best purely narrative literature in the language." This was not only a useful and accurate assessment, though it is to be doubted Twain had even a rudimentary knowledge of Caesar or Latin, but it was also subtle. One of the few military books Grant had ever read was *De Bello Civili,* in translation, at West Point.

Twain didn't presume he was doing the General a favor, and the General didn't accept his praise as such. Their friendship became profound, marked by a series of intimate dialogues. In the course of one of these discussions Grant confided that if he had time left after he finished the book, he intended to write an article for *The Century* arguing for a single six-year term for the presidency.

In late March, Twain brought the young sculptor Karl Gerhardt to East 66th Street. Twain had financed Gerhardt's study in Europe and helped support his studio in Hartford for no other reason, he noted, than that one man should help another if he can. While not without talent, Gerhardt was a manipulative young man, already a genius at exploiting his patron's reputation. He had recently won a commission from the Connecticut legislature for a memorial to Nathan Hale. The committee wanted assurance from Gerhardt that for its $5,000 it would have a horse to go with the martyr, but the sculptor refused to comply. He withdrew into his studio in a sulk, and busied himself with the bust of Mark Twain that appeared in the frontispiece of *Huckleberry Finn.* And when Gerhardt and the Connecticut legislators continued to remain at odds, the sculptor conceived the idea of fashioning a bust of Ulysses S. Grant from photographs. Twain was so impressed with the likeness he asked Gerhardt to come to New York so that the Grant family could point out defects in the sculpture before Gerhardt took molds.

Julia, Ida, and Jesse's wife, Elizabeth, were as excited as Twain when Gerhardt uncovered the small statue. The nose and the forehead were nearly right, they agreed, but not quite. Chattering, the ladies led Gerhardt up to the library, where the General was stretched out in his reclining chair, his feet propped up. He was muffled in his dressing gown and covered by an afghan; a scarf was wound around his neck, and his skating hat pulled down on his head.

While his wife and daughters-in-law turned his face this way and that for Gerhardt's inspection, the General never uttered a word. When Julia demanded, "Ulyss! Ulyss! Can't you put your feet on the floor?" the General complied. Gerhardt promised that it would take him only fifteen minutes to correct the defects in the bust. The ladies left as Gerhardt began his modeling. Twain and Faithful Harrison kept to the back of the room. The General watched Gerhardt work. One of his eyelids drooped, then the other. Quiet crept over the room. Grant fell asleep, the first sleep he had managed in weeks without an anodyne. Surveying the scene, Twain was led to remark that night in his notebook: "One marked feature of General Grant's character is his exceeding gentleness, goodness and sweetness. I wonder that it has not been more spoken of."

When Gerhardt finished his work, he displayed the bust to the enthusiastic family. Faithful Harrison pronounced judgment: "That's the General. Yes sir, that's the General. Mind! I tell you that's the General."

Fred Grant refused Gerhardt one more sitting, saying the bust was nearly perfect. If Gerhardt touched it again, he was likely to refine excellence out of it, rather than add excellence to it. Fred pointed to an oil painting. "That was a perfect portrait of my father once," he said. "It was given up by the family to be the best that was ever made of him. We were entirely satisfied with it but the artist, unhappily, was not. He wanted to do a stroke or two to make it absolutely perfect. After he finished, it didn't resemble my father or anyone else. With that lesson behind us, we will save the bust from a similar fate."

So the family did. Gerhardt's bust, reproduced in terra-cotta, adorned thousands of fireplace mantels and bookshelves in the coming decades. Twain, Sherman, and many others thought Gerhardt's little bust the most nearly correct likeness of Grant. It is as expressive as any of the Brady or Meserve photographs taken in the camps. Grant's head is slightly bowed. A military tunic covers the upper chest with general's insignia on the shoulders. What Gerhardt captured was the General's agony, but he transformed it into the thoughtful agony of the Civil War commander.

Stubbornly, tenaciously, Grant worked away at volume two. He was still capable of dictating or writing 10,000 words but now the effort exhausted him and for a day or two afterward he could only work fitfully. Sometimes a heavy injection of morphine made it impossible for him to work at all. But the General knew by the beginning of spring that Mark Twain had in hand actual payment for 60,000 sets of the memoirs. And the canvassers had only begun to solicit.

Twain estimated the number of books the country would require—300,000 sets of two volumes each. He wrote Webster: "If these chickens should really hatch according to my account, General Grant's royalties will amount to $420,000, and will make the largest single check ever paid an author in the world's history. Up to the present time the largest one ever paid was to Macaulay on his *History of England*, £20,000. If I pay the General in silver coin at $12 per pound it will weigh seventeen tons."

On February 16, 1885, by a vote of 158 to 103, sixteen less than the two thirds needed, the House of Representatives refused to suspend the rules to consider a bill placing Ulysses S. Grant on the retired list of the United States Army. "Thus," editorialized *The New York Times*, "four Confederate brigadiers, eleven colonels, one lieutenant colonel, one major, five captains, two lieutenants, and twelve enlisted men did to Grant in Congress what they couldn't do in the field."

Actually, the South rather admired Grant after the war; though following his presidency his name became synonymous with Reconstruction. However, in this instance, the veterans of the defeated Confederacy were joined by an embittered old Union general, William Rosecrans. A one-time classmate of Grant's and now a congressman from California, Rosecrans not only spoke against the bill, but said Grant's qualities of leadership were overrated. Rosecrans was smarting from a wartime dressing down by Grant, an incident that had just been publicly revived, and he was eager to take a potshot at the General.

Sherman, Drexel, Childs, Cyrus Field, A. T. Stewart, and ex-Secretary of State Hamilton Fish had all worked assiduously for the past six weeks, exerting their considerable influence to have the Senate pass this bill reinstating the General. Reinstatement would entitle Grant to a lieutenant general's salary. Upon his death, Julia would receive a pension of $5,000. George Edmunds of Vermont, who had written the bill prohibiting polygamy in the Territories, brought the original resolution before the Senate, where it did not find smooth sailing. Some senators opposed passage because reinstatement was a privilege reserved for officers suffering disabilities incident to their military service. Others argued incorrectly that Grant enjoyed an income of $15,000 a year that had been provided by his friends. There were few who realized how sick the General was, or how impoverished the Grant and Ward failure had left him. Edmunds argued that the question was not what Grant's friends had done for him, but what the country had done for him. It was a convincing argument. The Senate passed the bill.

But the House proved neither as responsible nor as generous. Apparently Grant's friends had failed. It was a profound letdown. Grant's physicians, in the first bulletin they ever released on the actual conditions of his illness, wrote, "The action of Congress in refusing to pass the bill restoring him to his honors has been very depressing." Badeau, in *Grant in Peace*, said that the General had looked upon this bill as some reparation for the injury his reputation had sustained. Its passage would intimate that the country still believed in him and had not forgotten his valor. "When the reparation was withheld," wrote Badeau, "he suffered proportionately." All Grant said was that the bill had failed on the anniversary of his capture of Fort Donelson.

This was not the first time a bill to reinstate Ulysses S. Grant as a lieutenant general had failed. In 1880 a similar bill was introduced in the House by Joe Johnston, the Confederate general Sherman had pursued through the Carolinas. But Grant's friends, who were readying him for a third term, saw to it that the bill died in committee. In the early spring of 1884 President Chester A. Arthur had vetoed a bill that placed Grant and General Fitz-John Porter on the retired list. Arthur insisted that Congress had usurped presidential nominating powers, and had offered "advice which was unnecessary and ineffective and able to serve no useful purpose upon the statutes." Chester A. Arthur acted on principle, but it was hard for the General to sympathize with this principle. The bill for his reinstatement had been introduced and passed before the Grant and Ward debacle and vetoed afterward.

It seemed now, in February, 1885, that he was never to be reinstated. Senator William Mitchell of New York thereupon proposed a pension of $3,000 a year, to take effect from the date of the General's retirement from the presidency. This measure, if passed, would guarantee the General $27,000. But upon hearing of Mitchell's plans, the General quickly wrote to advise he would not accept such a pension.

Senator Chaffee told a reporter that the General could not consistently accept a pension because he had vetoed such measures when he was in the White House. The General also saw that a pension would not provide for Julia after his death. But perhaps his last consideration was paramount: the General did not consider himself a pensioner.

Sherman told his cohorts that they had cut their way in once and they could cut their way in again. All they had to do was to persuade the House to reconsider the measure that had already passed the Senate. He began petitioning members of the Congress he knew. Very probably he petitioned William Rosecrans.

Childs editorialized in his newspaper that it was not only possible to reward a national hero, it was also customary. Meanwhile, the New York State Assembly instructed its congressional delegation to vote unanimously for any bill reinstating General Grant.

Hoping to persuade those Confederate veterans who had voted against the bill, Honorable James Speed of Kentucky made public a letter describing how Grant had preserved the paroles of the men of the Army of Northern Virginia. Speed, who had been one of Andrew Johnson's attorneys general, recalled that when General Bradley Johnson returned to Baltimore after Appomattox, he was arrested and indicted for treason. Grant had come to the President's office and insisted that this soldier had to be released, that military paroles were not to be violated by civil arrest. The President wanted to know how they could proceed to indict Robert E. Lee if they had to release the Confederate Johnson. Grant replied that they could never proceed against Lee as long as he did not violate his parole. He went further. He said he had granted the paroles, and before those paroles were violated he would resign as general-in-chief.

By the beginning of March the newspapers learned that the General was fatally ill. This sad news shamed Congress. Democratic Speaker of the House Samuel J. Randall promised Childs he would reintroduce the bill. But he saw little chance of its passage, because the 48th Congress would adjourn on March 3, the day before the new President, Grover Cleveland, took the oath of office. Randall did, however, ready the bill, in case the House found time to consider it. S. 2530 authorized the President to appoint one general to the retired list of the United States Army.

In its pell-mell rush to finish off pending legislation, the House did not consider the bill on March 3. But the House had not found time either to deliberate about appropriations that would establish the Brooklyn Navy Yard and an Indian Reservation in Montana. The House also had to resolve a disputed election in Iowa's Fifth Congressional District. The Speaker ordered the House to convene again on March 4 and date all business as having been transacted on March 3.

In New York, Childs assured the General the bill would pass. Grant said, "Mr. Childs, you know during the last day of a session everything is in turmoil. Such a thing cannot possibly be passed. If anyone in the world could pass such a bill, I think Mr. Randall could. But I don't think it is at all likely, and I have given up expectation."

Constitutionally, the House could not continue past noon. At that moment Grover Cleveland became President and the new Congress assumed its powers. A few minutes after 11 A.M., Randall surrendered the chair and made a motion for a suspension of the rules to consider the Grant retirement bill. With the business of the disputed election still before it, the chair ruled the motion out of order.

The dispute was between James Wilson and George Frederick. Frederick had been certified by the Iowa Board of Elections. Wilson argued that the board was in error. Now Wilson rose from his seat and asked for the floor. He promised to withdraw his objection to the seating of Frederick if, by this sacrifice, the House would consider the Grant bill.

Tumultuous cheers broke from the galleries.

The Grant bill passed with one bellowing, roaring "Aye!"

Randall rushed from the House to the Senate. Though the Senate had not convened that day, the senators were in the Capitol awaiting the inauguration ceremonies. Hurriedly the senators rushed to their chamber. As they scrambled for their seats, they awoke dozens of people who, unable to find hotel rooms, had used the gallery for a night's sleep. The president *pro tem* chased carpenters away from the platform they were building for Cleveland's joint address.

Outgoing President Arthur had not yet joined the inaugural procession. Instead, he had waited in one of the Senate offices in hopes the House would find a way for him to reinstate General Grant. Now he added his signature to the bill. The last act of his administration was to send to the still-convened Senate the name of Ulysses S. Grant for confirmation. The last business transacted by the 48th Congress was a resolution directing the president *pro tem* to send a telegram to General Grant informing him of the action.

The General read the telegram and said to Childs, "I am grateful the thing has passed."

Julia entered the library and cried, "Hurrah! Our old commander is back."

Mark Twain was also there. In his notebooks he records, "Every face there betrayed strong excitement and emotion—except one, General Grant's. . . . The volume of his emotion was greater than all the other emotions there present combined, but he was able to suppress all expression of it and make no sign."

A few spiteful enemies charged that, with his retirement secured, Grant would quickly get well. Many thought this canard beneath contempt. By no means were Grant's admirers shocked into silence. The ardent Republican publisher of the *Marion Star*, Warren G. Harding, editorialized:

A cowardly, sneaking copperhead in Van Wert County in a newspaper says: "I expected to see General Grant recover as soon as he received his pension." If that low-down pup knew the contempt he brought for himself by that utterance he would feel so small that a thimble could contain him and then show no evidence of being filled.

The first official act of the new Cleveland administration was the President's nomination of his cabinet. The second was Cleveland's signature on Ulysses S. Grant's now confirmed commission. The papers had been brought to him by Robert Lincoln, the son of the martyred President and the outgoing Secretary of War. Cleveland signed it. Now the commission needed the countersignature of the Secretary of War. Cleveland suggested that perhaps Lincoln would like to sign this paper, his father having signed Grant's first general commission. Lincoln thanked the President for the offer, but thought countersigning the commission was properly the duty and the pleasure of the new Secretary, Mr. Endicott.

The passage of the bill caused a slight relapse of the General's vigor. The doctor explained that surprises sapped him. But he was well enough to tell Childs he was going to wire his acceptance immediately. "The law," he said, "is to date the commission from the time one accepts. In the early part of the war I saw in the newspapers I was appointed to a higher rank and I wrote at once and accepted on the strength of the newspaper report. In about two months' time, through red tape, I got my appointment, but I got my pay from the time I wrote."

As a retired lieutenant general, Grant earned a salary of $13,500 a year. The General began counting the days until March 31, which worried Fred. He thought his father morbid, because a popular astrologer had predicted Grant would die on that date. But the General was anxious only for his paycheck.

Out of this money he repaid the loan advanced by Charles Wood of Lansingburg, who had lent it "on account of my share for services ending April, 1865."

Wood donated the money to charity.

The *Tribune* of February 21 reported: "We are gratified to learn from Grant's physician that all signs of the epithalioma have passed away. Whatever may have been the cause of the disease, it is a matter of great congratulation that all fears of grave complications are for the present at an end."

[171]

A week later, however, the *Tribune* learned the truth. On Saturday, February 28, it reported, "It is a fact that should no longer be concealed from the public that General Grant is rapidly breaking down and apparently without hope of reaction, and unless there should be some unexpected relief, he will not be long among the living."

To confirm this report, the *Tribune* included a statement from Fred Grant that admitted the true nature of the disease and another statement from Dr. Douglas. Douglas qualified his with the reminder that few physicians ever treat or see a lingual epithalioma.

The other newspapers picked up the story. On March 1, the *Times* headlined, "Grant Is Dying!" The *Herald* announced, "Sinking Into Grave: Grant's Friends Give Up Hope." The *World* noted, "General Grant Sinking."

Though Douglas had tried to explain that the length of time remaining to the General was conjectural, the editors collectively sensed a dramatic story with national importance. They were sure Grant was going to die soon and they did not want to miss one moment of his final agonies. The *Journal, World, Herald, Tribune, Sun, Post, Times, Brooklyn Eagle, Daily News,* and *Telegram* assigned around-the-clock reporters to the General's house on East 66th Street. They were joined by men from the wire services and occasionally by reporters from the Washington, St. Louis, Philadelphia, and Chicago papers. For the next eight weeks these reporters detailed what the General did each day and whom he saw. They all printed the two daily medical bulletins issued by the doctors. They editorialized on Grant's role in American history. They kept guessing how long he had to live.

In the beginning, the newspapermen tried to get their stories from the family itself. Julia and Fred quickly closed the door to them. When the door did open, it was Faithful Harrison who met reporters. Hair neatly brushed, whiskers trimmed English fashion, wearing a standing collar with tie and somber livery, Harrison answered every question with a polite, "He's better today, thank you. I think he grows better every day."

When Harrison was attending the General, the Grants' housemaid, an Irish girl, answered the door. She was dressed in black, her dark hair parted and combed smoothly. She never smiled. She followed Julia's instructions with a vengeance softened only by her brogue: "The General is neither better nor worse. He is about the same." The newspapers described her as "a tight-mouthed daughter of the Emerald Isle."

March was wet. Rain and cold followed one day after another. Yet people came to stand in the rain and the chill to stare at the general's house. The compulsion to stand before the gates of a stricken king or the home of a dying President is as ingrained as it is morbid. Police Chief Adam Gunner informed Julia that because the street was so crowded with mourners, he was stationing policemen to keep the throng moving.

Sometimes a dozen carriages waited along the curb while their occupants paid their respects inside. On weekends, the carriages were accompanied by farm wagons and mule-drawn carts. One of the policemen told a reporter that so many people asked which was the general's residence that he said, "The first house on the left" to all who approached, whether they wanted to know or not. The same policeman also noted that the school children were noticeably quieter when they turned down East 66th Street on their way home.

The clearing house for the reporters was in the basement of a small dwelling on the east side of Madison Avenue south of 66th Street. The publishers had rented it to better receive the news from their men on the spot. Each paper had strung a special wire to its downtown office. Three bulletin boys from Western Union, the Associated Press, and the United Press waited at the house for any dispatch, with which they would run to the nearest office.

The working reporters congregated on the sidewalk opposite the Grant residence. One of them gained a tactical advantage over the others by sweet-talking a neighbor's chambermaid who let him have access to a commanding window. Another climbed over fences into the Grants' backyard and tried to bribe the Irish maid.

Reporters gained exclusive interviews with Shrady and Douglas by presenting themselves as dummy patients at the doctors' offices. They feigned symptoms similar to Grant's and asked about the course of the disease and its usual termination. The newsmen pounced on everyone who came to call on the General or Julia, and bombarded the visitors with questions as they left the house. In stormy weather, the reporters worked in relays, two or three of them seeking refuge in the areaways under the stoops.

Once again the General had become a subject of absorbing interest to the public. While Grant told his doctors he did not like the probing reporters, he viewed them as a matter of course. He, Julia, and the doctors agreed that it was in their interest to issue the newsmen bulletins describing actual conditions. Despite this accommodation, many of the newspapers carried elaborate, fulsome, and exaggerated accounts of Grant's behavior. For the most part, however, the stories were accurate enough. The reporters learned that Grant coolly and matter-of-factly discussed the progress of his disease, that he observed and described his symptoms, took his own pulse, and carefully charted his temperature several times a day.

What complicated matters was that often the reports were too accurate. Barker, Douglas, Shrady, Fred, and Julia never discussed the General's deterioration in front of him. They would answer his questions, but they took pains not to pass on to him the information they discussed with each other. But when they confided medical information to the General's friends, the friends often let items slip before the newsmen, and these confidences found their way into the papers. The General was a devoted reader. He read six newspapers every day. He read news about himself that could not help but depress him. After reading one such bulletin, he turned to Shrady one day and said, "Doctor, you did not give a very favorable account of me yesterday."

The urgency of the newsmen and the concern of the doctors for accuracy had its genesis in the uninformed, uninspired, and cavalier way other doctors had treated both the press and the public when President James A. Garfield had been assassinated four years before. Garfield had been wounded in the back in the Washington railroad depot on the morning of July 2, 1881, by Charles Guiteau. After the assault, Garfield chose Dr. D. W. Bliss to take charge of the case. Bliss was a garrulous and self-important man. He chose three doctors to assist him: Surgeon General Joseph K. Barnes (who had attended Lincoln), Dr. J. J. Woodward, and Dr. Robert Redburne.

Bliss, however, took unto himself the duty of informing the

press and the public about Garfield's condition. He insisted that the President was improving, that his recuperation was satisfactory. Whenever the President was ill or feverish, Bliss attributed it to afflictions unrelated to his wound. His reports were misleading because they were optimistic. Not only did Garfield waste away from 210 pounds in July to 135 in September, but Bliss and the other doctors presumed the bullet to have penetrated Garfield's liver, which made chances of survival one in a hundred.

Garfield lingered until September 19. The autopsy, performed by Shrady for a coroner's jury, occasioned a medical scandal. Four eminent pathologists testified that the bullet had never entered the liver at all. The wound Garfield suffered was not enough to kill him; but, because it had never been cleaned, Garfield developed pyemia (pus in the blood) and died of a hemorrhage when the blood exploded an aneurism and flooded the peritoneal cavity.

Bliss had made what amounted to a political decision by his reassurances that Garfield was well and recovering. The President in fact was seriously disabled. A responsibly informed constituency might well have insisted then and there that its representatives develop a constitutional mechanism to provide for the accident of presidential disability.*

Shrady was particularly aware that the Garfield case had tarnished the reputation of the medical profession, and that forever after a "public" patient's condition was news to feed the public's curiosity. Any attempt to still that curiosity would lead to gossip, rumor, and speculation no one could control.** The medical

* One who saw this issue clearly was Ulysses S. Grant, who told a Chicago reporter that President Garfield was "clearly disabled," but conceded that the Constitution made no provision for succession or responsibility in this instance. Vice-President Arthur, Grant reasoned, could hardly take the initiative. Grant proposed that Garfield's physicians inform the cabinet about the President's incapacity and the cabinet invite Arthur to serve. In the end nothing was done, in part because Garfield and Arthur represented two wings of the warring Republican Party and in part because no grave problems confronted the country that summer.

** Twelve years later, President Grover Cleveland felt an ulcerated patch on the roof of his mouth. He sent for copies of the newspapers that described Grant's symptoms, read them at a sitting, and immediately summoned Dr. R. M. O'Reilly, the surgeon general. O'Reilly diagnosed an epithelial tumor, probably malignant, and recommended an immediate operation. On June 30, 1893, Cleveland boarded a private yacht in New York harbor. Boarding with him were two surgeons, an anesthetist, and a dentist. The yacht steamed up the East River into Long Island bulletins that Shrady wrote and the General approved were models of integrity, striking a balance between the need of the public to know and the need of the patient for privacy. Despite this, the newspapers often encroached upon the General's privacy and just as often manufactured news, some of it sensational.

There was a good deal more for the papers to print than the twice-issued daily bulletin. Sixty-sixth Street was sometimes a tumult. Numbers of people, unknown to the family, attempting to gratify a craze for notoriety, would ostentatiously present themselves to Harrison. They would leave their calling cards, then happily submit themselves to the reporters.

A fanatic named John Hansfelt tried to storm the Grants' front stoop. When a policeman restrained him, Hansfelt launched into a harangue that the General would live if he abstained from coffee. He had written Mrs. Grant to tell her of this. "The Lord moved me to write," he told the policeman, "but He did not move her to respond."

"Well," said the officer, "now I'm moving you."

Wallace Brown, a quack cancer specialist, also appeared unbidden. Fred Grant turned him away at the door. When the reporters converged upon him, Brown said he had a mysterious concoction that would kill tissue. When the reporters asked what was in the concoction, Brown guaranteed it wasn't arsenic.

Daily the doctors and the family received letters and packets and vials of home remedies. The backyard was piled with arcane nostrums, pulpy medicines, herb extracts, and strange waters. Piled beside them were useless gifts to the family, such as horse blankets and warbonnets, that tumbled from delivery carts every day.

General W. B. Darr, president of the California Grape Growers, offered the General and his family a vineyard complete with a modest house at Napa Soda, California.

One noon a middle-aged man knelt on the sidewalk and prayed with such fervor and intensity that not only the pedestrians but the reporters skirted him as though he had hallowed the spot.

On another morning the *Tribune* reporter interviewed an

Sound, where the operation was performed. On July 5, Cleveland disembarked, fitted with an artificial jaw made of vulcanized rubber. During his term of office no one save the participants ever knew such an operation had been performed.

elderly man with a missing arm who limped along with a cane. The man said he was passing out of respect for the General. "He's my old commander and I love him. When the Battle of the Wilderness was over and the Rebs had taken to their heels, I was a-lying in a shady spot I had a-crawled to, when the General rode by. My arm and my leg was a-hanging by a thread and as he passed me I shouted, 'Hooray!' and the General's face lit up with a smile of joy and sadness. That was my last battle and I never saw him again."

What fascinated the reporters and their readers were the reputations and positions of the many men who called. John C. Frémont, Grant's first commander in the West, came to see him; as well as Thomas L. Crittenden, the major general relieved of his command after Chickamauga, but later honorably acquitted by a military court of inquiry. Comfort V. Lane, who knew Grant in St. Louis, came, and so did Edwards Pierrepont, who had been one of Grant's attorneys general.

Pierrepont described Grant's working quarters: "There are forty-five or fifty huge manuscript volumes containing all his military papers, notes, orders, references, and points jotted down at the moment of occurrence. And there are hundreds of maps. The General's manner gave me the impression of a man who was expecting to take a steamer for a long voyage."

The newspapers discriminatingly paired those who visited Grant or sent messages of sympathy. The *Times*, for instance, reported that the sons of Robert E. Lee* and Albert Sidney Johnston, whose Confederate father fell at Shiloh, proffered their good wishes on the same day. Roscoe Conkling and Benjamin Bristow were paired. Conkling, an ex-senator, now a New York lawyer with a grizzled beard like Grant's, had promised the General the Republican Party nomination in 1880. Conkling counted 306 delegate votes when the convention opened in Chicago and after the thirty-sixth ballot, when Garfield was nominated by 399 votes, Conkling still controlled 309 for Grant. Clean-shaven Benjamin Bristow, one of Grant's cabinet members, had wanted the nomination in 1876. Exposing the widespread corruption of the Whiskey Ring doomed his chances.

* The Robert E. Lee Post of the Veterans of the Confederate Army mailed him a resolution of sympathy from Richmond.

The last months of the General's life were made easier by these men who put aside partisan differences, who banished their own bitterness, and chose to forget the disasters many of them had encountered.

Mrs. Hamilton Fish, whose own husband was ailing, sent round turtle soup to Julia. Without question one of the ablest secretaries of state who ever served, Fish was in retirement when Grant summoned him to Washington. He was not only the sole cabinet member to serve through both Grant administrations, but provided the President with invaluable advice. Twice Grant wanted to nominate Fish for a seat on the Supreme Court bench and twice Fish demurred because he sensed how desperately he was needed in the cabinet. Grant strongly urged Fish to seek the nomination to succeed him, but Fish shrugged off the suggestion saying he was too old. Yet he outlived the General by eight years, dying at eighty-five in 1893.

Another caller was General Ely Parker, a full-blooded Indian whose courage at Vicksburg so commended itself to Grant that he made then-Captain Parker his assistant adjutant general. Parker was the officer Lee confused as a black at Appomattox. But Marse Robert shook hands with him anyway.

General John A. Logan, called "Black Jack," visited. Logan had fought at Vicksburg, where his services earned him a major generalcy. He had spent twenty years in Congress and as a member of the House had arranged the impeachment proceedings against Andrew Johnson. As a senator he introduced the legislation that made Memorial Day a legal holiday. Logan was James G. Blaine's running mate in 1884. He and the General talked over the battles in which they had fought, and Grant let him read over some of the memoirs. "His physical suffering," Logan said to reporters, "seems to have nerved his mind for its best efforts."

Zealous B. Tower, one of Grant's instructors at West Point, spent an afternoon going over what Grant had written about the Mexican War, in which both had served.

And Horace Porter called, perhaps the most accomplished of Grant's subordinates. A West Pointer, Porter was one of the first men to win the Medal of Honor—for helping check the Confederate attack at Chickamauga—although the medal wasn't awarded him until thirty-nine years later. He was one of Grant's aides-de-camp and became indispensable by speaking for Grant on public occasions during the postwar years. He had served as a military secretary in the Grant administration until 1872, when he left the army to become a vice-president of the Pullman Company. As the president of the New York, West Shore & Buffalo Rail Road he had invented the "ticket chopper," a glass receptacle whose bottom was lined with rotored razors that shredded the passengers' tickets. Later, as the United States ambassador to France, he spent his own time and money to locate the grave of John Paul Jones; and in 1905 arranged for the disinterment of our first naval hero and his subsequent reburial at Annapolis.

Porter told the press: "To see him wasting and sinking in this way is more touching and excites deeper sympathy among his friends than if he made some sign of his suffering, as ordinary men do, by grumbling and complaining." In a short time—and for a short time—Ulysses S. Grant in his agony had become the apotheosis of his generation.

Some friends came and went every day, among them Senator Chaffee, Mathias Romero, Mark Twain, and Adam Badeau.

Badeau told the reporters that the General wasted his energy by incessant movement during the night. He was restless and unable to sleep. He would move from his chairs to his table to the hall and back again over and over.

Senator Chaffee quoted the General as saying, "No, Senator, I am not better. I am going to die. You know it as well as I do. So do the doctors. Every moment to me is a week of agony. The suspense is awful. I don't see the use of prolonging the struggle."

Mark Twain told them that Harrison had entered the library carrying a tray on which there was a glass of milk. Grant waved him off. But as Harrison turned away, the General called him back, dutifully and painfully drank the milk, not because he wanted or needed it, but to please Harrison.

The more inventive editors found a secondary source of copy. The *Boston Globe* called on Jefferson Davis for an opinion on Grant's career. "General Grant is dying," Davis told their reporter. "Instead of seeking to disturb the quiet of his closing hours, I would,

[179]

if it were in my power, contribute to his peace of mind and the comfort of his body."

A *Baltimore Sun* man tracked down Congressman William Rosecrans, who said, "No man can think of General Grant's deathbed without feeling that the country is losing a great man—and a soldier, a gentleman with a heart."

Learning of these statements, the General said, "I am very glad to hear this. I would much rather have their good will than their ill-will. I would rather have the good will of any man than his ill-will."

Confederate General P. G. T. Beauregard, who had ordered the firing on Sumter and later succeeded Albert Sidney Johnston on the field at Shiloh, refused to write about Grant for a Chicago newspaper. Beauregard regretted the General's sufferings and added, "Let him die in peace. May God have mercy on his soul." Unreconstructed Beauregard was the adjutant general of Louisiana and the manager of the state lottery.

General Edward Beale and General-in-Chief Phil Sheridan telegraphed their impressions of Grant to the *Tribune*. Beale remembered visiting Grant in Washington before his presidency. The two had returned late at night from a reception. As Beale went upstairs to bed, the General settled himself at a foyer desk on which were stacked a foot-high pile of notebooks left during the day by children who wanted Grant's autograph. Beale suggested Grant sign these in the morning but the General said, "No, I will sign them now. They belong to little boys and girls who will stop for them on their way to school."

Sheridan wired, "He was a far greater man than people thought him to be. He was always able, no matter how situated, to do more than was expected of him."

In St. Louis, William Tecumseh Sherman scolded an approaching reporter: "When General Grant dies, President Cleveland will have something to say. After that, the rest will have our say. Until that time comes, I will have nothing to say."

On March 25, the General was seized by a choking fit. Each night thereafter, the choking seizures grew more convulsive and lasted longer. The doctors relieved these spasms as best they could with cocaine and morphine. But anodynes did not stop them.

On March 30, Romero told the reporters, "The truth is the disease has gotten away from the doctors. It is possible he may die tonight and at the very best he cannot live ten days. As soon as the disease reaches a vital point, it will create a hemorrhage. As he is too weak, he cannot expectorate the blood and will choke to death."

The *Times* informed its readers that the doctors had decided against an operation to relieve the choking. It noted that in cases where the tongue was excised the mortality rate was 25 percent. Shrady himself said, "It is doubtful if the General's heart could stand another choking attack. We have decided he could not survive a tracheotomy for very long."

The press thought the General would die on March 31. The newspapers not only had the authority of Romero and Shrady but the astrologer who had predicted the General would not survive the night. Mark Twain wrote in his notebooks, "Many a person between the two oceans lay hours awake listening for the booming of the firebells that should speak to the nation simultaneously and tell its calamity. The bells' strokes are to be 30 seconds apart and there will be sixty-two, the General's age. They will be striking in every town of the United States at the same moment."

Grant fell asleep on the night of the thirty-first with a heavy dose of morphine. At 5 A.M. on April 1, the reporters saw the lights flame on in the library and then in other rooms of the house. Harrison came out, hailed a cab, and returned shortly with Dr. Shrady. Dr. Douglas soon appeared. Then Harrison again came out, this time proceeding downtown to the St. Cloud Hotel to return with the Reverend Mr. Newman and Buck.

In Chicago and St. Louis, the papers went to bed late as editors waited for the news of Grant's death. In the light mist that fell, a crowd began to gather in the gray dawn.

Inside, Julia wept.

But the General didn't die.

Having survived this crisis, he began to improve. The choking was subdued. Both Douglas and Shrady explained to those who would listen that the disease was marked by an ebb and flow. Each flow, however, was lower than the one that had preceded it. Where the General had been a man gasping his last on Wednesday morning, on Thursday afternoon he was hobbling back and forth across his room on the arm of Harrison. On Friday, Dr. Douglas snapped tight his medical bag with the promise, "General, we propose to keep to this line if it takes all summer."

In that brief spell of hope, Douglas heard laughter.

Most of the newspapers noted that Friday was the twentieth anniversary of Grant's taking Richmond. When Badeau reminded the General of the date, he sighed and said, "Twenty years ago I had more to say. I was in command then."

Badeau said, "Even then it took a year to win. Perhaps you may win still."

The General brightened at this and told Badeau, Shrady, and Douglas about Quartermaster General Rufe Ingalls's dog. It was a particularly mangy mutt that always sat at a particular spot around the headquarters campfire. The dog was a disgrace to the Army of the Potomac. Grant asked, "Rufe, do you intend to take that dog into Richmond?" Ingalls thought for a while, then said, "I think I shall. He belongs to a long-lived breed."

On April 9, the anniversary of Appomattox, Julia received a telegram from Queen Victoria's lady-in-waiting:

> The Queen who feels deeply for you in your anxiety commands me to inquire after General Grant.
> > Dowager Marchioness of Ely
> > Aix-les-Bains

Fred cabled:

> Mrs. Grant thanks the Queen for her sympathy and directs me to say General Grant is no better.
> > Colonel Frederick Grant

Porfirio Díaz, the Mexican dictator-president, wired his good wishes. The George C. Meade Post of the GAR sent the General a floral arrangement so large the horseshoe wouldn't fit through the front door. The General wanted to celebrate the occasion. He asked Shrady, "Do you think it would really harm me if I took a puff or two from a mild cigar?"

The request was so pitiable and Shrady saw so little harm in the venture that he said there was no reason why the General shouldn't enjoy one mild cigar. Eagerly Grant picked up a cigar from the mantel, settled himself in his chair, and began puffing away. Both Grant and the doctor had neglected to pull the shades. The next day the *Journal* ran the headline "Grant Smokes Again!"

Julia called this reporting vile. She charged the press with misrepresentation. She told Dr. Douglas there was no end to which the newsmen would not stoop. Prudently Grant and Shrady agreed with her.

One afternoon Jesse Grant and his daughter left the house. Grant was at the library window. Several men on the sidewalk saw him and lifted their hats. All told there was a crowd of forty people with every face upturned. The child studied them curiously until she reached the sidewalk. Then raising her head she followed the gaze of the crowd until she, too, saw Grant in the window. "There's Grandpa," she said, and with both hands blew him a kiss. The General blew one back.

On Good Friday, the General appeared at his window in his dressing gown and skating cap and saluted the men of the Ulysses S. Grant Post of the GAR. They marched up 66th Street to do him honor. Then, in full view of the watchers, he sat and read the newspapers. In the afternoon he took a ride in Chaffee's carriage. He walked slowly supported by a heavy cane, wearing a fur topcoat and a hat pulled low. He saluted the crowd and they in turn applauded his appearance.

When Mark Twain called the next afternoon, Grant said, "You would think the newspapers could get my weight right. While I was out riding, the thought occurred to me I would like to be weighed. When I got to a store, I got out and slipped on the scales. I did not say a word. The scales balanced at 146. Well, I read six newspapers this morning. No two of them have the same figures and no one of them is right."

Thirty-three members of the Excelsior Chapter of the Columbia Council, a masonic order, marched to the General's house on Easter Sunday to serenade him. The General came to the front stoop to tip his hat. As Sunday wore on there was more than the usual gathering on the street and on the opposite sidewalk. The General stood at his library window plainly gratified by this evidence of sympathy. Tired, he fell asleep in his chairs. While he slept, a cold shower dispersed the crowd, but when the General awoke, the rain had stopped and the street was more crowded than ever. Shrady, preparing the afternoon medical bulletin, suggested today would be a good opportunity for the General to express his gratitude to the people. On this Easter, every church in America had offered prayers for his recovery. Shrady urged him to couch the message in the first person.

Grant dictated: "I am very much touched and grateful for the sympathy and interest manifested in me by my friends—and by those who have not hitherto been regarded as my friends. I desire the goodwill of all, whether hitherto friends or not."

Shrady dispatched the message. A few minutes later Julia came into the library and the General told her what he had done. Hearing the text, Julia deplored its secular tone. This was Easter Sunday, she reminded her husband and his doctor. No amount of prudence would ride out her annoyance. Julia insisted Easter Sunday had its rights. Instead of rewriting an already dispatched message, Shrady suggested inserting "prayerful" before "sympathy" to give the text a religious tone. Julia was mollified.

Shrady walked around to the press bureau and added the required word. As he had predicted, some editors misunderstood when the change came through. Frank Mack of the Associated Press thought Grant had died after the transmitting and came by speeding carriage to 3 East 66th Street.

Fred Grant, Julia, and the doctors had warned and double-warned every caller to make as little comment as possible to the reporters. Visitors had to be on guard lest what they said be misinterpreted. But the press did not misunderstand or misinterpret what Senator Chaffee told them on April 17. "The diagnosis of the doctors might be wrong," Chaffee said. "Grant in my opinion has not been suffering from cancer but from an ulcerated sore throat. I have no doubt the General will pull through."

Chaffee's statement hardly represented informed opinion. Yet some papers, notably the *World*, treated it sensationally. "Not Cancer After All," headlined the *World* the next day. "The people rejoice that their great soldier Grant whose death a syndicate of doctors led them to expect at any moment for the past weeks is now apparently on the road to recovery."

The *Journal* pointed out that many doctors had always suspected Grant suffered from blood poisoning. The paper tested this opinion on a phalanx of lawyers, politicians, and bankers. Among the last, Henry Clews said, "Instead of an obituary on General Grant, the papers should offer congratulatory addresses. It appears the doctors have been mistaken."

Shrady knew why the papers leaped upon this possibility. The disease progressed slowly. The monotony of weary hopefulness is hardly news. The dramatic moment which would justify the time, inventiveness, and expense of forty working reporters seemed never to arrive. That savage cancer symptoms submerge and then erupt again is hard enough for a doctor to explain to his patient let alone a reporter to his readers. The press felt the public interest in Grant would fail to find sympathetic fulfillment.

The *World*, the *Journal*, the *News*, and the *Telegram* questioned the doctors' treatment of Grant. The reporters had learned that for the first time in months the General had eaten solid food, a cold chop and macaroni. This convinced them they had been misled.

"Grant Thinks the Doctors Will Pull Through," read one headline.

"The Doctors Still Gain Slowly," read another.

"A Bad Day for the Doctors. Grant Watches Them Closely," read a third.

The *World* began to call the doctors "the silent men" because they ceased issuing the bulletins. "Their pulses," said the paper, "are rising almost as high as their bills."

This was mischief. Julia Grant, reading the first stories, presumed they were official diagnoses. Friends elsewhere hailed the news with cables and letters which only made the General more poignantly aware of his impending death.

The *Tribune* did not join in this chorus. Its reporter sought out Shrady. Shrady said the doctors were now "but instruments to relieve the pain and lessen the suffering. Exhaustion and revival are characteristic of the disease."

The *Times* consulted a specialist who insisted on anonymity but who concluded, "General Grant has an epithalioma or else doctors have been working in the dark for eighteen centuries."

Grant was thoroughly conversant with the nature of his

malady. He never suspected the men who were treating him were incompetent alarmists. After the *World* had printed a virulent attack on Shrady's reputation, the General asked how the doctor felt about it.

Shrady said he knew he and the medical staff were right. He knew the newspapers were wrong. To which the General replied he was perfectly satisfied with his medical treatment and that he was the person, after all, with the most at stake. He went on to say he knew what it was like to bear the malicious libels of the press. He never read the papers when he was general-in-chief. He was too busy to credit "scribblers who were willing to give free and valueless lessons on matters of which they knew little or nothing. If a man assumes the responsibility of doing a thing," the General said, "he naturally does it in his own way and the result is the only proof that he may be right or wrong. One does the work and the other does the guessing."

Friends of the family covertly counseled a change in doctors. But the General became indignant when influential politicians openly suggested as much. He asked Dr. Douglas to release once again the facts of his case and gave him the following note for publication:

> This paper, the *World*, is a reformer in medicines. It is an advertising medium for quack medicines prepared by ignorant people. If I were left to their treatment, I would die within a few days, suffering the extremist [sic] agony in the meantime. I would not have the entire faith in the four doctors attending me, unsupported by the judgement of anybody else. But they are all distinguished in their profession. They reject no treatment because it is not given at their own suggestion.
>
> It is not true that they are experimenting on me with a single medicine about which they know little or nothing. It is not true they are persisting in a single treatment. With every phase of the disease, they have varied the treatment. The medicine alluded to as the one being "experimented with" is, I presume Cocaine. That has never been given me as a medicine. It has only been administered as an application to stop pain. It is well known that it accomplishes that result without leaving injurious effects behind. It is only applied when much needed.

[186]

Shortly after this memo was published, George Childs and Joseph Pulitzer halted their carriage before 3 East 66th Street. Childs got out and went into the house. Pulitzer, who had bought the *World* from Jay Gould two years before and who was in the process of making "yellow journalism" a phrase in the language, remained in the carriage. As well he might.

The General's sixty-third birthday fell on Wednesday, April 27. Twice during the day he went out for a ride in the park. In the afternoon, he stood at attention in front of the opened library window when New York's Seventh National Guard Regiment marched past in full dress and plumed shakos.

General James Grant Wilson, another who was to author a Grant biography, called with a birthday gift. He had an hour's talk with his old commander and read some of the memoirs. Wilson told the reporters that the General in his heroic efforts to meet his obligations surpassed the courage of Sir Walter Scott who, in his old age, had set a fierce program of writing for himself to avoid bankruptcy and pay off an avalanche of commercial debts.

Andrew Carnegie sent sixty-three roses.

Amid banks of flowers on the dining room table Julia set sixty-three tapers. He received birthday cards from six neighborhood children and a seven-year-old boy sent him a hand-painted pen wiper. The family held a private party, and Ulysses S. Grant, III, the West Point nominee, howled throughout the celebration.

The press guard relaxed. The editors sent the reporters off to more newsworthy assignments.

In the morning, Shrady, Douglas, and Barker saw that the gums and right side of the General's mouth were honeycombed with cancer.

The Reverend John Phillip Newman, who answered reporters' questions every time he went in and out of the Grant household—and he went in and out several times a day—was a celebrated Methodist minister. His first call was to New Orleans in 1862, where he blew both the "Federal and the Gospel trumpets." Later, he held the pulpit at the Metropolitan Church in Washington, D.C., when Grant, Vice-President Schuyler Colfax, Chief Justice Salmon Chase, and Senator John A. Logan filled the pews. He also served as chaplain of the Senate between 1869–1874. During this time he became a close confidant of Julia Grant and, because he was a friend of Julia, necessarily he became a friend of the General. When his term at the Metropolitan Church ended, in fact, Grant commissioned him as Inspector of United States Consulates. Thus the General afforded Newman and his wife a free trip around the world at government expense. In his turn, Newman made his friend Grant one of the trustees of the Central Methodist Episcopal Church of New York City, an honor that consumed considerably less of the General's time than visiting consulates had consumed of the Reverend's.

When the news of the General's terminal illness broke in the newspapers, Newman was in California to deliver the eulogy at the funeral of Leland Stanford, Jr., son of the railroad magnate. He received a fee of $10,000 for conducting this service. Newman left the graveside to hurry to New York. He felt the call to be with General Grant. "A great sufferer is passing away," Newman wrote in his diary. He also confided his dominating urgency—"to persuade General Grant to help redeem the world by leaving behind some immortal saying of his return to Christ." *

Newman wanted to get near Grant's soul to "call forth a clear religious experience." Thus he would insure the General a life everlasting. He arrived at 3 East 66th Street in mid-March, and found the General in better physical condition than he expected. He thought Grant manifested "more dependence upon God in prayer than I have ever known him to do." When Newman convened the Grant family for the evening's prayer service, Grant's "Amen" was delivered with such vigor that it spoke volumes to Newman. Since Newman thought the General in good physical condition when, in fact, his body was in dissolution, when he could barely speak, wore a scarf to cover the swelling the size of an egg in his neck, and had to limp painfully, it is quite possible that he did not understand Grant's booming "Amen" was delivered in relief rather than exaltation.

As a general and later general-in-chief, Grant got along well

* Newman's diary disappeared for over fifty years until the writer Stefan Lorant literally rescued it from an ashcan in 1951 and reproduced its illuminations for *Life* magazine.

enough with the clergymen and chaplains unless they encroached upon his military prerogatives. As President, of course, his affiliation was of moment to the constituency. It was impossible for a public man of that time to ignore organized religion. But Grant attended the Metropolitan Church no more often than he had to. More than occasionally he strayed from the true path. In 1868, Jay Cooke, the financier, protested to the Republican National Committee that Grant worked on Sundays. Cooke feared "God will not reward us unless our rulers are righteous." But Grant continued to labor in the vineyards of the War Department despite Cooke's very real concern. When a delegation of ministers called in 1872 to let Grant know they might endorse his renomination, the General said there were three political parties in America—Republicans, Democrats, and Methodists. It was obvious to most that Grant found little emotional satisfaction in religion.

He was not, however, exempt from the religious fervor that helped fan the war. There was no diminution of this ardor after Appomattox. Rather this ardor was assimilated by a people now suspended between a rural past and an urban present, their naïveté remolded by popular journalism, public education, and the hard sell of Dwight L. Moody. The little white church in the wildwood gave way to the massive auditorium called a tabernacle, an institution particularly suited to addressing the despair occasioned by the anonymous quality of the city.

Protestantism became an evangelical program. Ulysses S. Grant sat on the guest-laden platforms of Dwight L. Moody's tabernacles in Washington and Philadelphia. He was one of the successful with whom Moody bedazzled the plain folks who had come to think of salvation as a jostling, competitive land rush. Few were interested in or examined the theological core of faith—not Dwight L. Moody, certainly not Ulysses S. Grant.

It wasn't until now, mouth riddled with cancer, that Grant began discussing the verities with a man of God. When the choking seizures attacked him in late March, the General said to Newman, "I shall soon be through with things of this world, but it seems strange I must agonize for some days longer."

"It is the course of nature," said Newman. "The time will be brief to us."

[189]

"Yes," said the General, "brief to you who are without pain."

When the choking fits reached their crisis in the early morning of April 1, Julia summoned Newman. He arrived at dawn. She told him the General was dying. When Newman patted Grant's hand in reassurance, the General said, "I regret each moment I have to remain and regret leaving my family." Again he was wracked by violent coughing and choking.

"All supposed the General was dying," wrote Newman in his diary. "Mrs. Grant and Mrs. Corbin, the General's sister, were in doubt as to whether the General had been baptized and wished me to baptize him now. I said, 'I will baptize him if he is conscious: I cannot baptize an unconscious man.' As I began to pray the General opened his eyes and looked steadily at me. As the physicians believed he could not live five minutes longer, I prayed that God would receive his departing soul. . . . I then observed, 'General, I am going to baptize you,' and he replied, 'I am much obliged to you, Doctor. I intend to take that step myself.' I then baptized him in the Name of the Father, of the Son and of the Holy Ghost. He was conscious and wiped the water from his face. It was a solemn scene. Mrs. Grant knelt by his side and called for prayer and I offered the Lord's prayer."

Douglas had readied a syringe filled with brandy after the General told him, "If you doctors know how long a man can live under water, you can judge how long it will take me to choke when the time comes." As the General lay strangling, Shrady said the time had come to use the syringe, if they were to use it at all. He then injected the brandy into the General's right arm, both doctors continuing to watch the faltering pulse.

"As the pulse did not respond satisfactorily," Douglas wrote in his diary, "a second injection was resorted to, and at once the heart regained its action. Throughout this time the General was conscious, spoke clearly when addressed and was the least perturbed of those present."

In the coughing and choking that followed the injection, however, Grant in a massive vomiting dislodged a slough of diseased tissue from his mouth. Suddenly he could breathe easily. His throat was no longer clogged by secretions from his mutilated mouth and palate.

In the morning, Newman told the reporters that prayers had saved Grant's life.

Shrady told them it was the brandy.

While the press debated the issue of prayers versus brandy, and temperance groups begged the General to give up spiritous liquors, Grant was sure he had won a reprieve that would enable him to finish his book.

Newman later insisted that the Easter Sunday prayers of thousands in congregations across the country had been answered. Shrady, leaving the Grant establishment with Newman, heard this opinion with marked skepticism. When one of the reporters asked for his comment, the doctor said, "They mourned his death two weeks ago. Let them now rejoice in his resurrection."

Senator Chaffee declared to the press, "There's been a good deal of nonsense in the papers about Dr. Newman's visits. General Grant does not believe that Dr. Newman's prayers will save him. He allows the doctor to pray simply because he does not want to hurt his feelings."

Nor were Shrady and Chaffee the only of Grant's friends so annoyed. In his notebooks, Mark Twain doubted that Grant pressed Newman's hand and said, "Thrice have I been in the valley of the shadow of death, and thrice have I come out again." "Ten cents to a thousand dollars he never used that form of words," Twain added. "This piece of reporting comports with Newman, gush, rot, impossible." Among the notes Grant passed to Dr. Douglas, however, is one with that particular phrase—which does not prove Mark Twain imperceptive, only that Newman, who talked in chapter and verse, foisted his phraseology upon those around him.

Recalling the crisis later, Badeau remembered the General saying, " 'The doctors are responsible three times for my being alive, and—unless they can cure me—I don't thank them.' He had no desire to go through the agony again." The words sound more like Grant. As for Newman's influence, we have the testimony of W. E. Woodward, who interviewed the General's surviving sons and grandchildren in the 1920s. He reported agreement among them that the General said he did not care how much praying was done around him if it made his wife feel better.

[191]

In his diary, Newman wrote, "Oh, how grieved I was for God's cause. But I wrestled with God in prayer to vindicate His own cause and not let the General die until he had borne glorious testimony to Christ."

Newman was trying to convince the General that since some prayer and a degree of faith had returned him to strength, voluminous prayer and firmer faith would heal him. "I believe you will be raised up," he said to the General, "restored to health, to be a great spiritual person in the land. You are a man of Providence; God made you His instrument to save a great nation; and now He will use you for a great spiritual mission in a skeptical age."

"Can He cure cancer?" asked the General.

"Why not?" answered Newman. "You must hold on to him by prayer and faith."

But he was not convincing Grant. Several times Newman offered to give the General and Mrs. Grant the communion of the Lord's Supper, the Eucharist, a feast of Thanksgiving. Several times Grant refused, finally refusing irrevocably. He scribbled a note to Newman toward the end in which he said, "I would be only too happy to do so if I felt myself truly worthy. I have a feeling in regard to taking the sacriment [sic] that no worse sin can be committed than to take it unworthily. I would prefer therefore not to take it but to have the funeral service performed when I am gone."

Not only did Newman fail to convince Grant, in the end he failed to convince his colleagues, and was himself plunged into doubt. While prayer had led the General to renewed vigor, it was quickly spent. And when it was obvious that it was spent, Newman cried into his diary, "If God intends to heal him, why not now?" He was his own victim.

Whether his baptism did much for Ulysses S. Grant is a moot question. But it comforted Julia, and it certainly did a great deal for Newman. Hereafter he was always called "Grant's pastor." It was as Grant's pastor that Newman returned to the prestigious pulpit of the Metropolitan Church a year later. But he confessed in his diary that Grant represented his singular failure to bring a soul to Christ.

The newfound vigor that returned in April enabled the General to resume dictating for three and sometimes four hours a day. He was succinct and rarely made a false start. Dawson took down enough material every day to fill twenty-five printed pages. They were now well into volume two, and Grant, having planned how the material should be arranged, attacked it piecemeal. In writing his notes and in dictating to Dawson from them, he treated individual events and campaigns out of sequence. In the finished book everything could be put in proper order by Fred; for now the object was to get it down in writing.*

There was another object—to keep working while he could. When Newman asked him why he persevered so, he replied that it meant his life. "Every day, every hour is a week of agony," he said. "I am easier when employed." He recognized that the effort was costly. One of the notes preserved by Douglas reads, "I've said I had been adding to my book and my coffin. I presume every strain of the mind or body is one more nail in the coffin." But he continued to turn out a prodigious flow of words.

Senator Chaffee, who was privy to much of what he wrote, begged Grant not to emasculate the book by toning down any of his judgments about other generals. Grant proved to be kinder to General Benjamin Butler in his memoirs than he had been during the war. Late in 1864 he relieved Butler of command, complaining at the time that the enemy had corked up Butler's army as in a bottle. Chaffee argued against removing this vivid image from the memoirs. Grant replied that he had used the phrase then because it

* Grant's handwritten notes for his manuscript and the manuscript itself (some of the chapters in Dawson's writing) are in the Library of Congress in Washington, D.C. Grant's habit was to make notes from which he subsequently construed chapters. Toward the end, however, he simply connected his notes by transitional passages to make coherent chapters. Even in the first volume he did not always compose the book in chronological order, writing about Chattanooga before he wrote about Vicksburg; and now, in volume two, he wrote about Appomattox before he wrote about Sherman's March to the Sea. It is also worth noting that, as he got deeper into the book, he often made notes that ran to several pages which were to be inserted in already prepared chapters. During the ravages of the disease in March he wrote very little in consecutive order. He was at this time anxious to outline the remaining course of the book and his notes were for insertion here, there, and everywhere. When he got better he arranged these notes in sequential order.

stuck in his mind when he read it in his chief engineer's report. But he saw no need for it now. The General was a man who had himself known many humiliations. He was aware that his imminent death would leave these generals no redress after the book was published.

Grant had begun the book before his illness, and his rough manuscript mirrors his waning physical strength. In the beginning the manuscript is made up of neat pages with regular lines of inked script, easily legible. "The corrections," wrote Bruce Catton, "show a man rereading what he has written, striking things out here and there, looking for words and phrases that would more exactly express his words and thoughts, sometimes knocking out whole paragraphs." As the cancer ravaged him, Grant's pencil began to carve a skeletonized scrawl that is hard to decipher. Lined school pads replaced the bond paper. "The narrative no longer flows in smooth well-thought order," noted Catton. "From page to page the subject changes abruptly, as if the writer wants to get his ideas down and trust his editor to put things in order. Pain and the rising mist made it impossible to get every word in." Yet, despite the pain, there were doodles—triangles, squares, and flat-roofed houses—decorating the copy where the writer halted, as all writers halt, so that the words and sentences can regroup themselves and proceed in orderly fashion.

"The General was a sick man, but he wrought upon his work like a well one," Mark Twain remarked perceptively. The observation, which catches the essence of Grant's fortitude, may have been tinged with awe. Twain knew that the General was not only suffering, but was working in the midst of never-ending interruptions. There were constant callers, good friends who wanted to talk, reporters, publishers, the family, a religious missionary, and always the gnawing concern about money. These would delay and hamper an ordinary writer, let alone one who was conscious of impending death. The General's concentration surmounted everything.

So it was more than mischievous, it was libelous for the *World* to inform its readers on April 29 that Grant was not writing his own book after all. The *World* based this surmise on the authority of General George P. Ihrie, who had served with Grant in Mexico. Ihrie had inadvertently remarked to a Washington columnist that the General was no writer. From this ambiguous opinion, the *World* went on to declare, "The work upon his new book about which so much has been said is the work of General Adam Badeau. General Grant has furnished all of the material and all of the ideas in the memoirs but Badeau has done the work of composition. The most the General has done upon the book has been to prepare the rough notes and memoranda for its various chapters. He is so great that he can well afford to have the exact truth told about him."

Thundering and swearing, Mark Twain ordered Charles Webster to retain Clarence Seward for the libel suit. He called the *World* "that daily issue of unmedicated closet paper." He took the matter up with Fred Grant immediately. "The General's work this morning is rather damaging evidence against the *World*'s intrepid lie," he wrote. "The libel suit ought to be instituted at once. No compromise or apology will do. Press for punitive damages. Damages that will cripple—yes, *disable*—that paper financially."

To the reporters who checked on the story, Fred Grant said, "My father is dictating the Appomattox Campaign. And from his despatches and other data is enabled to give a perfectly straight and lucid account to the stenographer."

The General dealt directly with the libel. He sent the following letter to Charles L. Webster & Company:

May 2nd 1885

My attention has been called to a paragraph in the *World* newspaper of this city of Wednesday, April 29th of which the following is a part.

"The work upon his new book about which so much has been said is the work of General Adam Badeau. General Grant, I have no doubt, has furnished all of the material and all of the ideas in the memoirs as far as they have been prepared; but Badeau has done the work of composition. The most that General Grant has done upon this book has been to prepare the rough notes and memoranda for its various chapters."

I will divide this into four parts and answer each of them.

First—"The work upon his new book about which so much has been said is the work of General Adam Badeau."

This is false. Composition is entirely my own.

Second—"General Grant, I have no doubt, has furnished all of the material and all of the ideas in the memoirs as far as they have been prepared."

This is true.

[195]

Third—"but Badeau has done the work of composition."

The composition is entirely my own.

Fourth—"The most that General Grant has done upon this book has been to prepare the rough notes and memoranda for its various chapters."

Whatever rough notes were made were prepared by myself and for my exclusive use.

You may take such measures as you see fit to correct this report which places me in the attitude of claiming authorship of a book which I did not write and is also injurious to you who are publishing and advertising such a book as my work.

Both the *Tribune* and the *Sun* printed this disclaimer. The *Tribune* described Grant's letter as "A Characteristic Answer to a False Statement," and the *Sun* editorialized that no denial by General Grant was necessary. Grant had a telling English style, the *Sun* went on, and though Badeau was thoroughly conversant with the literary world, "the soldier is, in our judgment, immensely superior to the journalist."

No other newspaper picked up the *World*'s libel, so Mark Twain concluded it wasn't worth suing. He told Clarence Seward to desist. Twain had enough litigation on his hands as it was. He was suing John Wanamaker for selling *Huckleberry Finn* at cut-rate prices.

The gossip had a totally different effect upon Badeau. On the day Grant addressed his letter to Webster, Badeau entered the library, bowed, and handed over a sealed envelope. Not waiting for the General to open it, he left. He was an arrogant man, often discourteous, but this was the first time he proved mysterious.

Inside the envelope, which was addressed to General Grant, was a one-thousand-word letter. First, Badeau reviewed their original agreement that he was to receive $5,000 out of the first $20,000 and an additional $5,000 if the book made $30,000.* Badeau then proceeded to detail the sacrifices he had endured— giving up his own work for the General's memoirs; piecing

---

* The letters between Grant and Badeau were made public in the *Tribune* on March 13, 1888. On March 22, 1888, the *Nation* also reproduced them. Defending himself, Badeau later exchanged correspondence with the *Louisville Commercial* in April, 1889. Bruce Catton described the correspondence in *American Heritage,* June, 1968.

laboriously together disjointed and lengthy fragments into a narrative; and working without pay, for so far he had received only $250 of the "earnest" money paid by Webster on the signing of the contract. And not only was he without an income but, he complained, "I must efface myself," and I can have no reputation or consideration for my connection with the book."

> Your book is to have a circulation of hundreds of thousands, and the larger its circulation the greater its importance—the more completely it will stamp out mine [*Military History of U. S. Grant*]. . . . Yours is not and will not be the work of a literary man, but the simple story of a great general. Proper for you, but not such as would add to my credit. . . . Your name sells your work; your deeds are in its theme; your own story told by itself is what the people want. . . . Under these circumstances I am willing to agree to complete the work from your dictation in the first person with all the supervision you are able to give but in any event to complete it; to claim, of course, no credit whatever for its composition but to declare as I have always done that you wrote it absolutely.

For this Badeau wanted $1,000 a month, to be paid in advance until the work was done and afterward 10 percent of the profits. He concluded with the promise that he would transform the book into undying literature, "a monument such as no man ever put up to his own fame."

Ulysses S. Grant was not used to taking orders. For the first time in his life he turned severely businesslike. He replied to Badeau three days later in a letter of his own. He started out by saying he understood Badeau's letter better than Badeau who had written it and that, therefore, "you and I must give up all association so far as the preparation of any literary work goes which bears my signature."

Point by point the General went on to consider Badeau's complaints and dismiss his demands. He noted that Badeau had prepared his military history while he was a member of Grant's staff with the rank of colonel, three grades above his special rank; that Badeau's colonelcy gave him access to papers and documents other writers could not use; that these very documents were Grant's own, and that he himself had read and corrected every chapter.

If Badeau had indeed devoted his body, mind, and all working hours to the memoirs, still he was not keeping up with the stenographer; for that matter, he wasn't keeping up with the handwritten passages. The General wanted it remembered that Badeau had not checked or gone over either the Chattanooga or the Wilderness articles before they went to *The Century*. It was obvious, the General said, that Badeau could not fulfill his contract by publication date, and the expense of the failure would fall on the General and his publisher.

Nor had he ever expected more than two months of Badeau's time. Five thousand dollars seemed adequate recompense for this, with an additional $5,000 if the book sold widely. Never did the General expect Badeau to write. Rather, in the event of his death, Badeau was to put together what the General had written. As for the disjointed episodes, all were clearly designed to be inserted in the completed manuscript. As for their being fragmentary, only those the General had written while he struggled for breath fitted this description. He doubted Badeau would ever complete the book in the case of his death while $1,000 a month was coming in. "You are petulant, your anger is easily aroused, and you are overbearing even to me. As an office holder you quarreled with your superiors until you lost your office."

> My name goes with the book and I want it my work in the fullest sense. . . . I do not want a book bearing my name to go before the world which I did not write to such an extent as to be fully entitled to the credit of authorship. I do not want a secret between me and someone else which would destroy my honor if it were divulged. I cannot think of myself as depending upon any person to supply a capacity which I am lacking. I may fail but I will not put myself in such a position.
>
> . . . I have to say that for the last twenty-four years I have been very much employed in writing. As a soldier, I wrote my own orders, plans of battle, instructions and reports. . . . As President, I wrote every official document, I believe, usual for Presidents to write, bearing my name. All these have been published and widely circulated. The public has become accustomed to my style of writing. They know it is not even an attempt to imitate either a literary or classical style; that it is just what it is and nothing else. If I succeed in telling my story so that others can see as I do what I attempt to show, I will be satisfied.

Grant concluded with the observation that if he issued Badeau another contract, Badeau would become a partner with his family as long as the book found a sale. As an afterthought, the General said Badeau would always be welcomed as a friend at East 66th Street.

Badeau replied in a letter:

> As I stated to you in my letter of Saturday I have no desire, intention or right to claim authorship of your book. The composition is entirely your own. What assistance I have been able to render has been in suggestion, revision or verification.

Then, in a third letter, he told the General he would send for his trunk and possessions. He said he was going ahead with his plans for a book on the postwar Grant—which indeed he did. From the moment Mark Twain saw this letter, he worried. He was sure Badeau would produce a defamatory and hateful biography. That Badeau did not do so merely meant there was one less litigant in the big courtroom Mark Twain kept repopulating in his mind.

A variety of causes motivated Badeau's unexpected demand. Dawson, the stenographer, had come between him and the General. In addition, there was an ever-growing enmity between him and Fred. They worked and lived together under trying and discouraging circumstances. Though Badeau had made himself useful to the family during the General's crisis, that enmity never softened. Lastly, Badeau recognized the book's prospects. He knew it would have a success past all expectations. The root of Badeau's disaffection was that he wanted to participate equally in the General's financial returns and, more sadly, equally in the author's fame.

Badeau and Grant never met again. The rupture cost Badeau Julia's friendship and regard. More than causing the General grief at a time when he needed comfort, Badeau performed a vast disservice to his friend. Because of his demands, Badeau laid the book under a cruel suspicion, a suspicion not that he, Badeau, had written it, but that Mark Twain had. The rumor had a half-life for several decades until an editor named T. Ellsworth came across a neglected folder of Grant's notes to Mark Twain. Ellsworth published these and a commentary in the *Bookman,* a trade journal for the publishing industry, in January, 1931.

The notes make it clear that Grant wrote his own book. "There is much more I could do," the General had scrawled, "if I was a well man . . . if I could read it over myself many little matters of anecdote and incident would suggest themselves to me." Another note read: "Have you seen any portion of the second volume? It is up to the end or nearly so. As much more work as I have done today will finish it. I have worked faster than if I had been well."

Yet, in a certain sense, Badeau's impetuosity and arrogance sharpened the General's perceptions. Catton observed of this correspondence that Grant had become a writing man and was driven by a writing man's compulsions. He was proprietary about his work because a book is simply and eternally that—a work. The General came to realize that he himself, and what he himself saw and thought, was the central focus of this work.

One of Grant's sisters had provided Mark Twain with a long-forgotten daguerreotype taken when Grant was a young lieutenant about to leave for the Mexican War. Twain reproduced this for the frontispiece of volume one. Immediately afterward, the daguerreotype disappeared from the Webster office.

Twain saw the villainous machinations of the pirates. He and Charley Webster spent an entire night, from dusk until dawn, getting in touch with every managing editor in New York City, threatening them with criminal proceedings if the daguerreotype appeared in their newspapers. Either the editors feared Twain's wrath or the daguerreotype had been mislaid. It never appeared in the papers.

The jacket for volume one was also finished. It portrayed a sad-eyed, gaunt, forty-three-year-old bearded general.* The portrait was developed from a spoiled negative taken shortly after Appomattox. With these and the title page set in galleys, Twain hurried up to East 66th Street. The General told Twain that he originally hoped to put in the book the portraits of the generals who played a prominent part in the war—Sherman, Meade, Halleck, Thomas, and McPherson. But since the project was

* Of the many, many photographs of Grant, this author cannot remember seeing one of him smiling.

announced he had received so many letters from colonels and brigadiers who wanted inclusion that he decided to do without any.

Fond of reducing literature to weights and measures, Twain wrote in his notebook, "Macaulay's grand edition weighed 45 tons. Our first edition ought to weigh 330." That much paper tied up a substantial sum of money. The cost of ink ran into thousands of dollars. But Twain was unworried. "I am merely a starving beggar," he wrote Howells about this time, "standing outside the door of plenty—obstructed by a Yale timelock which is set for January 1st."

Twain was not, however, so introverted or expectant that he failed to see the agony that afflicted his friend. "It is curious and dreadful," he recorded, "to sit up in this way and talk cheerful nonsense to General Grant and he under the sentence of death with that cancer."

"A verb is anything that signifies to be; to do; or to suffer," Grant wrote in a note to Douglas. "I signify all three."

Dr. Fordyce Barker, whose own health was lately impaired, came to say good-bye in May, before leaving for a European stay of two months. The General thanked Barker for his professional competence. He had found his friendship in these last eight months a meaningful one. "I suppose you never expect to see me again," Grant remarked to the physician.

"I hope I may," said Barker.

"You do not say 'expect' but 'hope,' " said the General sadly.

Both were well aware that this might be the last onslaught of the disease.

Since the hemorrhage in early April, the General had made prodigious progress with his book. With the cancer eating away again at his mouth and throat, the effort cost him dearly. After finishing the account of Sherman's March to the Sea, he was in a state of near collapse. Douglas made the formal entry in his diary that the total weakening of his patient "resulted from cerebral exaltation attendant upon literary endeavor."

Restlessness late at night drove him to his work. He asked

Harrison for paper and pencil, which Harrison brought reluctantly. From May 6 into June he wrote for several hours into the night before trying sleep in his chairs near dawn. Douglas warned him that activity increased the pain as well as adding to the swelling of the neck. He suggested that the General rest more and give over preparations of the materials for the book to Fred. For the time being, the General ought to leave off weaving the narrative. He could not. The questions that bothered him late at night, the General explained to Douglas, were the questions of authenticity— the dates, the names of towns and roads, the battalion and artillery commanders. He had always answered questions best when they worried him.

Nighttime writing became his routine. Insomnia now always attended him. "I could do better," he scribbled to Twain, "if I could get the rest I crave."

Unfailingly, Douglas and Twain found bell-like clarity in what Grant had written. "I have been writing up my views of some of our generals and of the character of Lincoln and Stanton," the General said in one of his notes to his physician. "I do not place Stanton as high as some people do. Mr. Lincoln cannot be extolled too highly." He showed Douglas his text, in which he maintained that Lincoln and Stanton were polar opposites in every particular except that both possessed great ability: "Mr. Lincoln gained influence over men by making them feel it was a pleasure to serve him. He preferred yielding his own wish to gratify others, rather than insist on having his own way. . . . Mr. Stanton never questioned his own authority to command unless resisted. He cared nothing for the feelings of others. In fact it seemed to be pleasanter to him to disappoint than to gratify."

His humor surfaced on those rare occasions when the pain relaxed. He told Shrady about a night shortly after the war when he was walking in the rain to a reception given in his honor. A passing stranger offered to share an umbrella. The stranger was also bound for the reception. "I have never seen Grant," the stranger said, "and I go merely to satisfy a personal curiosity. Between us I have always thought Grant was a very over-rated man."

"That's my view also," Grant had replied.

[202]

He told Shrady that nothing ever gave him such quick delight as the sight of that stranger's face on the reception line.

On May 7, the Society of the Army of the Potomac reelected the General as its president. Later that month, and unbeknown to the General, Twain interceded with Fred on behalf of the sculptor Gerhardt, who wanted the commission to make the death mask. Fred agreed. "It is so much better," Twain confided in his notebooks, "that Gerhardt who is honest and whom the family know should do it than some tricky stranger." It never occurred to Twain to wonder who would own the death mask. No one, in fact, asked that question, not Fred, not Julia, not Gerhardt, an oversight that would have distressing complications.

On June 8, the General told Twain he had finished a rough draft of volume two. It remained for him to mold the book into a chronological narrative and to fill it out where the skeleton needed flesh. Twain's bet had paid off. He recorded, "The General says he has made the book too long by 200 pages—not a bad fault. A short time ago we were afraid we would lack 400 of being enough."

Accordingly, Twain released the prospectus to canvassers and to the public both in the United States and in Canada and England. Volume one would be published on December 1, 1885, and volume two in the following March. Twain also engaged twelve more presses, making twenty in all to work on the memoirs, and he let contracts to seven more binderies, one of which could turn out 1,500 volumes in a day. He even established his own bindery, renting a building, buying the machinery, and importing from Philadelphia the hands to run it. Charles L. Webster & Company was the envy of New York publishers, who had to send their large printing and binding jobs to other cities. Once the presses started to feed the binderies, Twain boasted, they would produce one book every second.

Yet Grant would not surrender the manuscript to Twain. He wanted to work on its completion himself, to do everything on it he could. "He is going to stick in here and there," wrote Twain to Howells, "no end of little plums and spices."

With the advent of the summer, Douglas suggested that the General leave the city. The swelling in his neck had subsided somewhat, and now and then, in moderate quantities, the General could eat solid food. The heat of the city would quickly aggravate and seriously weaken him. Julia thought the family could move to Long Branch, but Douglas said the Jersey seacoast was too damp and humid.

Several newspapers reported that the General would leave New York soon, and this news prompted a dozen hotel proprietors to offer the General and his family free room and board. These offers issued from men with mixed motives. Grant's presence at a summer place would do much for business. Among these offers was one from Joseph W. Drexel, the financier and philanthropist, who knew Grant, and whose brother Anthony was a close friend. J. W. Drexel had recently purchased a cottage at Mt. McGregor in upper New York State, twelve miles from Saratoga. Drexel was an investor in the Balmoral Hotel at Mt. McGregor and in the ongoing construction of the Saratoga, Mt. McGregor & Lake George Railroad.

When Fred reported the offer, Douglas, a long-time summer resident of Saratoga, said at once, "That is just the place I have been looking for. There is little heat there, it is on the heights, it is free from vapors, and above all it is among the pines, and the pure air is especially grateful to patients suffering as General Grant is suffering."

The Grants accepted the offer. Drexel gave orders that the cottage, more accurately a summer house, should be put in order at once. Drexel even sent a quantity of bric-a-brac and pictures from his residence to make the cottage as attractive as possible. The Grants intended to remain there through mid-September.

Douglas would spend most of his time at the cottage. He also arranged for a male nurse to come with the General to Mt. McGregor. As the preparations got under way, the General asked Shrady to promise he would be with him at the last. "So anxious was he," wrote Shrady in *The Century*, "that nothing would interfere with such an understanding that he questioned me concerning my whereabouts and my future plans. On learning that my summer home was my farm on the Hudson near Kingsbridge, he was particular to learn how long it would take me to reach him in response to an urgent message. After crossing the river, the railroad starting point would be Barrytown. He wished to know the distance from that point to Poughkeepsie, where a special locomotive could be obtained. Then in order to master every detail of the trip, he indicated the route on a piece of wrapping paper and smilingly styled it 'a working plan of battle.' "

The family moved from the city to Mt. McGregor on June 16 in a train furnished by William H. Vanderbilt. It consisted of an engine, a dining car, and Vanderbilt's own coach. Workmen removed three of the lounge seats from the coach so that the General could take along his two leather easy chairs. Along with the family came five grandchildren, the nurse, Henry McQueeney, Harrison, and the "tight-mouthed daughter of the Emerald Isle."

Early in the morning the General left his East 66th Street home for the last time. He wore a Prince Albert coat, now many sizes too large, bedroom slippers, and a scarf. A reporter described the General's wrist as skeletal when he adjusted the white silk around his throat. His hair and beard were white. To the many who had awaited him on the curb and sidewalk he appeared dazed. Before he got into the carriage, he looked back at the house longingly and sadly. At Grand Central depot, the General disembarked and tipped his silk hat to Albert Hamilton, the black driver whose carriage had waited outside the door these many months to ferry visitors and run errands.

At stations along the way, crowds gathered to see "General Grant's train." As the train chugged past stations, reporters threw off bulletins to the telegraph clerks. The General was news again.

It was a warm, quiet, hazy June day. Shrady noted that the Hudson was so glassy it reflected without distortion the sails of the boats. The shadows of clouds floated on the steep hillsides. In the fields cows stood as stationary as rocks.

The General dozed fitfully until the train neared West Point, when Julia awakened him. Blinking against the glare, the General stared at the castellated buildings and their embattlements until the train began to curve away and the trees obscured his vision.

PART V

I CANNOT STAY TO BE A LIVING WITNESS

There should be no real neglect of the dead, because it has a bad effect on the living; for each soldier values himself and comrade as highly as though he were living in a good house at home.

William Tecumseh Sherman
Memoirs

JUNE 16 WAS AN OPPRESSIVE DAY. THE HEAT SOARED TO 105 DEGREES along the Hudson Valley. The only relief afforded the passengers in the General's special train was by opening the coach doors and windows to let in the air. In with the rush of air came the cinders, the grime, and the heavy smoke of the engine. To spare the General's throat, Fred and Harrison reversed his chairs so that he was riding backward. Heat aggravated the swelling in his neck. He kept touching it beneath his scarf. His motions were reflexive, his hands tremulous.

At 2:40 P.M. the train pulled into the Saratoga yards and came to a slow, shushing stop beside the platform. The Wheeler Post of the GAR had constituted itself an honor guard, and prepared to stand for the General's inspection. But when the General got off the train, though he got off unassisted, he looked so wan and weak they could not bear to put him through the ceremony. The well-wishers who had turned out at the depot raised a cheer at the General's appearance and he responded with a wave of his cane.

The tracks of the narrow-gauge Saratoga, Mt. McGregor & Lake George Railroad ran parallel to the main line. The transfer from one train to another was a simple passage across the platform. The smaller train was already steaming. Its engine looked like a toy beside the Vanderbilt locomotive. In bold, gold letters, the little 2-4-0 proclaimed it was the J. W. Drexel. The General crossed over and, without help, swung himself up into the single coach.

Fred and several others who lent a hand had a harder time manipulating the easy chairs from the larger to the smaller car. They labored in the sun, the chairs made slippery with their sweat.

At one point the General himself came out on the coach platform to supervise their efforts. Finally, with an "all aboard," the little train began its serpentine route up and around the mountain to the depot at Mt. McGregor twelve miles away.

A cot awaited the General at the depot. He shuffled by it and walked the length of the platform to the embankment, at the top of which was the Drexel cottage. Detective John Fryer and Constable James Minnick followed him with a chair. At the bottom of the embankment steps the General halted and allowed Minnick and Fryer to carry him up. He got out at the top, walked down the path, mounted the eight steps of the cottage alone and entered the house with Harrison close behind. The guests at the Balmoral Hotel watched the General's progress from their windows and from the lobby.

The entourage that trooped behind him was as large as any staff he had ever assembled. To those who had accompanied him from New York were added Joseph W. Drexel and his wife, W. J. Arkell and other members of the Mt. McGregor Corporation, elected officials of Saratoga County, a police chief, the manager of the hotel, and a crowd that had come up from Saratoga below.

The General let Harrison help him change and brush the cinders from his hair and beard. Fifteen minutes after he had gone in he came back out to the broad porch that circled the cottage on three sides. He walked its distance several times, then, hands on hips, stood there taking in the scene. Wearing his top hat and black coat, he sat in the wicker armchair at the top of the steps until dusk, when the mosquitoes chased him inside.

Douglas examined his throat and found a minute collection of grime, which he cleansed. Grant had weathered the trip better than expected. The General expressed pleasure with his new quarters and asked Douglas if the mountain air would restore his voice. Even his husky whispering, when he could manage as much, was indistinct. The temperature went down to 40 degrees that night and the swelling on his neck began to subside. He slept for ten hours.

The mountain to which the General had come was named for Duncan McGregor, who had first sensed its commercial possibilities as an adjunct to the flourishing vacation resort of Saratoga Springs. McGregor hewed a road up the mountainside to the summit, opened a modest boarding house and restaurant, and prospered. In 1881 other men saw even more alluring prospects in the mountain as a woodland spa. A syndicate headed by J. W. Drexel and W. J. Arkell, publisher of the *Albany Evening Journal,* bought out McGregor for $50,000. The Saratoga and Mt. McGregor Improvement Company broke ground for the narrow-gauge railroad in 1882. By the end of the year coaches ran from the world-famous springs in Saratoga to the crest of the mountain. But the Saratoga, Mt. McGregor & Lake George Railroad never made it to Lake George.

The view from the mountain's summit took in the Adirondacks to the north. To the east were the Green and White mountains of Vermont and New Hampshire. One hundred and ten miles away was Mt. Washington, the tallest peak in the American northeast. To the south, the foothills of the smaller Catskills were visible.

In 1883, the company built the Balmoral Hotel, a four-story building in the shape of a "U" with sides facing east, west, and north. Every room let onto a balcony; the cuisine was excellent; and the appointments were luxurious. The Balmoral Hotel described itself as a dew-free, malaria-free, and mosquito-free oasis, and guaranteed that a week's stay relieved hay fever.

Joseph W. Drexel purchased Duncan McGregor's boarding house and restaurant, and renovated the building for his own use. He and his family summered at Saratoga Springs; the mountaintop cottage was intended as an occasional retreat from the social fever and the valley heat. Nights were always cool on Mt. McGregor. The daytime temperatures rarely went above 80 degrees.

Arkell suggested to Drexel that he tender the use of the cottage to the Grants. Drexel, a genuine humanitarian, made the offer immediately. In *The Captain Departs,* Pitkin quoted Arkell's reminiscences: "I thought if we could get him to come here to Mt. McGregor, and if he should die there, it might make the place a national shrine—and incidentally a success."

The cottage in which the General was to spend his last days was a two-story structure in Queen Anne style. It housed a dozen rooms, six of them upstairs bedrooms. Its exterior was painted a golden brown with dark brown trim. The interior walls were papered, and the ceiling downstairs was decorated with gold stars. Every room was carpeted and furnished comfortably, even to the breakfast, luncheon, and dinner settings of Dresden and Minton china. There was enough stemware to serve a thirsty battalion and enough bric-a-brac to qualify the cottage as an antique shop. There was a new fireplace with andirons, grate, and screen.

There was to be no cooking in the kitchen, which would save the General discomfort. Instead, the hotel agreed to send meals down to the cottage. After a few days this proved such a vast inconvenience to everyone that the Grant entourage dined in a small reserved room off the main restaurant. The General took milk and an egg and beef tea in the cottage.

On the cottage grounds was a tent pitched by Captain Sam Willett of the Lew Benedict Post of the Albany GAR. Willett had stationed himself to guard the privacy of the General and he proved occasionally efficient. He was a godsend for the General's grandchildren and Douglas's two little girls. They played in his tent most of the day and Willett had a gift for amusing them constantly.

The General occupied the corner room on the first floor. Two tall windows opened to the west. He placed his two easy chairs in the center of the room, beside his felt-covered working table, which held a Rochester kerosene lamp. A cabinet in the corner contained linens, medicines, and writing materials. It was a brighter room than the library at East 66th Street, but in another way it was more barren, for there were no deliveries of flowers.

Officially the Balmoral Hotel did not open for the summer season until July 1. But on the evening of June 16 it was well populated by reporters from the metropolitan newspapers, Saratoga dignitaries, and Albany legislators. They had come to pay their respects, if not to the General at least to the mountaintop he now occupied. The Balmoral had already booked a convention of pharmacists who trooped *en masse* past the cottage the next morning. One of them broke off from the rear and walked up the path to the porch where the General was sitting. He deposited a package of medicinal chewing gum in Grant's lap. The daughters of three of these pharmacists, little girls no more than six, approached the porch later to present the General with a bunch of daisies.

There was a thunderstorm on the night of the sixteenth and the next day the air was permeated by the odor of balsam. The temperature was barely 70 degrees. Grant decided on a walk. He summoned Harrison and, leaning on his servant's arm with one hand while picking his way with the cane in the other, he followed the path to Eastern Lookout, a knoll that afforded a panoramic view. From the hewn bench on which he settled himself, the General could look across the valley toward the Schuylerville Monument. It was in this valley that Benedict Arnold, Thaddeus Kosciusko, and Horatio Gates defeated the British army led by General John Burgoyne, winning one of the most decisive battles of the Revolutionary War. Ulysses S. Grant was to be the one famous soldier to die near this battlefield.

The distance he had traversed that afternoon was the equivalent of five city blocks. "More walking," said the *Herald's* correspondent, "than the General had done in five months." But it exhausted him. He lay for a long time in the chairs in his room before he asked Harrison for some pencil and paper. He wrote two notes, the first for Douglas, the second for Fred.

The one to Douglas read:

Dr., since coming to this beautiful climate and getting a complete rest for about ten hours, I have watched my pains, and compared them with those of the past few weeks. I can feel plainly that my system is preparing for dissolution in three ways; one by hemorrhage; one by strangulation; and the third by exhaustion. The first and second are liable to come at any moment to relieve me of my earthly sufferings. The time of the arrival of the third can be computed with almost mathematical certainty. With an increase of daily food, I have fallen off in weight and strength very rapidly for the last two weeks. There cannot be hope of going far beyond this period. All my physicians, or any number of them can do for me now is to make my burden of pain as light as possible. I do not want any physician but yourself, but I tell you, so that if you are unwilling to have me go without consultation with other professional men, you can send for them. I dread them however, knowing that it means another desperate effort to save me, and more suffering.

To Fred, the General wrote:

I have given you the directions about all my affairs except my burial. We own a burial lot in the cemetery at St. Louis and I like that city, as it was there I was married and lived for many years and there three of my children were born. We also have a burial lot in Galena, and I am fond of Illinois, from which state I entered the Army at the beginning of the war. I am also much attached to New York, where I have made my home for several years past, and through the generosity of whose citizens I have been enabled to pass my last days without experiencing the pains of pinching want.

He had heard promises of what the climate and the change would do for him. But the intense effort it took to get back and forth from Eastern Lookout had convinced him the promises were written on water.

Fred was dismayed by the note. While he disliked talking about the subject, he did tell the General that it was far likelier he would be buried in Washington. After thinking this over, the General scratched another message:

It is possible my funeral may become one of public demonstration, in which event I have no particular choice of burial place; but there is one thing I would wish you and the family to insist upon and that is that wherever my tomb may be, a place shall be reserved for your mother.

The General's note pierced Julia. The truth against which she had tried to shield herself brushed her defenses away. She never left the cottage after this; not for her meals, not to play with her grandchildren, not even to take walks to relieve her anguish. The General refused to let her nurse him, relying instead on McQueeney and Harrison, but Julia was at his bedside the first thing in the morning. When they sat on the porch, her chair was as close to his wicker as she could move it and she held his hand for hours when he dozed. Sometimes she prayed. He awoke once to see her hands thus clasped. He wrote, "Do as I do. Take things quietly. Give yourselves not the least concern. As long as there is no progress there is hope."

Douglas judged that Grant's death was not really at hand, but he worried that hopelessness and the sudden exhaustion that hopelessness engenders would hasten the end. He wired his colleague Dr. Henry B. Sands to come to Mt. McGregor as soon as possible. This was a psychological ploy. He did not expect Sands to tell the General he was getting well, but he expected that Sands's objectivity would convince the General he was not going to die immediately.

Sands took the midnight train for Albany. Reporters in New York City learned of his departure and, when Sands said he had no new information, one of the reporters went to Shrady's house, woke him, and asked what was going on at Mt. McGregor.

The General was in a better mood when Sands arrived. He was dressed, fully awake, and taking the morning sun on the front porch. Sands told him he wasn't going to die right away and the General believed him.

W. J. Arkell's commercial acuity regarding the presence of Ulysses S. Grant was soon realized. Visitors came to the mountain by train, by carriage, by horseback, and by foot. The newspaper watch in March and April had quickened the interest of the world, for the General was a famous American whom people in foreign capitals had seen. Now the world was interested in his fate. People sensed that his agony was every man's agony. The General unconsciously was teaching every man how to bear such agony.

Long lines of visitors walked past the cottage. Often Grant was on the front porch, preoccupied with his newspapers or his pencil and clipboard. He and his family submitted themselves to a great many photographers, and the Grants, Drexel cottage, and Mt. McGregor were reproduced in the popular magazines of the day. Now and then the General would look up at the curious who passed by and nod. For the most part he would stick to his business. One attractive young woman in a bright yellow dress carrying a yellow parasol trimmed with white stopped in the path and waved her yellow handkerchief. The General saw her, stood up, and tipped his hat in response.

Many local dignitaries simply presumed they were welcome — this despite the inability of the General to indulge any conversation at all. Congressman Francis Hancock, District Attorney Martine, and Judges Andrews and Rapallo mounted the steps one morning and started to chatter away. The General bore it. In the afternoon, these gentlemen were succeeded by Judge Hilton and Dr. John Gray, superintendent of the Utica Insane Asylum. A reporter described Gray as a man who could play Falstaff without stuffing. Grant noted on his pad how much larger Gray's shadow was than his. Affably Gray laughed and he and the Judge went on talking until Grant abruptly withdrew to the living room, where he penciled a note to Fred: "They will talk me to death if I stay out there." Somehow Fred revealed the note to one of the reporters, who included it in his story. This necessitated an apology: "It was the desire of the family to save the General from the common run of visitors but he was pleased to see Judge Hilton and Dr. Gray, neither of whom annoyed him."

One afternoon, an elderly well-dressed vintage politician called. Douglas had never seen a head with so much hair, nor a face with so much beard. Grant knew the man and apparently liked him, for he settled himself to hear what this visitor had to say. When the visitor left, Douglas commented on how unkempt an appearance he presented. Grant wrote, "Mr. N. is a Texan, but before he went to Texas in '44, he was a great admirer of Mr. Clay. In the contest of '44 between Clay and Polk, he took a vow never to cut his hair until Mr. Clay was President."

Not all of the visitors were as amusing. One man brushed by Sam Willett, rushed up on the porch and, taking the General by surprise, began pumping his hand. Extricating himself, Grant furiously wrote, "My doctors positively forbid me to converse." To which the stranger replied he would do all the talking. The General had to withdraw into the house to spare himself.

On June 21, the General worked on his book for an hour and on the twenty-second for several more. He had with him the manuscript of volume two and the page proofs of volume one. Dawson would read aloud from these and the General would stop him to make insertions or to rearrange passages. To the majority of writers, proofing galleys is a *pro forma* operation. It is done mainly to correct printers' errors and typos, sometimes to rewrite clumsy sentences. But the General was adding as many as twenty pages to the book each day with his additions and corrections. He was undertaking extended commentaries and revisions on what he had already written. Yet his gift for brevity, clarity, and simplicity never failed, and nothing he wrote at this time was ever excised. As a matter of fact, he was writing enough to keep Fred and Dawson up past midnight entering revisions on the galleys and transcribing the new material in its proper place in the manuscript.

The writer who continually picks at and worries what he has supposedly finished is not unusual. But the constantly revising writer is a bane to his publisher. Resetting proofs costs time and money. The ever-floriating manuscript pushes back publishing dates. Twain and Webster begged Fred to see if he could get the book out of the General's hands. Fred wanted nothing more. Tenaciously the General clung to his memoirs.

One cool day he suddenly found a measure of strength in his voice. He collected his notes and in a hoarse but audible whisper began dictating to Dawson. He wrote a completely new chapter to be added to the one already written on Appomattox. The efforts he made now were the equal of those he had made for *The Century* articles, and they brought on fatigue and weakness. He confided in Douglas, "I have worked off all I had notes of, and which kept me thinking at night. I will not press to make more notes for the present."

When he wasn't writing, his day was monotonous. Unable to amble through the surrounding forest of oaks, maples, pines, and firs, he was bored on the porch. He needed occupation. At Douglas's suggestion, Julia bought a copy of Oliver Wendell Holmes's *The Autocrat of the Breakfast Table* and read it aloud to him. He had in the past always read aloud to her, because her eyesight was poor. During their married life, they had read through most of Dickens and all of Thackeray.

Douglas's treatment was more intensive now. Grant wrote, "I feel worse this A.M. than I have for some time. My mouth hurts me and cocaine ceases to give me the relief it once did. If its use can be curtailed I hope it will soon have its effect again."

Cocaine was still in its experimental stages as an anesthetizing drug (doctors were not yet aware of its addictive qualities). In March, 1885, in fact, a young Viennese doctor named Sigmund Freud had experimented with its anesthetizing properties and concluded in a monograph that the drug might prove useful in eye operations. Freud did not pursue this investigation, but passed his monograph on to a colleague named Carl Koller, who did indeed pursue it and go on to win the Nobel Prize as the inventor of local anesthesia for surgery. John Douglas, though appreciably older than either of these doctors, was working along the same track. Douglas had used cocaine extensively in treating Grant and, because the General was so articulate and sensitive a patient,

Douglas probably had learned as much about the effects of cocaine as anybody else in the world.

Grant was clear in describing these effects. For instance:

> I have tried to study the question of the use of cocaine as impartially as possible considering that I am the person affected by its use. The conclusion I have come to in my case is: taken properly it gives a wonderful amount of relief from pain. Gradually the parts near there when the medicine is applied become numb and partially paralised [sic]. The feeling is unpleasant but not painful. Without the use of it the parts not affected with disease are pliable but of no use because their exercise moves the diseased parts and produces pain. When the medicine is being applied the tendency is to take more than there is any necessity and oftener. On the whole, my conclusion is to take it when it seems to be so much needed as it was at times yesterday. I will try to limit its use. This latter you know how hard it is to do.

The gift of a Bath chair, an English-made rickshaw, enabled the General to make a few trips to the veranda of the hotel after June 25. Harrison pulled at the tongue and some small boys pushed at the rear. When the veranda was reached, the manager asked the General if he wanted the Bath chair brought up with him. Grant looked at the Bath chair and back at the manager and said, "I guess my horse won't run away." The reporters asked Harrison if the General was improving. Harrison said, "He's getting better. He's not about to climb these rocks, but mind, he's getting better."

One of the cherished moments of his stay at Mt. McGregor came when a middle-aged man in dark suit, straw boater, and country shoes came down the path, a broad smile on his face, hand extended. It was Charles Wood of Lansingburg, who had sent Grant $1,000 "on account" when the Grants were penniless. The General got up from his wicker to meet him halfway on the steps. When Wood left, he had a treasured note from Grant: "I am glad to say that while there is much unblushing wickedness in this world, yet there is a compensating goodness of soul."

After two weeks at Mt. McGregor, Grant was a fixture. Guests at the hotel could look down at the cottage from the piazza. They saw him come out onto the porch at noon in his heavy coat and skating cap. Pillows were piled behind him on the high-backed chair. A shawl covered the right side of his face, and his neck was wrapped in a scarf. Then Julia, Fred, Harrison, or McQueeney draped a robe about his waist and legs. He would often spend as much as four hours there in concentrated writing. Sometimes he wore a top hat when his family gathered in midafternoon.

At night the guests often heard the Reverend Mr. Newman praying for the deliverance of Grant's soul. Another minister said the sight of Grant was the most eloquent and suggestive sermon he had ever met with.

Mark Twain spent summers at Quarry Farm in Elmira, New York. He was there June 27 when he received a telegram from General Grant asking him to come to Mt. McGregor. Twain left the hilltop the next morning at 6 A.M. and did not arrive at the cottage until after 8 P.M.

As a result of reducing the Vicksburg article, the editors of *The Century* asked the General to insert transitional sentences. They wanted him also to verify, authenticate, and explicate certain passages. To make this new work for the magazine consonant with the copy in the book, the General needed Twain's help. It could not have been extensive, because Mark Twain and Fred Grant accomplished it in one sitting which lasted from midnight until daybreak.

Twain nourished high hopes that on this visit he would wrest the manuscript away from Grant. He put it to the General that perhaps his work was done. The General penciled, "If I could have two weeks of strength I could improve it very much. As I am, however, it will have to go as is, with verifications by the boys and by suggestions which will enable me to make a point clear here and there."

The last sentence meant that he was going to keep it. In describing Twain's visit, one of the newspapers noted, "General Grant's part of the work is really over except for an occasional correction." Admitting defeat, Twain prevailed upon the General to let him take the maps. Later, Twain admitted that the General was right. The longer he kept working on the manuscript, the more he improved it. During Twain's visit, in fact, the General wrote the 500-word preface. He began it, " 'Man proposes and God disposes.' " He went on to describe his illness. "I have, however," he informed his future readers, "somewhat regained my strength and am able, often, to devote as many hours a day as a person should devote to such a work." Grant dated this July 1, 1885, and Twain and Webster sent it to the newspapers. The press gave this simple preface great play.

Twain waited on the mountaintop to see Jesse Grant, who came up from the city on weekends. Mark Twain and Jesse were gripped by the excitement of a monumental business deal. The year before, Governor Leland Stanford of California had dined with the sultan of Turkey, who offered him the franchise to run a railroad from Constantinople to the Persian Gulf. Stanford started to capitalize this project, having set his son up as the president of the corporation. Then the young man died and Stanford lost interest. He gave the franchise to Jesse Grant, who was now in the process of assembling the substantial capital to underwrite the venture. Twain was an eager enough investor to write a letter to the sultan. Grant wrote one, too.*

After discussing their business deal, Twain, Jesse, and Buck Grant sat beside the General on the porch to keep him company for the afternoon. The day before, James D. Fish of the Marine Bank had been sentenced to seven years in prison. The judge remarked that except for his gray hairs Fish should be serving a sentence seven times seven. Buck said seven years was too short. Jesse cursed Fish, too. Twain, summoning his bluest language, helped swell the chorus. The General listened impassively, then penciled, "He was not as bad as the other." It was his only comment. He looked off to the hills and the conversation about Fish promptly ended. "Even his handwriting looked gentle," remarked Twain describing the event in his *Autobiography*.

Over a three-day period the General wrote twelve notes to Fred, all of them about the book. Among other concerns the General wished he could have an objective opinion about the style and arrangement; he asked if the latest attempt to describe the

---

* Fortunately, or unfortunately, nothing ever came of this. The sultan, it seems, handed out railroad franchises as European monarchs handed out honors. Twain was subsequently inspired by the vision of buying the remains of Christopher Columbus for interment in the base of the Statue of Liberty—"No," he stormed in his notebooks, "in the Rotunda of the Capitol at Washington! !"

Petersburg campaign was good enough; he warned Fred to take care of himself: "Your services are too important now to have you break down."

Robert Underwood Johnson came to Mt. McGregor to claim the revisions for *The Century*. He himself had made the deletions on the Vicksburg article, a task he did not relish. This conference with Fred would be the last before the piece was set in print. Johnson knew the family had sent dozens of telegrams to friends asking them not to come to the mountain and he did not expect to see the General. Once Grant learned of Johnson's presence, however, he asked him forthwith to come over to the cottage. The General could no more not see certain people than he could stop writing his book. "I told the General," Johnson wrote, "that we had willingly acceded to his son's request that we should relinquish that part of the long Vicksburg narrative that preceded the siege—an article in itself. [Grant] smiled faintly and bowed his acknowledgement, and as I rose gave me his hand. I could hardly keep back the tears as I made my farewell to the great soldier who saved the Union for all its people and to the man of warm and courageous heart who had fought his last long battle for those he so tenderly loved."

Fred was shortly to write Johnson that his father's connection with *The Century* had been pleasant and that the General was gratified in having done business with gentlemen. "You have been generous," he concluded, "and if in the future I am able to do anything for your interest you will find me acting with you."

On June 25, Shrady came for a short stay. The General had dictated aloud the day before and now Douglas had put his voice under house arrest. He was not allowed even to whisper. "I do not suppose," the General wrote to Shrady, "I will ever have my voice back again at all."

Shrady who had not seen Grant since he left New York was quickly aware of a noticeable weakening. The General was now unable to clear his throat by coughing, expectorating, or vomiting. He needed swabbing and cleansing every four hours. When Shrady asked if the air was doing him any good, the General wrote, "I cannot at this moment get my breath through my nostrils."

Morphine quieted this panic, enabling the General to sleep. But often he disdained the injection because the drug interfered with his concentration. When Shrady took over from Douglas for a few days, he noticed that the General's arms were nevertheless swollen from the needles.

The General enjoyed Shrady's company. The doctor had an electric intelligence and a lively sense of humor. While it would be impolite to describe the profoundly devoted Douglas as dour, he was still a solemn man. Shrady liked to laugh. One morning, he lacked a tongue depressor. As he rummaged for one, the General took his pad and wrote, "I said if you wanted anything larger in the way of a spatula—is that what you call it?—I saw a man behind the house here a few days ago filling a ditch with a hoe, and I think it can be borrowed."

Shrady was also realistically direct. The General wanted to know the exact details of the climax of his disease. He wanted to know, and he wanted to know without hedging, whether he would die by choking or by hemorrhaging. Shrady said his end would probably be a peaceful one, relatively free from pain. Cancer victims invariably succumbed to ailments induced by their weakened condition. Shrady was pretty sure the General would live through the summer and into the winter months.

"It is postponing the final event," the General wrote. "A great number of my acquaintances who were well when the papers commenced announcing that I was dying are now in their graves. They were neither old nor infirm people either. I am ready now to go at any time. I know there is nothing but suffering for me while I live."

As long as he read the papers every day, it was hard for him to escape the thought of his own death. At least one journalist had him dead by nightfall. "The *World* has been killing me off for a year and a half," he wrote Shrady. "If it does not change, it will get it right in time."

Whenever Newman appeared, Shrady went to the Balmoral. Newman liked to read, and the General liked to hear passages from Chapters 8 and 9 of Matthew: "When he came down from the mountains great multitudes followed him," and "I am a man under authority, having soldiers under me, and I say unto this man, Go, and he goeth; Come, and he cometh; and to my servant, Do this, and he doeth it," and, "The harvest truly is plenteous but the laborers are few."

On the twelfth Newman held Sunday services on the piazza of the Balmoral. From his seat on the porch, the General could hear the familiar hymns. When Governor David Hill of New York and W. J. Arkell walked down to the cottage afterward, the General said he did not feel as much of an invalid as he looked.

After these two gentlemen withdrew, Newman sought out the doctors—Douglas had returned—and suggested they post an "imperative edict" that the General suffer the intrusion of no more visitors. This the doctors had no intention of doing. While visitors fatigued the General, he usually welcomed them, which was, after all, his prerogative. Often visitors helped lift his depression. Certainly they distracted him from the fury of concern he indulged in completing the memoirs. When Newman left, Shrady remarked to Douglas that there went the voice of one who crieth in the wilderness.

Father Raymond Didier of St. Vincent's Church in Baltimore arrived to pay his respects. Grant said he would see him. The priest brought the good wishes of his archbishop, James Cardinal Gibbons, and said, "We are all praying for you." The visit and the statement visibly pleased the General. As President, Grant had proposed in his second inaugural that Congress repeal the tax exemption of religious institutions. It was a proposal that would have severely penalized the Roman Catholic Church with its burgeoning system of parochial schools. The hierarchy let it be known they considered such a policy bigoted. Now bygones were bygones. "General Grant had no enemies, political or sectional, in these last days," Twain told his biographer, Alfred Bigelow Paine. "The old soldier battling with a deadly disease yet bravely completing his task, was a figure at once so pathetic and so noble that no breath of animosity remained to utter a single word that was unkind."

A group of twenty Mexican journalists and editors also came to Mt. McGregor. Physical restraint alone would have kept the General from seeing them. They clustered around him on the porch, one of them conveying in English the respect of all.

Grant wrote for their release:

My great interest in Mexico dates back to the war between the United States and that country. My interest was increased when four European monarchies attempted to set up their institutions on this continent selecting Mexico as their territory. It was an outrage on human rights for foreign nations to attempt to transfer their institutions and their rulers to the territory of a civilized people without their consent. They were fearfully punished for their crime. I hope Mexico may begin an upward and prosperous way. She has all she needs for these ambitions; she has the people; she has the soil; she has the climate; she has the minerals. The conquest of Mexico will not be an easy task in the future.

The Mexicans were patently gratified by Grant's courtesy and appreciated the effort it cost him to see them. His short paragraph was widely reprinted.

Of all the friends who had stopped to pay their respects, the one who most excited the General was Simon Bolivar Buckner. Avidly, he looked forward to Buckner's visit. To Douglas the General excitedly wrote, "General Buckner—Fort Donelson will be here on the next train. He is coming up especially to pay his respects."

Buckner, a year younger than Grant, had just married, and was returning with his bride from a Niagara Falls honeymoon. His ties with Grant went back farther than Donelson, to West Point and Mexico. It was Buckner who had rescued Grant in New York, when the destitute and disgraced ex-captain wanted to return home. After the surrender of Fort Donelson their roles momentarily reversed. "Grant," Buckner remembered, "left the officers of his own army and followed me, with that modest manner peculiar to himself, into the shadow, and there he tendered me his purse."

Later in the war Buckner commanded at Mobile, led a corps at Chickamauga, and wound up heading the Confederate forces in Louisiana. He returned to Kentucky after the war and became editor of the *Louisville Courier*. Two years after this final meeting with Grant he would be governor of Kentucky. And he would live until 1914, the last surviving Confederate general.

Twain, who was also at Mt. McGregor that afternoon, recalled in his notes some of their conversation. "I have my full share of admiration and esteem for Grant," said Buckner. "It dates back to our cadet days. He has as many merits and virtues as any man I am acquainted with but he has one deadly defect. He is an incurable borrower and when he wants to borrow he knows of only one limit—he wants what you've got. When I was poor, he borrowed $50 of me; when I was rich, he borrowed 15,000 men."

Reporters followed Buckner and his wife to the Mt. McGregor railroad platform. Buckner said his visit was "purely personal," and that as a gentleman he couldn't very well discuss what had passed between him and the General without the General's permission. Arriving in New York City, Buckner learned the General did indeed think the tenor of their conversation had public import. He fished from his pocket one of the slips on which Grant had penciled a message and read, "I have witnessed since my sickness just what I have wished to see ever since the war—harmony and good feeling between the sections. I have always contended that if there had been nobody left but the soldiers we would have had peace in a year. Jeff Davis and Beauregard are the only two I know of who do not seem to be satisfied on the Southern side. We have some on ours who failed to accomplish as much as they wished or who did not get warmed up to the fight until it was all over."

This hoped-for harmony was one of the compelling reasons the General had undertaken the book a year before. The work is dedicated to the "*American* soldier and sailor," and one of its concluding paragraphs states, "I feel that we are on the eve of a new era, when there is to be great harmony between the Federal and Confederate. I cannot stay to be a living witness to this prophecy; but I feel it within me that it is so."

Buckner's visit sharpened within the General a sense of his own worth. His career had been one of spectacular ascents and precipitous plunges. He had seen farmboys from plains that didn't catch two inches of rain a year fell forests to build pontoon bridges over savage rivers; and insurance clerks from Boston skin mules through the treacherous passes of Raccoon Mountain. They had fought to keep the nation whole. And now, even though his own body was in dissolution, he saw the nation becoming integral. His life had become inextricably a symbol of his nation's history.

No awareness of this colors the *Personal Memoirs*; Grant did not think of himself this way. But his life was coming to an end, and he

[225]

had opportunity enough to consider its meaning. In a memo he wrote to Douglas on July 8, he mused about destiny:

> If I live long enough I will become a sort of specialist in the use of certain medicines if not in the treatment of disease. It seems that man's destiny in this world is quite as much a mystery as it is likely to be in the next. I never thought of acquiring rank in the profession I was educated for; yet it came with two grades higher prefixed to the rank of General officer for me. I certainly never had either ambition or taste for political life; yet I was twice President of the United States. If anyone suggested the idea of my becoming an author, as they frequently did, I was not sure whether they were making sport of me or not. I have now written a book which is in the hands of the manufacturers. I ask that you keep these notes very private lest I become an authority on the treatment of diseases. I have already too many trades to be proficient in any. Of course I feel very much better for your application of cocaine, the first in three days, or I should never have thought of saying what I have said above.

When Shrady left Mt. McGregor in the middle of July, Douglas confided, "I fear the worst the day the General completes his book." Simultaneously the General was instructing Fred to embalm his body and keep it for burial—he spelled it "buryal"—in the fall. "Keep to the publisher's deadline. Do not," the General underlined, "let the memory of me interfere with the progress of the book."

Sometime before the twentieth, the General put down his pencil and said he was finished. He told Dawson he had done all he was going to do. Dawson remembered the joy with which the General informed his family and his physician that the task was done. He had completely revised the galleys of volume one; volume two was ready to go to the printer. He qualified his completion with the reminder that he could profitably work on the book until he died. He said he was finished with the book because better than all of them he knew that death was at hand.

He studied himself in the mirror for the first time in a week and wrote to Dawson, "I look like a bloat or a ghost." Then he wrote his last note to Douglas:

> After all that however the disease is still there and must be fatal in the end. My life is precious of course to my family and would be to

me if I could entirely recover. There never was one more willing to go than I am. I know most people have first one and then another little something to fix up, and never quite get through. This was partially my case. I first wanted so many days to work on my book so the authorship would be clearly mine. It was graciously granted to me, after being apparently much lower than since, and with a capacity to do more work than I ever did in the same time. My work has been done so hastily that much was left out and I did all of it over from the crossing of the James River in June/64 to Appomattox. Since that I have added as much as fifty pages to the book, I should think. There is nothing more I should do to it now, and therefore I am not likely to be more ready to go than at this moment.

When Douglas was dressing Grant's throat that night he asked what kind of day it had been. "Quiet, almost too quiet," whispered the patient.

On the twentieth, the General indicated he wanted to go to Eastern Lookout once more. There was no weakness in his pulse or in his appearance. There was no vital tension, either. There was nothing now to feed the General's mind, to make him rouse himself for a definite goal. Douglas assented.

With Harrison at the tongue of the Bath chair and Fred, Douglas, and others pushing, the party set out. They chose a new route and ran into difficulties when they reached the railway depot. Several tons of recently dumped coal barred their path. The General dismounted and picked his way up and down the pile while the others wrestled with the Bath chair.

At the point of Eastern Lookout, the General was deathly pale. After letting Harrison rest a few minutes, Douglas signaled the party to make their way back. Harrison pulled and the men pushed to get the General home as soon as possible. It was a tough uphill grind. The General managed to mount the porch. He dropped his cane before he made it to his easy chairs in general collapse.

He was quiet for eight hours. In the morning, Douglas felt his weakening pulse. The day was hot. Temperature on the mountaintop registered an unusual 85 degrees. The air was sultry. The General tried to take food. After a few swallows he began to cough and rejected it. He shook his head at a glass of wine. He asked for food again, forgetting that a few minutes ago he could not swallow. He began hiccuping.

Douglas feared a heavy dose of morphine would submerge him forever. He administered two minimal doses, which seemed to satisfy the patient. Several times Grant got up and sat on the bed while the pillows on his easy chairs were refreshed. He dozed.

He revived a little toward dusk of the twenty-first and ventured into the parlor, where he sat beside Julia for a few moments. At his gesturing she helped him back to his room and his chairs.

As night drew on, his room became stifling. Henry McQueeney suggested moving the General to the parlor where more windows would offer relief. Harrison and Fred moved the chairs while McQueeney supported the tottering Grant.

His temperature had risen. His pulse was faster, erratically pounding between 100 and 120 with no stability. There was no question in Douglas's mind that the General was dying. He wired Buck Grant in New York to come immediately and he informed Shrady and Sands they were needed.

Concerned over the growing weakness of his patient, Douglas administered two hypodermics of brandy. Temporarily the brandy steadied the flickering pulse. The General remained clearly conscious, fully aware of what transpired. He heard the voices of his family on the porch at 10 P.M. and whispered, "Tell them to retire. I wish no one to be disturbed on my account."

He remained composed. Douglas stayed with him while the others slept. The General was not resting, however. Douglas said the "dozing quietude was more that of extreme and growing lassitude than of restful repose."

When he arrived the next morning, Shrady saw that the General's struggle was drawing to an end. Sands and he conducted a superficial examination and reported in the bulletin a "critical weakness." Buck Grant saw at a glance the radical debilitation. Yet the General greeted Buck with a movement of his lips and an intelligent look.

Newman came and knelt beside the General's chair and prayed. Timidly he offered his hand after the "Amen." Gently Grant took it.

At noon, the clock tolled only eleven chimes. The General, who was facing it, wrote to Fred, "Fix the clock right. It only struck eleven."

Douglas felt the General's hands. They were growing cold. As the hours passed, symptoms of dissolution spread. The pulse remained weak and too frequent. Respiration was shallow and quick. But intelligence remained. The General knew his loved ones were around him.

When Fred asked if he was in pain, the General distinctly said "No." But he could no longer hold his head erect. Fred supported it.

"Death Coming Very Near" headlined the *Times*.

In anticipation, the *World* trimmed its front page with a black border.

Lieutenant General Phil Sheridan rode around Washington, D.C., with the Secretary of the Interior scouting a proper burial site.

William Tecumseh Sherman left St. Louis for Chicago, where he would make connections for New York and then to Mt. McGregor.

All this on the twenty-second.

That night, Fred asked his father if he wanted anything. The General whispered, "Water." Henry McQueeney wet a towel and placed it against the General's lips.

The General said he would like to lie down. He was surrendering, as surrender he must. His sons transferred him from the chairs to the bed. For the first time in many months, the General lay supine. Julia sat beside him, mopping his brow, never releasing his hand, staring sadly into his face. She, Nellie, the three sons, their wives, Harrison and McQueeney, and the three doctors waited until past midnight, when Douglas sent them to their rooms.

At dawn, Douglas took a short walk. When he came back, he heard the General breathing in a slow whistle. The whistle grew feeble, then more feeble. Harrison roused the family.

"There was no expiring sigh," Douglas wrote. "Life passed away so quietly, so peacefully that, to be sure it had terminated, we waited a minute."

Fred stopped the hands of the clock at 8:08.

Douglas stretched the sheet on the cherrywood bed over the General's face.

At 8:14 A.M. the *Times* posted the notice of the General's death in its window.

By 9:00 all the flags in the city were at half-mast.

By 4:00 P.M. Bloomingdale's had sold over 100,000 yards of black and white ribbon.

Mark Twain, at Quarry Farm, learned of the General's death a little after 10:00 A.M. He remembered his last sight of the General, sitting fully dressed with a shawl around his shoulders, pencil and paper at hand. Twain wrote in his notebooks:

> I then believed he would live several months. He was still adding little perfecting details to his book, and preface, among other things. He was entirely through a few days later. Since then the lack of any strong interest to employ his mind has enabled the tedious weariness to kill him. I think his book kept him alive several months. He was a very great man and superlatively good.

Later in the day, he wrote to Henry Ward Beecher, "One day he put aside his pencil and said there was nothing more to do. If I had been there I could have foretold the shock that struck the world three days later."

There were hundreds of messages sent to the family and hundreds sent by foreign governments to the United States's Chief of Protocol.

Sherman wrote Julia to say she had been as true to the General "as the needle to the thread, in poverty and in health, in adversity as well as exaltation."

The effect of Grant's death on the public was numbing, and people found it hard to express themselves. One of the most poignant attempts was that by Joseph Twichell, a Hartford minister, who wrote to his close friend, Mark Twain:

> I suppose I have said to [my wife] forty times since I got up here, "How I wish I could see Mark." My notion is that between us we could get ourselves expressed. I have never known anyone who could help me read my own thoughts in such a case as you can and have done many a time, dear old fellow.
>
> I'd give more to sit on a log with you in the woods this afternoon while we twined a wreath together for Lancelot's grave than to hear any conceivable eulogy of him pronounced by mortal lips.

T. C. Crawford, a reporter from the *World*, had accompanied Grant to Mt. McGregor, and there became friendly with Dr. Douglas. He was later to memorialize Douglas in an article for *McClure's Magazine* in which he urged Congress to reward the physician's devotion. Crawford quoted a letter Douglas wrote the day after the General's death:

> Nine months of close attention to him have only endeared him to me. I have learned to know him as few can know him. The world can know him as a Great General, as a successful politician; but I know him as a patient, self-sacrificing, gentle, quiet, uncomplaining sufferer, looking death calmly in the face and counting almost the hours in which he had to live, and those hours were studied by him that he might contribute something of benefit to some other fellow-sufferer. If he was great in his life, he was even greater in death. Not a murmur, not a moan, from first to last. He died as he had lived, a true man.

There was also a final message addressed to Julia from the General himself. Fred came across it unexpectedly, among items he was removing from his father's robe. These items included a ring Julia had given Grant many years before; it had come loose when the General's fingers shrank, and he secreted it in his clothing. There was also a lock of her hair, entwined with a lock of Buck's, that he had carried with him in Oregon and California. There was also the pencil he had gripped with such tenacity. And there was the letter he had written to Julia fourteen days before:

> Look after our dear children and direct them in the paths of rectitude. It would distress me far more to hear that one of them could depart from an honorable, upright and virtuous life than it would to know that they were prostrated on a bed of sickness from which they were never to rise alive. They have never given us any cause for alarm on this account, and I trust they never will. With these few injunctions and the knowledge I have of your love and affection and the dutiful affection of all our children, I bid you a final farewell, until we meet in another and, I trust, better world. You will find this on my person after my demise.

Fred's daughter, little Julia, aided by McQueeney, made a wreath of oak leaves for her grandfather's coffin.

"There was another morning for him," wrote the agnostic Shrady, "another light, glorious, infinite, immortal."

Julia prohibited an autopsy. Shrady and Douglas concluded that starvation was the actual cause of death. When the undertakers from Saratoga moved the corpse, they judged it did not weigh one hundred pounds.

Because they had to work in the cottage, the undertakers took two days for embalming. During this time, the corpse was preserved in an ice coffin. A few days after the General's death, a specially ordered casket arrived at Mt. McGregor. It was made of polished oak with a copper interior covered by a dark purple velvet. Solid silver handles extended along both sides. "U. S. Grant" was engraved on a gold plaque. The lid opened on a glass top that hermetically sealed the corpse within. Grant was dressed in a Prince Albert black broadcloth suit with a white standing collar around which a black scarf was tied in a bow. Gold studs lined the shirt and gold cuff links secured the sleeves. He wore patent leather slippers.

Though his uniforms and his swords were at the Smithsonian Institution, the family could have one of each for the asking. They did not ask. They draped the coffin with a flag on top of which they placed the now-varnished wreath little Julia had woven.

Though Fred and Julia knew the General was going to die, they had not guessed he would die so soon. Fred had a great many decisions that he could not make at a moment's notice. On hearing of the General's death, President Grover Cleveland had dispatched his adjutant general, R. C. Drum, to ask if the family preferred a military funeral and, if they did, where it was to take place. Up until now it was customary to bury ex-Presidents in their home state. Fred informed the President that the family wanted the General buried with military honors. Since very little of his father's career had transpired in either Ohio or Illinois it would take the family a short while to decide upon an appropriate site. Until then they would keep General Grant at Mt. McGregor.

This decision annoyed social Saratoga. The season was in full swing and an extended period of mourning would inhibit the festivities. A committee of prominent citizens called on J. W. Drexel to protest and ask his help in moving the General as quickly as possible, to restore Saratoga to its glory. Drexel sent them back crestfallen.

The local newspapers joined by the New York *Tribune* charged this was a profit scheme planned by Drexel and Arkell to promote Mt. McGregor as a summer resort. Drexel vigorously and speedily corrected this impression. He pointed out that he had never relied on the bizarre to make money and that it had cost him and Arkell $1,000 a week to tender generous considerations to the dying General. The newspapers apologized to Drexel, the *Tribune* among them.

On the afternoon of the General's death, the members of the Wheeler GAR Post of Saratoga presented themselves as a self-constituted guard of honor. They wore full uniforms. One of these men displayed a sword he had worn at the funerals of Lincoln, Farragut, and Garfield. Another, H. M. Knight, was one of the soldiers who helped carry the moribund Lincoln from Ford's Theater to the William Petersen house on 10th Street.

The U. S. Grant Post of Brooklyn also arrived on the twenty-third as a guard of honor. Diplomatically Fred accepted both contingents. The Brooklyn Post guarded the porch and the room where the General reposed; the Saratoga Post guarded the grounds. Three reliefs around the clock marched at attention with polished rifles. They pitched their tents on either side of the cottage, ran up their colors, and provided their own mess. It was easy for the hundreds of visitors during the next weeks to spot the General's cottage. It was the small building besieged by soldiers. Their presence proved more than ceremonial. Without them, the relic hunters would have carried away the cottage splinter by splinter and the surrounding woods leaf by leaf. As it was, one greedy souvenir hunter made off with the lightning rod and the cottage was struck on the thirtieth. The bolt collapsed part of the ceiling of the nursery room and, although Ulysses S. III escaped injury, three soldiers were shocked and burned.

Soon after Grant's death, Sheridan wired the family that they could bury the General in the park surrounding the Soldiers' Home in Washington. The governor of Ohio promised that the legislature would provide a site at either Point Pleasant or Georgetown.

Sure that the family would remain in the east and remembering his father's last preference for a site in New York City, Fred wired Mayor William Grace. Grace promptly responded. He sent Chief Clerk W. L. Turner to Mt. McGregor with the information that the City Board of Aldermen had voted to appropriate a site in one of the public parks. On the twenty-seventh Fred returned to the city with Turner, Jesse, and General Horace Porter.

Julia wanted the General buried in Central Park. Central Park's 840 acres between 59th and 110th streets and between Fifth and Eighth avenues had been acquired by the city in 1856. By 1885 Central Park looked much as it looks now, with its winding paths, open fields, reservoir, and arched bridges. It contained an Egyptian obelisk, called Cleopatra's Needle, a zoo, a mall, a museum, an arsenal built in 1848 and a blockhouse dating from the War of 1812. The park was already enclosed by the city on all sides. Grace took the two Grant brothers and General Porter on a complete tour of all available sites. They chose one tentatively in the Watch Hill area near 110th Street.

Then Grace suggested they go on to the Claremont area on Riverside Drive. Known as Riverside Park, the area extended northward from 86th Street, gradually ascending a high bluff that ended at 122nd. The bluff fell away precipitously to the Hudson River below. It commanded an impressive view of the Palisades stretching north and the Jersey piers and railroad terminals to the south. The Claremont area was completely undeveloped. The character of Riverside Drive was not yet formed. This was the determining factor for Fred and Porter. The monument to the General could take whatever form its architects chose, uninhibited by a preexisting architectural environment.

"Mother takes Riverside Park," wired Fred on July 28. "Temporary Tomb had better be at the same place."

The plans for this temporary tomb were drawn in twenty minutes by J. Wrey Mould, the city architect. It was a brick vault with a semicircular roof, the form of a World War II Quonset hut. It was closed by a barred door with an embossed "G" in its center. The rims were ornamented with bluestone. A runic cross at its entry was finished in maroon and gilt. Although Mould ordered more than a sufficient amount of bricks he found he needed twice as many: the masons sold bricks as souvenirs and passersby made off with them as often as they were able.

When the funeral arrangements were finally decided General Drum announced the formal schedule from Mt. McGregor. On August 4, a funeral service would be held on the mountain. Then the General's body, with an accompanying cortege, would travel to Saratoga, switch trains, and move on to Albany, where the General would lie in state at the Capitol for one day. On the sixth the casket would go to City Hall in New York. On the eighth, a Saturday, a funeral procession would accompany the General to the vault on 122nd Street, where he would be interred after public services.

Julia did not view the body, which was kept in the parlor. She spent the week in her room, prostrate with grief. When she finally descended the stairs on Fred's arm, the GAR guards came to attention and departed, leaving mother and son alone for a long time. Outside of his immediate family, the only visitors who had viewed the body were Mathias Romero, who had arrived on the twenty-fourth, and General Joseph B. Carr, a personal friend who was involved in the massive planning for the funeral as New York Secretary of State.

The flood of thousands of messages from every corner of the country and from foreign capitals never abated while the casket was at Mt. McGregor. Messages came with such frequency to the small telegraph office at the Balmoral that the reporters complained they could not send their news dispatches. Fred Grant asked the newsmen to announce that it was impossible for him now to acknowledge these condolences but he would in due time.

During this period the nation's newspapers were filled with Grant lore. Newspapermen hunted down Grant's friends and fellow soldiers for anecdotes and summaries of the great man's life and career. Sherman was a particular target. "The *Century* and *North American Review*," he wrote his wife in July, "are persecuting me with telegrams and personal messages to write something sensational about Grant, but I *will not*. . . ."

On the second Saturday the General lay at Mt. McGregor, the guests of the Balmoral Hotel were allowed to view the body. This privilege was extended as a token of the family's appreciation for favors large and small. The guests had respected the Grants' need for privacy and now the ladies at the Balmoral were stitching the rosettes that would bedeck the special train leaving Mt. McGregor on August 4.

Once the people in Saratoga learned of the open casket, they jammed the next train to the mountaintop. Soldiers admitted them by twos to the cottage.

General Winfield Scott Hancock, senior major general of the army, presented himself to the family on August 3. President Cleveland had detailed him to take charge of the formal arrangements. He had been a classmate of Grant's and he had repulsed Pickett's charge at Gettysburg. Under Hancock's command, Company E of the Twelfth Infantry came to Mt. McGregor accompanied by two batteries from the Fourth and Fifth Artillery.

Military honors consist of the escort, carrying reversed arms; the flag; and the volley. Because Grant was a general, the cortege would include the riderless horse, boots backwards in the stirrup. Because he was a President, he would be accorded a twenty-one-gun salute.

At dawn on the fourth the guns fired across the valley every half hour in Grant's honor. At 10 A.M. the clergymen appeared. They were W. L. Harris, the Methodist Episcopal Bishop of New York, Reverend Dr. Benjamin Agnew of Philadelphia, and the Reverend Mr. Newman. The cannons boomed a thirteen-gun salute as Hancock followed them. Accompanying Hancock were William T. Sherman, Admiral Stephan C. Rowan, Joseph Drexel, Hamilton Fish, Senators Warner Miller, William Evarts, and Thomas P. Ochiltree. They joined General Horace Porter, ex-Postmaster General John A. Creswell and his wife, and Mr. and Mrs. Arkell on the porch. The pulpit, a lectern on which rested a plain black Bible, faced the open doors into the parlor where Grant's family sat. Romero was there with General Rufe Ingalls and the General's sister, Virginia, and his niece, Clara Cramer. Mrs. Potter Palmer and Nellie Dent Wrenshall, Julia's sister, comforted her. On the porch steps was a choir formed by the Brooklyn Post. They sang "My Faith Looks Up to Thee." Guests from the Balmoral and some from Saratoga formed a semicircle on the lawn.

The Reverend Dr. Agnew delivered the convocation. Newman then proceeded with the eulogy. He spoke for an hour and twenty-five minutes. He apostrophized Grant the soldier, the statesman, and the genius. He described the General's happy family life telling mourners Ulysses was the Doric column that persevered while Julia was the Corinthian that beautified. Newman saved Grant the Christian for the peroration: "He knew that Christianity had nothing to gain from him beyond the influence of a well-ordered life and godly conversation, but he had everything to gain from the power and promises of our Lord. More than all things else, he was taciturn touching his religious faith and experience. The keenest, closest, broadest of all observers, he was the most silent of men. He loved within himself."

Bishop Harris pronounced the benediction.

At noon, the GAR choir sang "Nearer My God to Thee."

Bugles sounded a dirge as the GAR men in a death-march step carried the casket to the railway platform. Here it was placed in an open observation car covered by a canopy bedecked with the emblems of mourning. The entourage filled the coaches coupled behind this. Julia remained behind at Mt. McGregor. She said that what she would see in New York would only wound her sorrow while it would not relieve her grief. Mrs. Newman stayed with her; and Harrison, who would remain in her employ until his death.

General Grant at sixty-three was on his way home forever. Going down the mountain, General Hancock ordered the coffin opened so that the men of the Wheeler Post could see the gray face of their commander for the last time. Sadly they circled.

At Saratoga the coffin was transferred by its escort to the larger train, which reached Albany in the late afternoon. The General lay in state at the Capitol until noon of the next day. Then the escort took the coffin to New York City. As the funeral train passed West Point, the entire Corps of Cadets came to present arms. The Cadet Captain who brought the Corps to the salute was John J. Pershing, America's next four-star general. Cadet Frank Winn remembered that, after the train passed, lightning, wind, and rain swept down from Storm King Mountain, making the afternoon black.

The public began to file by the catafalque in the Governor's Room at City Hall beginning at 8 A.M. on Thursday morning.

Two hundred and fifty thousand people came to say good-bye. City Hall was draped in black. Three hundred and twenty policemen controlled the long lines. Workmen passed carrying lunch pails and pretty shopgirls waited in shabby dresses and worn shoes. There were delegations from every GAR post in the nation. Many nearby posts attended *en masse*. The members of the Wilson Post in Baltimore bore a floral crown of white pinks and asters. Factories were quiet. Chimneys were smokeless. The *Times* said:

> The outward manifestations of a common sorrow are by no means confined to the costly decorations on the houses of the rich and to the abundance of material festooned and draped with all the care. In the narrow streets and the tall crowded buildings where the poor make their homes the sign of grief is on nearly every door post. In many cases it is nothing but a narrow strip of cheap black cambric fluttering in the breeze from the topmost story of some tenement house or a small flag bordered with a piece of folded crepe stripped from a wornout bonnet.

Members of the Brooklyn GAR Post and soldiers from the Twelfth Infantry who had come down from Mt. McGregor stood guard detail. At 1 A.M. on the morning of the eighth they closed the coffin and draped it with the flag.

Military contingents who had camped at Governor's Island began landing from their ferries at Battery Park while the moon shone. A reporter noted that when the sun rose and first glanced off the brass and silver of the uniforms, the electric lights of the city went out as by ethereal command. Martial sounds echoed throughout the city. There was the steady clop of the horses' hooves, the tread of marching men, and then ceasing with the sudden crash of rifle butts on the pavement as the soldiers came to parade rest.

By daylight the ferries from Hoboken and Jersey City were crowded with guests journeying from as far away as Washington, D.C. Thirty policemen from Jersey City were added to the New York complement at the Hudson ferries to facilitate the constant flow of disembarking spectators.

Every available coach had been pressed into service by the Pennsylvania, the Central, the New Haven, and the Harlem River railroads. Most of the trains pulling into the terminals were so long they were drawn by two locomotives.

Brooklyn Bridge was a teeming mass of humanity as thousands upon thousands, unable to board the elevated cars, took the footway over to Manhattan. The New York elevated subways transported over 600,000 spectators. The only time similar stress had been laid on the elevateds was at the opening of the Brooklyn Bridge, when half that number traveled to the ceremonies. Yet on this August day not one elevated broke down or caused any congestion along the tracks. It was the only summer day that Coney Island was deserted.

Every horse and every stable in Manhattan had been commandeered by the military escort commander. Not only had the government hired every hansom cab, but it had borrowed as many carriages as it could from city residents.

On the Hudson, from Stevens Point in upper Manhattan around to the Narrows on the East River, hundreds of sailboats had dropped anchor. Their masters peered through binoculars at the spectacle transpiring in the city.

Five men-of-war were in the line on the Hudson. Heading the line was the *Despatch*, the flagship of Admiral Jouett. Behind it were the *Omaha*, *Swatara*, *Alliance*, and the *Powhatan*, which had been Commodore Matthew Perry's flagship when he landed at Nagasaki, Japan, in 1853. Closing the line was the revenue cutter *U. S. Grant.*

At dawn the bo'sun piped "All hands on deck," which began the ceremony of "cockbilling the yards," the mariners' sign of grief. The "yards" are the spars which support the sails. At the command "Sway," the forcyard of each ship was lowered to port and the mainyards to starboard and there made fast. The colors were dipped to half-mast. The sailors were piped down to don mourning —white cap, white jacket, and black trousers.

The escort commander, General Hancock, mounted on a spirited black stallion, arrived at City Hall at 8:30 A.M. Hancock was a fine figure of a man, a splendid horseman, and his chest glittered with a gold sash. He was followed by the mounted members of his staff and eight brigadiers, including Fitzhugh Lee, the grandson of Lighthorse Harry and the nephew of Robert E. Their gold helmets with white plumes, their gold epaulets, white gauntleted gloves, and shiny medals became incandescent in the bright morning.

Superintendent of Public Works William Murry told Hancock's aide, Colonel Beck, that the city was ready to transfer the casket to the government. The Liederkranz Society on City Hall's steps sang Schubert's "Geisterchore"—the song of spirits over the water—and the "Pilgrims' Chorus" from *Tannhäuser* as Colonel Beck reported to his chief that the procession was ready to start.

Bishop Harris and the Reverend Mr. Newman, leading eight other ministers, descended to the sidewalk. Behind them came Douglas, Shrady, and Sands wearing wide mourning sashes of black and white.

The funeral car clattered up to the steps. It was drawn by twenty-four black horses in drapery. Each horse was tended by a black groom dressed in black broadcloth and wearing a black silk hat. Albert Hawkins drove the hearse. He was a black coachman who had chauffered Grant as Secretary of War and later as President, and had stayed on at the White House as a driver. He had asked President Cleveland for this honor.

While the ministers, the doctors, and the escort waited, the Brooklyn honor guard carried the casket down the wide steps and onto the catafalque in the hearse. A black canopy shielded it. Four black plumes rose at each corner of the catafalque.

Hancock ordered, "Forward march," and the escort started. Behind it came the David's Island Military Band playing Beethoven's "Marche Funèbre," then keeping time with muffled drums.

The rank of officers was a varied panoply. They were in raiment. The army was experimenting with new uniforms at the time and had not yet standardized the officers' dress blues. Hancock wore a gold-trimmed admiral's hat and knee-length coat. Others wore a belted tunic and a German-style steel helmet, with either a spike or white plume. Still others wore the open field jacket with cummerbund and forage hat. White-gauntleted hands tugged at bridles decked with shiny brass or steel rivets. Medals glistened over every heart. The officers riding behind Hancock looked equally as distinctive in their uniforms as ever Grant had in his unadorned flannel shirt and muddy boots.

The order of march in a military funeral consists of the escort, the band, troops, the colors, the chaplains, the hearse, beside which march the bearers, the honorary pallbearers, the family, members of the executive and judicial arms of government, enlisted men and officers from the command of the deceased, delegations from the legislative arm of government, then from the states, then the municipalities, lastly delegations from societies and fraternities.

The line of march was up Broadway from City Hall to 14th Street, west to Fifth Avenue, north to 57th Street, again west to Broadway, which traverses Manhattan at an angle, north again to 72nd Street, then west to Riverside Drive, proceeding north to the vault at 122nd Street. Over a million spectators assembled along this line.

They had begun flooding downtown in the morning and by noon they were backed up along the bluffs above the Hudson. Windows of large warehouses along the way had been cleared of goods so spectators could look out from them. Hundreds sat on the roofs of buildings at Union Square while from the balconies below proper ladies viewed the procession through lorgnettes. At 18th Street two young men knocked together three-legged wooden stools, which they sold for twenty-five cents. The purchasers used these to stand on tiptoe for a better view. Men shimmied up telegraph poles. Boys crawled out on the branches of overhanging trees. Nearby statues were dark with climbers. The stoops of the rich, who were away in August, were particular vantage points for the poor. Gentlemen wore watchchains with a "Grant" pennant while ladies sported "Grant" medallions sold by Bloomingdale's for souvenirs. A spectator said:

> Broadway moved like a river, a river into which many tributaries were poured. There was one living mass choking the thoroughfare from where the dead lay in state to the grim gates at Riverside open to receive him. From 14th Street to the top of the hill—pavements, windows, curbs, steps, balcony, and housetop teeming. All walls and doorways were a sweep of black.

From City Hall, which was at the juncture of Broadway and Park Row, past Cortland, Chambers, Worth, Broome, Charlton, Greenwich, West 4th up to 36th, more than fifty side streets were filled with uniformed soldiers, deployed east and west of Broadway, waiting for the escort commander to pass. Armed troops, carrying weapons reversed, traditionally precede the catafalque. As Hancock rode by, the men on the side streets wheeled in behind him, and then the troops on the next northward street behind them.

It was a marvel of military drill, planned and organized by General Henry Shaler of the New York State Militia. Sixty thousand armed men paraded the length of the city. Not only did they have to fall in at the right instant, but they had to maintain their rank in the line, so that they could march to their original points for transport that evening.

At Broome Street, four companies of the Virginia State Guard and men of the First Massachusetts Infantry shared the close-order space. These two units had fought against each other at the battles of first and second Bull Run. Now only their insulting witticisms concerning each other's military bearing clashed. Each state paid for the transportation and pay of its militia. The First Massachusetts cost the Commonwealth of Massachusetts $10,000.

The escort included the Twenty-second Infantry with four battalions of artillery. Behind them marched detachments of sailors in blue uniforms with white leggings and hats. Then came a marine division in white trousers, blue coats with yellow epaulets, and white caps with black brims. There were National Guard regiments and brigades from every state that had fought for the Union. Black troops from the Southwest marched behind Pennsylvania Zouaves in red pantaloons followed by the governor's foot guards from Connecticut in colorful uniforms with criss-crossed white chest belts. When the last of these had joined the line at noon, the command stretched for two and one half miles. The men marched with fixed bayonets, an endless sea of rigid steel slivers in the bright day.

Then came the catafalque with the honor guard. Behind them in carriages rode the honorary pallbearers named by President Cleveland. They were General William T. Sherman, Lieutenant General Philip Sheridan, Admiral David H. Porter, Vice-Admiral Stephan T. Rowan, Hamilton Fish, George Boutwell, Senator John A. Logan, George Jones, and Oliver Hoyt. At Julia's direct request, Cleveland also named Confederate Generals Simon B. Buckner and Joe Johnston.

Grover Cleveland shared a carriage drawn by six bay horses with Secretary of State Thomas Francis Bayard, who wore a white silk hat and did all the talking. Ex-Presidents Rutherford B. Hayes and Chester A. Arthur were directly behind. Members of the Supreme Court followed. The carriages of the governors were arranged in the order in which their states had entered the Union.

From City Hall, spreading southeast and west, were eighteen thousand men of the GAR led by Major General Dan Sickles, who had lost a leg in the Peach Orchard at Gettysburg. The units he led were as varied as the Loyal Legion, of which Grant had been a member, to the Columbo Guards, half of whose Italian recruits had died at Cold Harbor, to the Virginia Grays, who wore blue and gray ribbons fluttering from shields bearing images of the General's face. Carriages for disabled veterans lined the length of Canal Street three abreast. The Atlantic City guard marched with the Union Veterans Corps of Washington, D.C. There was even a complement of the "Old Guard," soldiers mustered out before the Civil War began. They marched in bearskin caps, white coats, and blue trousers. These units and men all paid their own way. The parade, in fact, cost the United States government only $30,000.

This was the second great parade for most of these veterans. The first had come in May, 1865, when for two days the victorious Union armies had marched through Washington, with President Andrew Johnson, Grant, and Sherman taking their salutes on the reviewing stand.

Bringing up the rear were the carriages of eight thousand civil and municipal dignitaries led by Mayor William Grace. The line of march stretched half the length of Manhattan. Forty-five thousand traveled the streets to the Riverside bluff. They kept time to dozens of marching bands. About two hundred fife and drum corps bands and musical units marched in the line. Each one of these struck up at the Fifth Avenue Hotel on 21st Street, in deference to both the Cleveland entourage and Grant family who were registered there. "Nearer My God to Thee," commented a *Herald* reporter, had been played more in New York state since Grant's death in July than "God Save the Queen" in England. The bands also played Sullivan's "Lost Chord," Beethoven's "Hymn to Night," Civil War songs and marches, including Rudolph Aronson's "Memorial March" composed especially for this occasion, until the brass and the pipers were too tired to blow any more and left the beat to the drummers.

Vendors patrolled the route selling doughnuts, pretzels, peanuts, and fruit from baskets. Other peddlers dipped gallons of lemonade, barley water, and cider from pewter tanks mounted on two-wheeled carts.

When Hancock's escort broke upon the knoll at Riverside and 72nd Street, they could see the white pavilions of Fort Lee across the river. A sailor with semaphore flags signaled the warships. Their guns began booming a final salute. Hancock ordered "Route March" and the men shifted their weapons more comfortably. Detachments stopped along the route for their lunch and officers often dismounted to stretch their legs, letting privates ride the horses.

Meanwhile workmen on 122nd Street hurriedly completed the vault by throwing sand over the arched roof still moist with tar. The walls were wet with new enamel. Carpenters drove finishing nails into the half-acre expanse of the wooden platform that would accommodate the honored guests. Tons of gravel dumped during the week had transformed the bluff into a hard-packed parade ground. They had no sooner finished than a bugle blast announced Hancock. Behind him the men picked up the step. The files dressed.

By 2:30 P.M. Hancock was in place. The only considerable delay in passage came when the catafalque could not pass under the elevated railway structure at 72nd Street and had to make a detour of several blocks. At 4:30, to the strains of Chopin's "Funeral March," Hancock led the honorary pallbearers into the tomb. The honor guard carried the casket, which they laid on two steel beams supported at each end by blocks of marble. They folded the flag and presented it to Colonel Grant. One of the noncommissioned officers placed little Julia's oak wreath on top of the coffin.

"God of battles," thundered Hancock, "Father of all. Amidst this mournful assembly we seek Thee with whom there is no death." Bishop Harris then the Reverend Dr. Newman conducted a simple Methodist service.

A soldier closed the barred gate. A bugler paced alone to its center. As he placed the gleaming instrument to his lips, William Tecumseh Sherman was wracked with sobs. Then the bugler sounded the notes of farewell:

> Day is done.
> Gone the sun.
> From the lakes, from the hills, from the sky.
> All is well.
> Safely rest.
> God is nigh.

EPILOGUE

The Americans are too self-laudatory, too apt to force the tone and thereby as Sainte-Beuve says, to give offence; the best way for them to make us forgive and forget this is to produce what is simple and sterling. Instead of Primers of American Literature, let them bring forth more Maxims of Poor Richard; instead of assurance that they are "the greatest nation upon the earth," let them give us more Lees, Lincolns, Shermans, and Grants.

Matthew Arnold
General Grant

MARK TWAIN WITNESSED THE FUNERAL PAGEANT FROM HIS OFFICE windows on 14th Street. The procession lasted five hours. Afterward, he plowed through the sidewalk crowds to Fifth Avenue and on uptown to the Lotus Club on 40th Street. There, later that evening, he and Sherman talked about the Grant each of them knew and loved.

Twain was fifty years old and at the peak of his powers when Ulysses S. Grant died. His publishing firm was worth $500,000.* His three great books, *Life on the Mississippi*, *Tom Sawyer*, and *Huckleberry Finn*, would sell more than two million copies by the end of the century. Yet hard times were ahead.

In 1887 he published a *Life of Pope Leo XIII*, with the imprimatur of His Holiness himself. The biography, written by Father Bernard O'Reilly, commemorated Leo's golden jubilee. Multiplying the number of priests in the United States by $3, Twain figured that the book would have to return a profit of at least $100,000. Inasmuch as no Catholic home could be without the book, there was another $500,000, at least, guaranteed. Unfortunately, many an American priest not only did not buy the book, but didn't even read it. And the number of Catholic homes that managed to do without the book turned the anticipated profit into a sizable loss.

Next Twain advanced Henry Ward Beecher $5,000 for his autobiography. Three weeks later the famous preacher dropped

* This figure was arrived at by careful computation when Jesse Grant wanted to buy into the firm at 10 percent.

dead in his library. The loss to Christendom was great, said Twain, but the loss to Charles L. Webster & Company was greater.

Twain's company published memoirs by McClellan, Burnside, Hooker, and other generals, but none generated the excitement, or the sales, of the Grant book. Nor did the company publish any writer who secured a large audience. Subconsciously perhaps, Twain never signed a writer who could compete with him. He had a chance to publish George du Maurier's *Peter Ibbetson* and Thomas Hardy's *Tess of the D'Urbervilles*, but Twain always saw greater profit in tedious books.

The company went under in 1894, sunk by the production and distribution costs of the multivolume *Library of American Literature*, edited by Twain and William Dean Howells. "Get me out of business!" Twain pleaded to his friend H. H. Rogers, a Standard Oil partner. The financier arranged to sell the firm's list to the Century Company. Twain accused Charley Webster of having "chouseled" him out of thousands of dollars. But it was not Webster, broken in mind and body and long out of the firm, who did Twain in. Nor was it really any of the unsalable books. It was a mechanical monster, an infernal machine, that almost destroyed Mark Twain.

Something called the Paige typesetting machine swallowed the profits made by the Webster Company, gobbled up the royalties earned by Twain's books, and consumed the savings of a lifetime. In all, the machine cost Mark Twain more than the quarter of a million he admitted to losing. It cost him time that might have been spent more profitably writing; and it cost him peace of mind. There was very little peace of mind for Mark Twain in the last third of his life.

The machine was the invention of a smartly dressed, smooth talker named James W. Paige. He was, wrote Twain, "an extraordinary compound of business thrift and commercial insanity." His complicated and sophisticated typesetting machine appeared at a time when all type for newspapers, magazines, and books was still set by hand. Twain, who had refused to invest $5,000 in Alexander Graham Bell's telephone company, saw possibilities in the typesetting machine, and financed its inventor with all he had.

"There are 11,000 papers and periodicals in America," Twain

wrote in his *Notebooks*. "This typesetter does not get drunk. He does not join the printers' union. He does not distribute a 'dirty case.' He does not set a 'dirty proof.' A woman can operate him." Once the machine was perfected, it was Twain's plan to rent models, rather than sell them outright. But the Paige typesetter was never perfected, and was always in disassembly as its inventor strove to make it ever more sophisticated. Where Twain went wrong—and he should have known better, since he had been a printer's devil in his youth—was in not recognizing that Paige's machine was adding steps to the typesetting process, rather than simplifying it. Besides, there was a simpler and more efficient machine already available— the linotype, patented by Ottmar Mergenthaler in 1884. It would sweep the market. Robert Paige took Mark Twain much as Ferdinand Ward had taken Ulysses S. Grant. To the end of his life Twain entertained a fantasy of watching Paige's death struggle while locked in a steel cage. The one and only typesetter can still be seen on exhibit in the Twain mansion at Hartford. It is all Twain had to show for his money.

In his late fifties, Mark Twain found himself a bankrupt. He determined to pay off all his debts one hundred cents on the dollar. And he managed it—in a frenzy of writing and a hateful grind of traipsing around the world on lecture tours. One must admire the times as well as the man. Loss and failure were not paralyzing. Men swore to themselves they would "come back," and they did. Twain did, but the effort embittered his later years.

William Tecumseh Sherman moved to New York City shortly after Grant's death. Within months of the move, he was a widower. Thereafter he became a noted bon vivant. He had once told Grant his avocation in peace would be balls and cotillions, because he loved to see young people happy. He loved the theater and was always in attendance at Shakespearean productions. He would go to Acts I, II, and III one night, and Acts IV and V the next. With Mark Twain he founded the Players Club.

Some of his later years were embittered by religion. His wife, Ellen, was a devout Catholic and before her death a world-famous almoner. Her faith created a barrier between them. Thirteen-year-old Willie Sherman, his father's high hope, died of smallpox during the war, and they lost another son in infancy. When Sherman's third son, Tom, took vows as a Jesuit his father could not accommodate the decision. "I can't get over Tom," he wrote eleven years after young Sherman had begun his novitiate. "Why should they have taken my splendid boy? They could have brought over thirty priests from Italy in his place."

Sherman was in St. Louis when he was stricken by a cerebral hemorrhage. He lingered for a week, rising once from his sickbed to stagger to a chair and say, "Tom, I want to see Tom." His passing was attended by a minor religious controversy. A priest visited the sickbed during his last hours, which led some St. Louis newspapers to conclude that the Catholic clergy were trying to pull the old general into heaven against his will. John Sherman, his brother, quieted this ugly charge. He pointed out that Sherman's daughters were Catholics, and that if seeing a priest made them feel better, William Tecumseh was only too happy to talk to a kindly neighborhood father.

At Sherman's funeral, General Joe Johnston, an honorary pallbearer, caught cold and succumbed a week later to pneumonia.

The money earned by the great success of the *Personal Memoirs* secured Julia's widowhood. With it she paid off $187,900 of Grant and Ward debts that bore the General's endorsement. If this seems an alarming generosity, the chief losers in the firm's collapse had been Ulysses and Julia, Fred, Buck, Nellie, the General's sisters, and Julia's brother. But the money also augmented her travails as a widow.

She turned down an offer by the noted American sculptor Augustus Saint-Gaudens to make a death mask of the General. Saint-Gaudens had been commissioned by *The Century*. Julia turned him down because Mark Twain had already interceded on behalf of Karl Gerhardt. But when Julia asked for the mask, Gerhardt asked for $17,000. It was an outrageous demand, and Julia refused to pay it.

The situation distressed Twain, who insisted that Gerhardt surrender the mask on the promise of later exclusive use. Gerhardt said he wanted the money. Fred said he would take the matter to court. Twain sided with the Grants, but worried that a court scandal would injure sales of the memoirs to the extent of $100,000. (It has been remarked that $100,000 was Twain's favorite figure in estimating losses; profits were always figured in the millions.) In the end, Twain resolved the quarrel at his own expense. When Gerhardt handed over the mask, Twain gave him a receipt in full for $10,000 the sculptor owed him, and paid off an additional $8,000 of Gerhardt's obligations.

Julia was threatened by Adam Badeau with a suit for monies due him. Certainly Badeau was owed something; he had signed a binding contract with the General. Fred, at first, refused to pay him anything, then offered $1,500, and finally $8,000. The matter was complicated because Fred and Badeau would communicate only through their lawyers. Even the publication of Badeau's paean to the General, *Grant in Peace*, failed to soften Fred. The two of them vented their anger in the newspapers, calling each other illiterate. In March, 1888, they went to court. There—actually, on the courthouse steps—Fred agreed to a settlement of $11,253. This represented the sum originally specified by the General plus interest. Fred had retained Roscoe Conkling to represent him. After the settlement Conkling walked home—into the Blizzard of '88. He collapsed in the snow and died soon after from the effects of overexposure.

Because she was rich, and because she had always been thrifty, Julia was accused of parsimony. The accusation surfaced venomously when Dr. John Douglas lay dying in a charity hospital. A newspaper charged her with ingratitude. But Julia had paid Douglas $7,000 for his services and an additional $5,000 that the General wanted the doctor to have as a gift. After the General's death, Douglas was beset by poor health and bad luck. His wife was reduced to running a boarding house in Bethlehem, Pennsylvania, while the doctor tried unsuccessfully to make his way back.

Julia Grant continued to live in Washington and New York, and to travel frequently through Europe. She lent her energies to the cause of women's suffrage, and always advised the young to vote the straight Republican ticket. She became a close friend of Varina Davis, the widow of Jefferson Davis. They agreed that posterity had made up its collective mind about their husbands, and consoled each other over any aspersions cast on the Confederacy or the

Grant presidency. Within the family, Julia devoted herself to mothering her twelve grandchildren.

She died in 1902, in her seventy-fourth year, and was interred beside the General.

Jesse and Buck Grant moved to California and made themselves wealthy in real estate. They built and operated the U. S. Grant Hotel in San Diego. Buck became a well-known genealogist and served for many years as head of the Grant Family Association. In 1925 Jesse published *In the Days of My Father, General Grant,* containing an account of the family's life in Galena in 1860–1861.

Fred remained in New York City. He became president of the American Wood Working Company. In 1888, the New York State Delegation to the Republican National Convention proposed a ticket of Lincoln and Grant, Robert for President, Fred for Vice-President. Benjamin Harrison won the nomination and the election. He appointed Fred ambassador to the Austro-Hungarian monarchy. Vienna, remembering his father's visit, turned out to cheer Fred as he rode to the embassy. Fred served as ambassador until 1893. Two years later, he accepted Theodore Roosevelt's offer and became commissioner of police in New York City. In May, 1898, during the Spanish-American War, he was mustered into the volunteers as a colonel of the Fourteenth New York Infantry. By the end of the war he was a brigadier. He remained in the army and commanded a brigade in the Philippines, fighting the guerrilla insurrections of the early 1900s. As a major general he held territorial commands in Texas and Illinois. Fred Grant died in New York in 1912 and was buried at West Point.

His daughter, Julia, married Prince Speransky-Cantacuzene of the Russian royal court. With their children, and apparently some of the Speransky fortune, they fled the revolution to the United States. She became a socially prominent Washington grande dame, and wrote a series of magazine articles later published as *My Life Here and There.*

Fred's son, Ulysses S. Grant, III, the West Point appointee of 1885, was graduated from the Military Academy in 1903. He trooped with Pershing in Mexico and served in both world wars, retiring from the army as a major general. He was the author of

Washington: A Planned City in Evolution and a biography of his grandfather, published in 1969.

Dr. George Shrady died in 1908, shortly after finishing his articles on Grant for *The Century*. His journal, *Medical Record*, eventually forced the New York legislature to institute tests for the licensing of doctors. Shrady's son, the sculptor Henry Merwin Shrady, executed the Grant Memorial in the Mall in Washington, D.C., in 1922.

Neither William Henry Vanderbilt nor Senator Jerome Chaffee survived the General by six months.

James D. Fish served six years of his sentence and was paroled. Ferdinand Ward did not come to trial until after the General's death. The delay prompted rumors of a payoff. But Ward was tried and convicted; and, like Fish, served six years before he was paroled. During his imprisonment his wife died, and the courts placed his son, Clarence, with a maternal uncle who refused to send the boy back to his father. Ward sued for custody of his son, lost, later kidnapped him and was apprehended. In the late 1890s a reporter found him working as a town clerk in Geneseo, in upstate New York. But the suspicion that Ward had secreted the Vanderbilt money somewhere hung over him for all his days.

Grant's death made Mt. McGregor famous, but its further development never materialized profitably. There were once plans to chisel the General's face in the side of the mountain. W. J. Arkell said he and his family lost a fortune trying to turn the place into an elite summer resort. "Instead of making the place," Arkell reported in his old age, "Grant's death killed it absolutely. After his death, as people came to the mountain, the moment they stepped off the train they took off their hats and walked around on tiptoes, looking for something I never could find."

The cottage still stands, looking exactly as it did at 8:08 on the morning of July 23, 1885. For many years the GAR paid for its upkeep, until New York state took over its maintenance. The Metropolitan Life Insurance Company built a sanitarium for its tubercular employees on top of the mountain in 1913. In 1942 the sanitarium became a Veterans Administration rehabilitation center and still later a school for the mentally retarded. There are plans to close this school and demolish the obsolete buildings. Perhaps tourists will then flock to Mt. McGregor and Grant's cottage, just as thousands visit Grant's birthplace at Point Pleasant, the Hardscrabble farm in St. Louis, and the Galena House in Illinois.

THE
PERSONAL MEMOIRS

My family is American, and has been for generations, in all its branches, direct and collateral.

Ulysses S. Grant
Personal Memoirs

THE 295,000 WORDS OF ULYSSES S. GRANT'S *Personal Memoirs* FILLED 1,231 pages in two volumes. "The thick pair of volumes of the *Personal Memoirs*," wrote critic Edmund Wilson, "used to stand, like a solid attestation of the victory of the Union forces, on the shelves of every pro-Union home." Charles L. Webster & Company sold 312,000 sets at $9—624,000 books. In that decade, General Lew Wallace's *Ben-Hur* sold 290,000 copies, and *The Adventures of Huckleberry Finn* 500,000.

Julia Grant's first check was for $200,000. It is still on display at the Players Club in New York, where Mark Twain proudly and ceremoniously hung it. Twain had estimated his own profits to the nickle. Charles L. Webster & Company cleared $200,000 on the first edition, and $50,000 on each of two subsequent editions, published in 1892 and 1894. Eventually, in all editions, the work earned Grant's estate nearly half a million dollars.

The only contemporary book comparable to Grant's is Dwight D. Eisenhower's *Crusade in Europe*, which sold 301,000 copies when it was published in 1948, and considerably more in paperback reprints. It earned Eisenhower $600,000. Oddly enough, Grant was the first United States President to publish a book. James Madison had contributed thirty or more articles to *The Federalist Papers*, and James Monroe wrote an unpublished history and an autobiography, both in a code that has never been fully deciphered. After Grant, William McKinley, Theodore Roosevelt, Woodrow Wilson, Herbert Hoover, John F. Kennedy, and Richard Nixon all wrote books, mostly historical works. As governor, Calvin Coolidge wrote *Have Faith in Massachusetts*, a book as platitudinous as its author was taciturn. Presidents Truman, Eisenhower, and Lyndon Johnson wrote histories of their administrations. Kennedy's *Profiles in Courage*, the most successful of all these, won a Pulitzer Prize. But Abraham Lincoln remains the only President who could have been a great writer, the equal, say, of Twain or Melville.

The *Personal Memoirs* was widely and appreciatively reviewed when it first appeared. The New York *Tribune* devoted a full page to the event, its critic finding the book a "model of simplicity and directness." The *Times*, devoting almost equal space, reported that it was valid history. The magazines were equally enthusiastic. *Atlantic Monthly* said it was the story of the "first great and conquering commander developed by modern republican institutions." *The Nation* praised its literary qualities: "As to his style, it has the principal element of thoroughly good writing, since we are made to feel that the writer's only thought in this regard is how to express most directly and simply the things he has to say." William Dean Howells wrote to Twain, "I am reading Grant's book with delight I fail to find in novels. I think he is one of the most natural—that is, *best*—writers I ever read. The book merits its enormous success, simply as literature."

It was a book for which the public appetite had been so whetted that the reviewers hastened with their opinions as soon as it appeared. Heretofore newspapers and magazines had let their critics digest the substance of a book for several months before venturing to put their opinions in print. What would happen to publishing, a worried Twain wrote to Howells, if reviewers chastised a book without excellence before the public had a chance to buy it? Well he might worry, because the practice soon became ingrained custom.

Many reviewers leaped at the chance to reawaken old controversies: Why had Grant put Sheridan in relief of Warren before the Battle of Five Forks? Why hadn't he entrenched at Shiloh? Why hadn't he relieved Butler after the fiasco of the Bermuda Hundred? The subjects were compelling then, because the participating soldiers were still arguing both sides of the case. Most reviewers, like the one for *Harper's*, found "The chief value of the book must be in the revelation of Grant's own character, feelings, judgments and modes of thinking." And Grant's character has remained the major preoccupation of subsequent critics of the *Personal Memoirs.*

The first of many preeminent figures of modern literature to comment on Grant's memoirs was Matthew Arnold. He wrote a lengthy critique of the book for English readers, which was reprinted in a Boston magazine in 1887. Grant and Arnold had met at a dinner in London given in Grant's honor. The guests included Robert Browning, Anthony Trollope, and Thomas Henry Huxley. In such company, Grant hardly noticed the critic, while Arnold found Grant unimpressive. They met again in 1883, in New York, at a reception given for Arnold by Andrew Carnegie. Grant attended the Englishman's first American lecture at Chickering Hall. The squeaky-voiced critic was an unfortunate public speaker, and on this occasion inaudible. "Well, wife," Grant said to Julia, "we have paid to see the British lion; we cannot hear him roar, so we had better go home." But he complimented the *Tribune* on its written report of the lecture, and this gesture delighted Arnold.

The *Personal Memoirs* did not capture the imagination of the British book buyer. To the English, the hero of the war was Robert E. Lee, because he was a gentleman and a champion of the underdog. Arnold informed his countrymen that Grant deserved better consideration, and undertook a clear and comprehensive review of the memoirs and the man who wrote them.

He found in the book a man "strong, resolute and businesslike . . . with no magical personality, touched by no divine light and giving out none . . . a man of sterling good sense as well as of the finest resolution; a man withal, humane, simple, modest. . . ." He also found "a language all astray" in its grammar; "an English without charm and high breeding." But the General possessed "the high merit of saying clearly in the fewest possible words what had to be said, and saying it, frequently, with shrewd and unexpected turns of expression."

Arnold traced Grant's career through the Civil War. He accurately and admiringly described the Vicksburg campaign; and, like so many others, found Grant's account of the meeting with Lee at Appomattox worth quoting in full. He also explained succinctly the root causes of the Civil War, and concluded that the great value of the memoirs lay "in the character which, quite simply and unconsciously, it draws of Grant himself."

This eminently fair, reasonable, sensitive, and thorough account deeply annoyed the American public. In 1887 Americans considered any criticism of Ulysses S. Grant sacrilegious. For this English schoolmaster to take the heroic General to task for imperfect grammar was worse than objectionable. In addition, Arnold had used a disquisition on General Grant to comment condescendingly upon American manners at a time when Americans were insecure and neurotic about their culture.

Americans took umbrage, and their chief spokesman was Mark Twain. He pointedly remarked on Arnold's own grammatical lapses. As for Grant's, Twain noted: "If you should climb the mighty Matterhorn to look out over the kingdoms of the earth, it might be a pleasant incident to find strawberries up there; but, great Scott, you don't climb the Matterhorn for strawberries." Grant's book was great, said Twain, "a unique and unapproachable literary masterpiece . . . and great books are weighed and measured by their style and matter, not by trimmings and shadings of their grammar."

Twain himself had actually voiced some second thoughts about the book. When Henry Ward Beecher asked about the General's drinking, Twain replied there wasn't a hint of it in the *Personal Memoirs*. "I wish I had thought of it," he wrote Beecher. "I would have said to General Grant: 'Put the drunkenness in the memoirs—and the repentance and reform. Trust the people.' "

The *Personal Memoirs* were Gertrude Stein's favorite reading. What she found in the book was an American voice writing a prose barren of ornamentation. Grant was able to compose two volumes of fairly intricate subject matter without recourse to too many Latinisms, circumlocutions, or euphemisms, or too much military nomenclature. He was unafraid of repetition. By relying on a basic though extensive Anglo-Saxon vocabulary Ulysses S. Grant kept his prose uncluttered, clear, and new. Gertrude Stein saw Grant as undisturbed by the passions and confusions of either battle or composition, phlegmatic, a man who had intuitively found the mask she wanted writers to wear.

The *Personal Memoirs* and the *Memoirs of General William Tecumseh Sherman* are the foundations for our understanding of the military history of the Civil War—important because the Civil War was the first modern war. And Grant's memoirs have proved more than a source of military history. Lloyd Lewis depended upon their early chapters for his biography *Captain Sam Grant*, which has become, since its publication in 1950, one of the supreme evocations of American frontier life. Bruce Catton has used these memoirs as skillfully for understanding American political history as Gertrude Stein used them for understanding American prose.

In *Ulysses S. Grant and the American Military Tradition* Catton described the physical look of the memoirs and how their physical presence revealed the man behind their composition. Alone of Grant's critics, Catton saw their political implications, noting that they "contain the key to everything [Grant] was driving at in the reconstruction program." Catton said the *Personal Memoirs* were a record of what Grant saw when he looked back from his deathbed, and "apparently what he saw was very good."

Surely no critic ever discussed the *Personal Memoirs* with the balance, precision, and perspective of Edmund Wilson in his chapter on Grant in *Patriotic Gore*. Wilson's maximum opus among many magna opera, *Patriotic Gore* is a series of essays on the literature of the American Civil War. In it he likened the *Personal Memoirs* to *Walden* and *Leaves of Grass*, as "a unique expression of the national character." Wilson also recapitulated Grant's life and career, but re-created the man through appropriate flashbacks, usually citing one of Grant's contemporaries. And he was astonished "to what extent the romantic popular legend has been substituted for the so much more interesting and easily accessible reality" of the Civil War.

Wilson noted two climaxes in the memoirs, the taking of Vicksburg and the surrender at Appomattox. He praised Grant's writing, and remarked:

> These literary qualities, so unobtrusive, are evidence of a natural fineness of character, mind and taste; and the memoirs convey also Grant's dynamic force and the definiteness of his personality. Perhaps never has a book so objective in form seemed so personal in every

line, and though the tempo is never increased, the narrative, once we get into the war, seems to move with the increasing momentum that the soldier must have felt in the field. What distinguishes Grant's story from the records of campaigns that are usually produced by generals is that somehow, despite its sobriety, it communicates the spirit of the battles themselves and makes it possible to understand how Grant won them. . . . The reader finds himself involved—he is actually on edge to know how the Civil War is coming out.

Wilson's primary purpose in *Patriotic Gore* was explicating the Civil War, discovering how the war was understood by the men and women who wrote about it as participants. What he found in the *Personal Memoirs* was drama, a moral drama—perhaps the best explanation of why Grant's book remains inspiring.

Twain, Arnold, Wilson, and others compared the *Personal Memoirs* to Caesar's *Commentaries*. Superficially, both books present a bald recitation of facts, so the comparison is apt. Stylistically, the books are twins, so the comparison is fruitful. Despite differences between the two books—Caesar uses the present tense and describes himself in the third person—the stylistic similarities are striking.

Caesar maintains pace, the speed with which his narrative proceeds, by an absolute reliance on verbs. He concludes each sentence, each subordinate clause with a verb. Typically, a paragraph ends with an asyndeton.* He sacrifices adjectives to include auxiliary verbs; he would rather use a verb than a noun; prefers a verb to the participle; and will go to the perfect tense rather than use an adjective.

Caesar understates action. In *De Bello Civili*, for example, he describes marching into Cingulum on his way to Rome. The citizens crowd into the streets and cluster around Caesar asking what they can do to help. "Caesar orders soldiers. They send. [*milites imperat: mittunt*]." That he recruited soldiers meant his march on Rome had popular support. But that is the unstated fact, the fact the reader must infer.

Caesar rarely includes direct discourse, quoted speech, in the *Commentaries*. Dialogue is almost always revealed through indirect discourse. Latin reflexive pronouns, of course, obviate the confusion

---

* Omission of conjunctions; the most famous literary example is Caesar's: "I came, I saw, I conquered."

attendant in such English sentences as, "His bull gored him," where the reader must wonder whose bull is goring whom. However, Romans were addicted to speeches. Most Romans had composed their dying words before the advent of middle age, and managed to deliver them not once, but many times before their death.

These three stylistic devices are typical of Grant. Grant, too, relies on verbs. He prefers the simple sentence to the compound and the compound to the complex, though he manages the last two often enough. This preference leads to a stunning literary execution. In describing a battle, Grant states his own actions simply: "I rode in person out to Clinton. On my arrival I ordered McClernand to move early in the morning on Edwards Station." He describes the action of his Confederate opponent in complicated and passive sentences. For example, while Grant is preparing for this attack, his opponent, Pemberton, is described as follows: "Receiving here early on the 16th a repetition of his order to join Johnston in Clinton, he concluded to obey, and sent a despatch to his chief, informing him of the route by which he might be expected." Grant identifies himself with verbal, active language and his opponents with adverbial, passive phraseology.

Because he is verbal, he is not often metaphorical. He does describe the trees on the crest of a Mexican mountain "waving like plumes in a helmet"; and says of the territory around Vicksburg: "The country in this part of the Mississippi stands on edge as it were, the roads running along the ridges except when they occasionally pass from one ridge to another." Yet he achieves many visual effects. When he describes the besieged troops at Chattanooga, he writes: "The fuel within the Federal lines was exhausted, even to the stumps of trees." He always sees where he is, and always orients the reader to what the land is like. Here is southern Texas: "The country was rolling prairie and, from higher ground, the vision was obstructed only by the earth's curvature. As far as our eyes could reach to the right the herd [of wild horses] extended."

Grant, like Caesar, is a master of understatement. Understatement is a form of ironic emphasis. Where the reader expects a surcharge of excitement, he finds instead surcease. When Grant takes Vicksburg he never indulges in exaltation.

> The Vicksburg paper which we received regularly through the courtesy of the rebel pickets, said prior to the fourth, in speaking of

Yankee boasts that they would take dinner in Vicksburg that day, that the best recipe for cooking a rabbit was "First ketch your rabbit." The paper at this time and for some time previous was printed on the plain side of wall paper. The last number was issued on the fourth and announced that we had "caught our rabbit."

The purpose of understatement is to build up reserves for the climactic statement. Understatement conserves attention, does not allow it to dissipate. The climactic statement in the memoirs is, of course, the meeting at Appomattox Court House. Grant devotes twelve pages to this. He describes Lee's elegance: the shiny boots, the red stitching on the new butternut gray uniform, the jeweled scabbard presented by the daughters of Richmond; and his own slovenliness: the private's blouse, the mud-spattered boots, the lack of sidearms or sword. Lee and Grant talk about their adventures in the old army. Twice Lee interrupts the conversation to call attention to the purpose of the meeting. At the second interruption, Grant asks for pencil and paper and writes out quickly the terms for the surrender of the Army of Northern Virginia. Lee reads it over, noting that officers can keep their sidearms. He tells Grant that in the Confederate army the cavalrymen and artillerists own their horses, and wants to know if these men can keep them. Grant replies that only officers can take their private property. Lee prepares to sign the paper.

> I [Grant] said to him that I thought this would be about the last battle of the war—I sincerely hoped so; and I said further I took it most men in the ranks were small farmers. The whole country had been so raided by the two armies that it was doubtful whether they would be able to put in a crop to carry themselves and their families through the next winter without the aid of horses they were then riding. The United States did not want them and I would, therefore, instruct the officers I left behind to receive the paroles of his troops to let every man of the Confederate Army who claimed to own a horse or mule take the animal to his home.

It is a stylistic device to end the story on this note; it makes a significant moment in history more immediate. Grant says, in effect, that history was made by the men who took home their horses, and by the Union soldiers who shared their rations, as he tells us, with their former foes.

And like Caesar, neither in this passage nor in others does Grant resort to direct discourse. He rarely quotes—with three important exceptions.

During the narrative, Grant is at pains to detail the rise of Phil Sheridan from lieutenant to colonel of a Michigan regiment, to brevet brigadier charging up Missionary Ridge, to commander of the cavalry of the Army of the Potomac. But Sheridan is allowed only one statement in his own person. Lee is about to abandon Richmond and pull back to North Carolina. Grant wants Sheridan to cut him off. He gives Sheridan his orders: "I told him that, as a matter of fact, I intended to close the war right here, with this movement, and that he should go no further. [Sheridan's] face brightened up, and slapping his hand on his leg he said, 'I am glad to hear it, and we can do it.' "

Grant quotes Lincoln on several occasions, principally because everything Lincoln had to say was eminently quotable. Lincoln spent his last weeks with Grant at City Point in Virginia. He spoke to Grant as much as he spoke to anyone. These conversations have been incorporated into too many books to bear repetition here, but they were original with Grant at the time he wrote the memoirs. When Fred was working over the manuscript of volume two, *The Century* learned about the Lincoln anecdotes and successfully importuned him for the rights to publish them. Mark Twain was vehement in his anger, but refrained from venting it on Fred.

Grant quotes Sherman often. And it is here that the memoirs take on the tension that transforms them from history into a literary achievement. Sherman's role in the memoirs is special. Grant, unlike Caesar, does not inveigh against enemies. He is almost polite and deferential in describing Lee; he is saddened by the spectacle of a valiant soldier surrendering a brave army that fought for a cause without justice. Pemberton and Buckner are not enemies. But in lieu of an enemy, the memoirs have a subsidiary hero, another champion—William Tecumseh Sherman.

The reader first encounters Sherman in a telling incident at the siege of Fort Donelson. Sherman is at the mouth of the Cumberland River to forward supplies and reinforcements.

> At the time he was senior in rank and there was no authority of law to assign a junior to command a senior of the same grade. But every

boat that came up with supplies or reinforcements brought a note of encouragement from Sherman, asking me to call upon him for any assistance he could render and saying that if he could be of service at the front I might send for him and he would waive rank.

At Shiloh, Sherman holds the right flank, inflicting heavy casualties on every Confederate raid that tries to turn it. And Grant writes: "A casualty to Sherman would have been a sad one for the troops engaged at Shiloh. And how near we came to this! On the 6th Sherman was shot twice, once in the hand, once in the shoulder, the ball cutting his coat and making a slight wound, and a third ball passed through his hat." After Shiloh, Grant gave up all "idea of saving the Union except by complete conquest." He says, in effect, it will be a long war and he will need Sherman to win it.

After the Confederate retreat, Halleck assumes field command and, jealous of Grant, shelves him. As the Union maneuvers to occupy Corinth, Grant, nominally second-in-command, has no actual command at all. He resolves to ask Halleck that he be relieved. "But," writes Grant, "General Sherman happened to call upon me as I was about starting and urged me so strongly not to think of going that I concluded to remain." This is Grant's crucial moment; his request would have effectively taken him out of the fight once and for all. Sherman, who previously offered to help Grant with a military obstacle, has now helped him surmount a serious political difficulty.

The reader of the *Personal Memoirs* can see the Grant-Sherman relationship develop. Sherman has begged Grant to give up his Vicksburg plan. But Grant perseveres and the victory is won:

> There was a little knot around Sherman and another around me and I heard Sherman repeating, in the most animated manner, what he said to me when we first looked down from Walnut Hills upon the land below on the 18th of May, adding, "Grant is entitled to every bit of credit for the campaign: I opposed it. I wrote him a letter about it." But for this speech it is not likely that Sherman's opposition would ever have been heard of. His untiring energy and great efficiency during the campaign entitle him to a full share of the credit due its success. He could not have done more if the plan had been his own.

Early in volume two, Grant reveals to the reader his proposed strategy. All the armies are to move together toward one common center; they are to act as a unit so far as it is possible over a vast field. The main object toward which they will work is to drive Lee from Richmond into the open field where he can be defeated. But Grant's generals fail him, except for Sherman—he moves, he fights.

As Grant meets Lee in the Wilderness, Sherman begins the flanking attacks that will force Johnston back into Atlanta. In September, Sherman takes the city. This insures the reelection of Lincoln and the continued prosecution of the war. Sherman then proposes the March to the Sea.

> His suggestions were finally approved, although they did not find favor in Washington. Even when it came to the time of starting, the greatest apprehension, as to the propriety of the campaign he was about to commence filled the mind of the President. This went so far as to move the President to ask me to suspend Sherman's march for a day or two until I could think the matter over. . . . I was in favor of Sherman's plan from the time it was first submitted to me. My chief of staff however was very bitterly opposed to it and, as I learned subsequently, finding that he could not move me, he appealed to the authorities to stop it.

In life, the relationship between Grant and Sherman had psychological implications for both men; in the *Personal Memoirs* it serves a literary purpose. It provides a dialogue, the only dialogue in the book outside of the one Grant conducts with Lincoln. Grant quotes Sherman and attends his movements, where he only reports the movements of the other generals. Thus does he lead the reader to one of his essential points. The purpose of this dialogue is not to define the Civil War—Grant clearly states in the book that the war was fought over the issue of slavery; nor is it to define any war—the whole book implies that war is a contest between people, not armies. The dialogue defines what it is to *soldier*, because soldiering is what made the Union victorious.

It was a people's war. Two citizens' armies fought it. From privates to generals, volunteers filled the ranks. Professional soldiers made fighters out of patriots, abolitionists, immigrants, bounty men, and draftees. Grant's internal theme, his core message, is that the successful conclusion of the Union cause was brought about not by religious fervency, gallantry, or historical necessity, but by force of arms expertly applied to the enemy's weakness. If it seems an obvious core, it is not what every general says. It is not what Eisenhower says in *Crusade in Europe,* witness the title.

The London *Times* complained that the *Personal Memoirs* did not contain a war story worth repeating. Its value to historians mitigates that judgment. But it is true the book is not always adventurous; nor is it ever linguistically innovative. These are literary considerations, and what the book ultimately provides is something more elemental. Mark Twain may not have precisely analyzed it, but he felt it when he told a cheering Hartford veterans reunion: ". . . we only remember that this is the simple soldier who, all untaught of silken phrase-makers, linked words together with an art surpassing the art of schools, and put them into a something which will still bring to American ears, as long as America shall last, the roll of his vanished drums and the tread of his marching hosts."

GRANT'S TOMB

Henry James visited Grant's Tomb and remarked that
the memorial was to him democracy in the all together—
an unguarded shrine where all could come and go at
their own will.

"The General's Last Victory."
New York State and the Civil War

THE *Personal Memoirs* IS GRANT'S SELF-COMPOSED MONUMENT. THERE would be others, by other hands, one especially familiar. Even before the funeral, on July 28, Mayor William Grace called a meeting of citizens interested in building a suitable memorial for Ulysses S. Grant. Influential friends and admirers of the General met at City Hall and proposed to raise $500,000 for such a memorial through a popular subscription. Subsequently, the Grant Monument Association won a charter from the New York Assembly. It numbered thirty-three trustees, headed by ex-President Chester A. Arthur. Assisting him on the executive committee were Hamilton Fish, Joseph Drexel, J. P. Morgan, Cornelius Vanderbilt, Jr., James Gordon Bennett, Frederic Coudert, and Joseph Pulitzer, among others.

The first subscriber to the monument was Western Union, which gave $5,000 through its president, Norvin Green. Western Union also offered the free use of its wires to anyone who wished to telegraph a subscription. Within a year, the Monument Association had collected $110,000. But Chester A. Arthur, an efficient and able administrator, died in November, 1886. He was succeeded by Sidney Dillon, a stockbroker, and a year later by Cornelius Vanderbilt, and then by William Grace. Half-heartedly administered, the subscription languished. Moreover, New Yorkers had just been solicited for funds to build the pedestal for the Statue of Liberty, which France had presented to the United States in 1884. It was completed in 1886. And they were being solicited for the

Washington Square Arch, the gateway to Fifth Avenue, designed by Stanford White. The arch was finally completed in 1895 at a cost of $128,000.

In the four years following the first solicitation, the Monument Association collected less than $25,000. Sherman, who visited the temporary sepulcher, noted: "Thousands visit it and gaze into the tomb containing the casket visible through the grated door; but as to a monument not a thing has been done." He had contributed $100 to the subscription, and that reluctantly. He didn't believe generals needed monuments. Mark Twain, in a letter to Charley Webster, wondered if building a barracks for the soldiers guarding the vault might not be a more worthwhile contribution. He was sure it was what the General would want.

In 1890, the Senate passed a bill authorizing the army to remove the General's remains from their temporary tomb in New York to the National Cemetery at Arlington. Julia Grant asked her friends to stop this. The New York delegation in the House defeated the Senate proposal, after heated debate and a promise that New York would build a memorial and build it soon. Toward this end, the Grant Monument Association asked General Horace Porter to become its president. Porter, who had proved himself an able soldier and a successful businessman, was about to prove himself a spectacular fund raiser. First, he determined that the subscription would be raised in New York City and that it would be raised within sixty days. From fourteen of the city's millionaires he solicited gifts of $5,000 apiece. Second, he then proceeded to set up 215 different committees composed of 2,487 committeemen, each equipped with a subscription book. There were committees for every business, profession, and trade; for each large mercantile establishment, church denomination, and university; for military, civic, and fraternal organizations. Committeemen solicited contributions in the stock and commodity exchanges and from passengers debarking from ships. There was a monument subscription box in every elevated railway station, every bank, every hotel, and every store on a main thoroughfare. Porter circularized the newspapers of the city and won their prompt and energetic support for the campaign, plus a sizable donation. Finally, the Monument Association sponsored essay contests in Manhattan and Brooklyn high schools, offering twenty gold dollars for the best essay on the life and career of Ulysses S. Grant and ten gold dollars for the second best.

Porter gave the Monument Association life and vigor and, though it took him considerably longer than sixty days, raised the money. A total of ninety thousand residents of Manhattan and Brooklyn contributed over $400,000. With the money already raised, plus the interest it had earned, the Monument Association could commission a memorial costing $600,000.

In 1890 the Grant Monument Association invited architects to submit competitive designs for the memorial. Sifting through five entries, it unanimously approved the design of John H. Duncan of New York City. Duncan's prototype was Hadrian's Tomb, in Rome—a square carrying a cylinder surmounted by a cone. There were two overriding merits to Duncan's design. First, it capitalized on the high bluff: the monument would rise to a height of 150 feet from the ground and 280 feet from the Hudson, making it a conspicuous landmark. Second, the monument would not look like an incomplete structure as the work progressed.

On April 27, 1892, the anniversary of Grant's birth, President Benjamin Harrison laid the cornerstone with a gold trowel manufactured especially for the occasion. Harrison, who had won a promotion to brevet brigadier during the Civil War, placed in the cornerstone a box containing a copy of the Constitution of the United States, the Declaration of Independence, the Articles of Confederation, and the Bible. The cornerstone also contained copies of eulogies delivered on Grant, a new American flag made of silk, a badge of the Grand Army of the Republic, the military order of the Loyal Legion, eleven medals struck at the United States Mint depicting events in Grant's life, one complete proof set of United States gold and silver coins, and copies of the New York newspapers of April 26 and 27.

The President led the parade in an open barouche drawn by four horses. At Riverside Drive fifty thousand people heard Chauncey Depew eulogize Grant. That evening the dignitaries toasted the General's widow at a commemorative dinner at Delmonico's. It would take five years to the day to complete the memorial.

Duncan wanted a structure that was clearly a memorial. He

wanted it to command the Hudson River, and he hoped it would become a meeting place for civic groups. The lower portion of the tomb was 90 feet square, rising to a height of 72 feet from the ground. It was finished with a cornice and a parapet. Statuary decorates and lends emphasis to the parapet's slope. Robed Grecian maidens, the work of J. Massey Rhind, pose at each corner and two are braced against the center tablature, which reads, "Let Us Have Peace." Above the square Duncan placed a circular cupola, 72 feet in diameter, surmounted by a pyramidal drum.

Symbolically, the tomb faces south. Steps 70 feet wide lead to a porch, protected by a portico that is supported by ten fluted Doric columns. Twenty Ionic columns form the shell of the cupola above it. Two 30-foot-high bronze doors of handwork design lead to the interior of the tomb. The interior is cruciform, though not in the shape of the traditional cross, but that of the equilateral "plus" sign. It is lined with marble. The points of the cross to the east, west, and north meet the ceiling with small lunettes, half-moon arches, on which mosaics depict the battles of Vicksburg, Chattanooga, and Appomattox. Above is the high dome. A rotunda 60 feet in diameter circles it with windows admitting light.

There are two display rooms on either side of the north stairwell. Originally these rooms contained hundreds of testimonials to Grant from foreign governments and state legislatures. More recently the displays have been changed to photographic histories of Grant's military and political career. Outside one room the Ohio state flag is on display, outside the other the Illinois. Between them is a stairwell at the top of which is a small equestrian model of the General sculptured by Paul Manship. On the wall to the rear is a tablet inscribed:

> Here is Buried
> the man whose Military Genius
> Saved the Union.
> For this a grateful Nation
> Elected Him
> To its Highest Office.

In the center of the tomb is the crypt, a well 20 feet in diameter surrounded by a marble balustrade. At the bottom of the crypt are the sarcophagi of Ulysses and Julia Grant. Each sarcophagus weighs ten tons and is 10 feet 4 inches long, 5 feet 9 inches wide, and 4 feet 8 inches high. The sarcophagi rest in the center of a circular gallery supported by square columns and reached by the stairwell. In the surrounding niches are busts of the General's contemporaries.

The sarcophagi were cut from single blocks of Montello porphyry in Wisconsin. Duncan selected this stone because it can be polished to a glistening red that resembles mahogany. Julia protested when she learned that the architect proposed her burial in the same sarcophagus as her husband. "General Grant must have his own sarcophagus," she insisted, "and I must have mine beside him. General Grant's identity must remain distinct. Hereafter when persons visit this spot, they must be able to say, 'Here rests General Grant.' "

For his building material Duncan chose granite, because it weathers the best of all stone. After seven months, he found a granite of light color, entirely flawless and durable, at a quarry in North Jay, Maine. Its granite was so light in color that in strong sunlight it passes for marble. So stringent were the contractual requirements of the Monument Association that $10,000 worth of granite was discarded in the selection process.

The Monument Association and the friends of General Grant expressed complete satisfaction with the tomb, but New Yorkers have never taken to it. While 250,000 pilgrims from out of state visit Grant's Tomb yearly, sophisticated city dwellers treat it as a vaudeville joke. New Yorkers found it a forbidding mausoleum, admitting light through purple glass that cast a funereal pall. Lately, orange glass has been substituted for the purple, and the amber glow creates a more comfortable interior effect. And the tomb was found wanting as a meeting place, because Duncan did not provide for toilets or adequate storage space.

The tomb was never completely finished. Steps leading from a river pier were never constructed, nor was extensive statuary erected in the plaza. In 1928 Manship was commissioned to execute his equestrian model as a colossal outdoor statue. The cost was estimated at upwards of $100,000, and the depression of the 1930s doomed the project. In 1959 the United States Department of the

Interior took over the tomb as the General Grant National Memorial. Its suggestion that the colossal equestrian statue of Grant in Brooklyn's Grand Army Plaza be moved to the tomb was received with less than enthusiasm by Brooklyn's borough president.

Grant's Tomb was dedicated on April 27, 1897, the seventy-fifth anniversary of the General's birth. It was a cloudy, bleak day, but the city offset the gloom by flying more flags than ever before. A parade as long and as impressive as the funeral cortege preceded the dedication. Once again a million people lined the streets along the route of march. The West Point corps of cadets led sixty thousand marchers, including two regiments of the regular army and three thousand schoolboys. The line of march, which started up Madison Avenue from 26th Street, took seven hours to pass in review at 122nd Street. The reviewing stand held two thousand people, including ambassadors from twenty-seven nations. Señor Romero represented Mexico. President William McKinley took the salute.

There were ten warships from the North Atlantic Fleet in the harbor, headed by the flagship USS *New York*. Alongside were British, French, Italian, Portuguese, and Spanish warships. They were all dressed in their ensigns, fifteen rainbows of color in midriver. Darting in between were eleven lighthouse tenders, five small ships from the Revenue Marine, and several merchant ships.

Five thousand GAR members brought up the rear of the parade, many of them, according to the *Tribune*, "bowed with infirmity." Among them was one man in a Confederate uniform. He was Charles Brown of Brooklyn, who had fought with the First Maryland Regiment. Brown said he was proud to have worn the uniform in the war, and he wore it today in honor of General Grant. As he marched along he swapped war stories with the Union veterans.

At the reviewing stand the wind raised huge billows of dust. It was a penetrating wind, one that howled as it tried to drown out the words of the speakers. "New York," said McKinley stoutly against the screeching, "holds in its keeping the precious dust of the silent soldier, but his achievements are in the keeping of seventy million Americans."

Shortly afterward McKinley departed, and the seventy thousand spectators gradually abandoned the plaza and the bluff. The tomb stood alone in the fast-gathering cold darkness. The next day sentries came to their last present arms before the temporary vault and began dismantling it. The bricks were distributed to GAR posts throughout the country.

In 1966 a sculptor, Pedro Silva, organized a mosaic workshop at Grant's Tomb. Over the next two years students surrounded the east, north, and west sides of the plaza with a continuous line of free-form inlaid concrete benches and tables. There are mosaic representations of the General, his battles, the flag, the Capitol, and whatever else struck the workers' fancy. Silva conceived the program as a celebration of the Centennial Year of the National Parks. Ulysses S. Grant had signed the bill creating Yellowstone National Park, the first in the world.

The neighborhood is now populated mainly by Puerto Ricans, and one suspects that Grant, who loved Mexico, would have liked his neighbors. Grant's Tomb has become a place for "happenings." Posters on the flagpole announce an evening of "Steel bands, street theater, dancers, food, folksinging, clowns, crafts, and people."

On the twenty-seventh of April the American Legion, the Veterans of Foreign Wars, and the Grant Monument Association place wreaths of flowers at the head of the sarcophagus. Then the men step back and smartly salute.

BIBLIOGRAPHICAL ESSAY

BOOKS AND AUTHORS ON WHICH I DEPENDED I HAVE IDENTIFIED IN MY text. I want to seize the chance here to make brief comment on some of them.

At least one biography of Grant, Bruce Catton's *Ulysses S. Grant and the American Military Tradition* (Boston, 1954), is certainly part of our literary tradition. It is instructive to compare Catton's book with Owen Wister's *Ulysses S. Grant* (Boston, 1900). Both authors approach their subject in the same way—Ulysses S. Grant as the American character. Both books are brief. Both cover the same ground. Wister's book was written as a reaction to the wave of militaristic imperialism that washed over the country after the Spanish-American War. Catton's book was written in reaction to the election of Dwight D. Eisenhower as President, a glorification of World War II.

Books about Grant tend to run in cycles. They often transform the General and his times to make comment on the prevailing milieu.

Between 1885 and 1898 a spate of books were quickly published about Grant. I say "quickly" because there was no end of capitalizing on this hero. The best of these are Adam Badeau's *Grant in Peace: From Appomattox to Mount McGregor* (1887) and Hamlin Garland's *Ulysses S. Grant: His Life and Character* (1898). Both are marred by sentimentality and an emotional partnership ill-befitting the biographer, but they are still valuable foundations for the Grant canon. George C. Childs's *Recollections of Ulysses S. Grant* was published as a pamphlet in 1888 after its appearance in the Philadelphia newspapers. It is a rich source of anecdotes about the

[279]

General's life in peace and it is an especially informative book on the General's last year. Badeau, Garland, and Childs had in common the urge to reveal Ulysses S. Grant not only as a leader and a good fellow but also as a pious American. Grant's Christianity was a theme in every biography or appraisal published up until the turn of the century. Gertrude Stein's essay on Grant in *Four in America*, though published in 1920, was the apogee of this cycle.

Owen Wister's biography did much to diminish the General's reputation. So did the historians reassessing the Civil War. In 1917, however, on the eve of our entry into World War I, Louis A. Coolidge published *Ulysses S. Grant* (Boston). It remains a fair yet sympathetic survey of Grant's two administrations. It is marred neither by sentimentality nor by excessive rhetoric, and there is much in the book that must be assimilated by any serious historian. It marks a rehabilitation of Grant's reputation, inspired perhaps by the need for a hero when the country was facing a grave danger. Books by Jesse Grant and Princess Cantacuzene continued this, capped in 1928 by the publication of W. E. Woodward's *Meet General Grant* (New York). While a hero worshiper of no mean proportions, Woodward included in his biography much firsthand information from Grant descendants and many heretofore uncollected accounts by Grant contemporaries. *General Grant's Last Stand* (New York, 1936) by Horace Green, which includes the Douglas notes and diaries, belongs to this genre.

Two of the best histories of the Grant administration were published in the mid-thirties. Both books are animated by a desire to define a responsible federal government which, of course, the Roosevelt administration was and the Grant administration was not. Allan Nevins's *Hamilton Fish: The Inner History of the Grant Administration* (New York, 1936) and William B. Hesseltine's *Ulysses S. Grant: Politician* (New York, 1935) reveal much of Grant, the President, but equally as much of Grant, the man. These histories, needless to say, are critical. Both writers are facile and both are thoroughly informed. There is no question but that both books transcend their time.

Captain Sam Grant (Boston, 1950) by Lloyd Lewis had its genesis in the 1920s, when Lewis began collecting material for his definitive

Sherman: Fighting Prophet (New York, 1932). Lewis's biography was as much about Grant as about Sherman. During the next eighteen years Lewis collected the research for a definitive three-volume work on the General. His death cut this ambition short. But his widow passed on the research to Bruce Catton, who authored *Grant Moves South* (Boston, 1960) and *Grant Takes Command* (Boston, 1969).

To correlate each book on Grant with a coextensive political or historical change would be foolhardy. But Ishbel Ross's *The General's Wife* (New York, 1959) may owe something to the feminist movement, which started in the 1950s. *The General's Wife* is one of the best biographies ever written about an American woman.

Thomas Pitkin's *The Captain Departs* (Carbondale and Edwardsville, Ill., 1973), which, along with Green's book, proved invaluable to this writer, is devoted half to the General's declining days on Mt. McGregor and half to the mountain's subsequent history. Mr. Pitkin is a retired supervisory historian of the National Park Service. The book grew out of essays relating the history of the Drexel cottage, and perhaps it owes something to the ecological and conservationist movements, which came to prominence in the 1960s.

Mark Twain dealt extensively with his relationship with Grant. He devoted a lengthy chapter to the GAR Festival of 1879 and an equally lengthy one to the *Personal Memoirs* in his *Autobiography*. His *Notebooks* (New York, 1924) also chronicle his friendship with the General and to this are added two more chapters included in *Mark Twain in Eruption* (Ed. Bernard de Voto, New York, 1939). *General Grant: By Matthew Arnold with a Rejoinder by Mark Twain* was published by the Southern Illinois University Press in 1966.

Where Ulysses S. Grant lived three different lives, Mark Twain lived two, both of them at the same time. This is the theme of Justin Kaplan's *Mister Clemens & Mark Twain* (New York, 1966). The book is a psychological study with penetrating insights accomplished without jargon or psychological nomenclature. There is no more amusing book to be read than Samuel Clemens Webster's *Mark Twain: Business Man* (Boston, 1946). The book includes the correspondence of Twain to Webster with interpretive commentary.

[281]

Albert Bigelow Paine's *Mark Twain: A Biography* (New York, 1912) remains the most informative source for Twain's life. About one third of volume two concerns Twain and Grant.

I made extensive use of the New York City newspapers of the time, particularly the *Times* and the *Tribune*, which are indexed, and drew heavily from periodicals, as Grant is indexed in *Pool's Periodical Index, 1880–1899*.

INDEX

gold, discovery of, 133
Gold Bugs, 95
gold market, attempted cornering of, 93–95
Goldsmith, Alden, 148–149
Gore, John, 56
Gould, Jay, 5, 10, 13, 93–95, 187
Grace, William, 234, 243, 271
Grand Army of the Republic (GAR), 108, 119, 123, 135, 182, 183, 209, 212, 233, 235, 238, 242, 253, 276
Grand Army Plaza (Brooklyn), Grant's statue in, 276
Grant, Clara, 30
Grant, Elizabeth, 164
Grant, Ellen "Nellie" Sartoris, *see* Sartoris, Nellie Grant
Grant, Fannie, 21
Grant, Frederick Dent, 11, 20, 54, 62, 109, 120, 130, 144, 149, 151, 152, 154, 155, 156, 157, 159, 160, 163, 165, 171, 172, 174, 182, 184, 193, 203, 204, 209, 217, 227, 228, 229, 231, 235, 250, 251
  as aide to father, 116–117, 128, 129, 153, 195, 199, 202, 216, 219, 221, 226, 265
  and father's funeral, 213–214, 226, 232, 233–234
  last years and death of, 252
Grant, Hannah Simpson, 29, 31–32, 36, 54, 55
Grant, Ida Honore, 117, 120, 149, 154, 164
Grant, Jesse, 29–34, 35, 36, 37, 43, 54, 59–60, 64
Grant, Jesse Root, 62, 65, 164, 183, 220, 234, 247n, 252
Grant, Julia, 231, 232, 244, 252
Grant, Julia Dent, 4, 16, 21, 22, 23,

Grant, Julia Dent *(cont.)*
24–25, 55, 57, 59–60, 62, 64, 66, 94, 95, 101, 102, 103, 116, 120, 129, 131, 141, 149, 150, 151, 152, 154, 159, 164, 167, 168, 170, 172, 173, 174, 176, 181, 182, 183, 184, 185, 187, 188, 190, 192, 199, 203, 204, 205, 217, 219, 229, 230, 231, 232, 233, 237, 242, 250, 257, 272, 275
  Grant's courtship of, 45–48
  last years and death of, 251–252
  marriage of, 53–54
  reaction of, to Grant's cancer, 144–145, 214
  Ward and, 109–110
  in White House, 91
Grant, Mary, 30
Grant, Orvil, 30, 64
Grant, Simpson, 30, 43, 63, 64
Grant, Ulysses Simpson:
  appointments of, 93, 95–96, 99, 110
  baptism of, 190, 192
  boyhood and schooling of, 34–36
  as businessman, 62–65, 119, 197
  cancer of: callers and messages during, 178–184, 187, 194, 215–216, 218, 221, 222–225; discovery of, 141–143; drugs used in, 143, 145, 180, 181, 217–218, 221–222, 226, 228; newspaper coverage of, 157, 169, 171–177, 179–181, 183, 184–187, 204, 205, 213, 215, 216, 222, 225, 229; religion and, 187–193, 222–223; suffering in, 146, 149–151, 154, 178, 179, 180, 185, 189–190, 193, 194, 201, 213, 217, 221–222, 231; treatment of, 143–147,

Webster, Samuel Clemens, 163*n*
Webster & Company, Charles L.,
    128, 129, 130, 157–163, 195,
    203, 248, 257
Wellington, Duke of, 148
Western Union, 271
West Point, 53, 117, 205, 237
    Grant at, 36–43, 141, 148
Wheeler, Joseph, 112
Whigs, 31, 50, 53
Whiskey Ring, 97–99, 177
Whitman, Walt, 139
Wilcox, Cadmus Marcellus, 54
Wilde, Oscar, 109
Wilderness campaign, 87–89, 142,
    148, 150, 177, 267
    Grant's article on, 114, 116, 118,
    198
Willett, Sam, 212, 216

Wilmington, N.C., capture of,
    90
Wilson, Edmund, 257, 261–262
Wilson, Henry, 97
Wilson, James, 169–170
Wilson, James Grant, 187
Wilson, Woodrow, 109*n*, 257
Winn, Frank, 237
Wood, Charles, 21–22, 171, 218
Woodward, Dr. J. J., 174
Woodward, W. E., 42, 191
Worth, William Scott, 52–53
Wrenshall, Nellie Dent, 236

Yates, Richard, 10, 67
"yellow journalism," 187
Yellowstone Expedition, 117
Yellowstone National Park, 277
Young, John Russell, 42, 110–111